# Made from Scratch

## RECLAIMING THE PLEASURES OF THE AMERICAN HEARTH

## JEAN ZIMMERMAN

FREE PRESS

New York London Toronto Sydney Singapore

FREE PRESS
A Division of Simon & Schuster, Inc.
1230 Avenue of the Americas
New York, NY 10020

Manufactured in the United States of America

10   9   8   7   6   5   4   3   2   1

Library of Congress Cataloging-in-Publication Data

Zimmerman, Jean.
Made from scratch : reclaiming the pleasures
of the American hearth / Jean Zimmerman.
p. cm.
Includes bibliographical references.
1. Home economics—United States—History.
2. Home economics—United States—Philosophy. I. Title.

TX23.Z55 2003
640'.973—dc21                          2003042403

ISBN 978-0-684-86960-5

For information regarding special discounts for bulk purchases,
please contact Simon & Schuster Special Sales: 1-800-456-6798
or business@simonandschuster.com

*For my mother,*
*my grandmothers, and our foremothers*

# Contents

# Introduction

I WROTE THIS BOOK for selfish reasons.

The family I was born into on my mother's side was a small-town dynasty where old-fashioned domesticity prevailed for generations. The culture of my grandparents could be called the last bastion of traditional Southern homemaking, a style of keeping house driven by country necessity. My mother's desire for psychic independence prefigured the Feminine Mystique, yet with all her education and strength she also chose domesticity as her primary occupation. That decision was a mystery to me as I grew up in a culture permeated with rhetoric about women's oppression by their homemaking role. The home, I believed along with many of my peers, was a dead end for women, a deception, a place not to become "trapped."

I reached midlife after working hard at my career, marrying, and starting a family with a sense of conflict about the place of home and hearth in my life, a feeling shared by many people I knew. It was to make sense of this conflict that I embarked on the research, observation, and interviews that went into *Made from Scratch*.

For years I had had a quietly percolating interest in all things domestic. Ten years ago, I happened upon a nineteenth century mansion in Upstate New York called Montgomery Place, the ancestral home of the prominent Livingston family, which was then in the process of restoration to its original appearance but was in the meantime open to visitors for guided tours. The views from the house's balustrade swept over the glittering river and the dusky Catskill Mountains beyond in what Henry James once called "the strong silver light" of the Hudson Valley. Inside, Bavarian crystal chandeliers floated above the original hand-painted wallpaper. Miniature portraits and Chinese urns and marble tables and teak chairs had the elderly women in my group murmuring like doves, "Oh, how beautiful."

The house's appointments interested me, but I found myself more engaged by the humbler quarters of the basement, our final stop on the mansion tour. As recounted by our guide—a distant relation of the Livingstons with tobacco-stained teeth who introduced himself as Jupiter—it was here in the depths of the structure that the family's last heir resided until his death in 1985. It was here, beneath the mansion that was too costly to heat, amid the 1950s-era appliances and worn linoleum, that he and his wife continued to make their home. Blue-blooded but cash poor, husband and wife spent their days cataloging and displaying the two centuries of treasured family belongings in the grander precincts upstairs. They were driven to preserve a whole, organic past in the midst of their truncated domestic present.

That image stuck with me, the basement life of the last of the Livingstons. Their story suggested how strongly these castouts continued to feel about home.

I grew interested in people's relationship with dwellings of the past. A friend of mine had refused to go with me to the Livingston property, saying of old houses, "I've always found them disquieting." I could see her point. The combination of all the antiques in the house, the broad drive edged by black locust trees that curved toward the mansion from the main road, and the rambling orchard with its heirloom apples and peaches offered an intoxicating whiff of an irretrievable moment. I too found it uncomfortable, the disparity between immersing myself in a simpler, more orderly, less mechanized style of domesticity, and then returning home to the rushed, chaotic, mass-produced, artificial elements of "real life."

How do you make time stand still? I didn't crave a mansion, but I dreamt of a different kind of domestic space, one not defined by take-out food and frenetic comings and goings, a place where things of the past were valued, where the tastes and skills of the past were kept alive in the carefully preserved fruit stock or the carefully divided rhizomes of the iris bed. I wanted a home that sang with tranquility and was rooted in, though not bound by, tradition.

Other people apparently felt the same way. I noticed that along with the corny nostalgia that permeates the atmosphere at many historic sites, there is something valiant about both the folks who run these places and those who visit, who want to touch what is essentially a relic—but, more than that, a way of life—and hold it close, if only for an afternoon or a weekend. I was impressed by what I then saw as the powerful lure of the past for so many Americans. Eventually, however, I saw something that was its inverse: the reason we are so drawn to older homes is to a great degree because we are dissatisfied with the quality of the home lives we lead. Where once I had seen genteel kitsch I began to recognize painful paradoxes. From the kitchen shelves at cheap antique stores I collected hand-carved wooden spoons, blue speckleware mixing bowls, funky one-of-a-kind plates. I found these objects beautiful, and they sharpened my longing for those earlier times when domesticity held a place of honor in our culture.

My home life became somewhat schizophrenic. Working on a book about the military while living out in the country, I juggled pickling cucumbers from my garden and phoning high-ranking Navy officers to interview them. More recently I've been both a professional and an old-fashioned suburban housewife, and I often don't know if I prefer assembling a fruit cobbler or doing the research for a book chapter. On vacations I bring along *Family Circle* for beach reading the way someone else would pack a gothic romance. I still long for a tranquil, uncluttered home, but find it difficult to keep up with the laundry and the towering piles of paper. Like everyone else, I try to determine priorities, but I want everything and often I just can't figure out how my ideal of home fits into my actual life. Having come of age in the mid-1970s when domesticity was broadly disparaged, I sometimes feel like a dinosaur attempting to integrate my work identity with my domestic interests. Why bother making it from scratch when it's just as easy to hire, buy, or order in?

SINCE THE GODDESS Hestia kept alive the hearth fires of ancient Greece, women have been the guardians of the domestic flame—feeding and clothing their families, not to mention writing all the thank-you notes—and society has benefited. In the last century homemaking has been eroded, however, and the role of homemaker gradually devalued. Today, companies spend vast sums marketing replacements for homemade items. Americans feel they can't be bothered to engage with the processes that used to define domesticity. Whether it's cleaning, cooking, or crafting, most of us agree it's easier if not better to purchase it or forego it rather than to do it ourselves. As a result, products and services that make it easier than ever not to perform the work of the home have proliferated, however enjoyable doing that work may be. Baking a pie, for example, is a source of pleasure now readily passed up because people prefer the convenience of a pie from the supermarket. We've bought the hype that has evolved to tell us we just don't have the time or energy to spend on the work of the home, effort that is thought to be, in the accepted parlance, "drudgery."

The future of domesticity is already upon us, coexisting edgily with the homemaking wisdom of our grandmothers. It may well obliterate the old ways at a time when they count more than ever in nurturing us and our children. Researching this book persuaded me that most Americans feel a passionate loyalty to their domestic heritage. What we also feel is guilt—guilt over not cleaning enough, not cooking enough, not spending enough time "cocooning" at home with loved ones. Convenience is a real and valuable commodity, but the question must be asked whether buying or hiring can fully satisfy our basic human needs—to nurture and be nurtured, to create, to craft, and to perform. When we bemoan the loss of values in our culture, doesn't this stem in part from the loss of the home?

Sometimes when I tell people I'm writing about the decline of domesticity, they jump to what seems to me a somewhat different subject, the destruction of the American family. *Made from Scratch* does not begin to untangle America's changing demographics or judge the current makeup of the family unit. In my estimation, reclaiming the pleasures of domesticity in no way implies reviving a cookie-cutter notion of family, one that features a nine-to-five husband and a housewife and two or three children, a model that seeks to replicate some kind of mythical golden age. Every person in every circumstance needs a home—a senior citizen as much as a baby in a brood of twelve, couples who may or may not be legally wed, single-parent families, roommates, blended families, foster families, and communities of like people under one roof, such as assisted-care facilities. No matter who lives in a home, the value of domesticity, it seems to me, is just the same: to offer sanctuary and shelter, to give comfort and creative satisfaction and the assurance of connection. Some of the people not described by conventional family arrangements may in fact have the greatest need for the succor and support a reinvigorated home can provide.

☙

WHAT STRIKES ME is that we don't appreciate to what extent our age-old domestic skills and traditions have already slipped away. My grandmother sewed all her family's clothes, as did all my fore-mothers, stretching back generation after generation, but rare is the 20-something today who can sew on a button. You can buy takeout because you choose not to make dinner, but when your child grows up, he won't have that choice, simply because he won't have learned to cook—in one generation, a broad swath of culinary know-how and experience cut to the ground. Yet we're not paying attention to the loss we suffer by this development. We're huddled in the basement, too psychically impoverished to reclaim the rich, beautiful pieces of our domestic heritage.

My aim has been to gather the remnants of a world that might soon be lost, honor it as best I can, and depict ways in which some people are working to keep that world alive. What is required to save the hearth as we know it is, strangely enough, not storming the barricades of Burger King or performing some other radical public act. The only thing that we must do is allow ourselves to reclaim the pleasures that domesticity allows. In the small private act of stirring a pot of homemade soup or knitting a scarf for a loved one we preserve the rich heritage of the home and keep back the swelling tide of mediocrity and commodification that is fast replacing it—and, most important, nourish our own souls.

Researching domesticity as an author entitled me as a woman to immerse myself in the age-old customs, techniques, and lore of my female elders. Learning about Mediterranean goddesses or colonial housewives, using source material that included cookbooks and quilts, fulfilled some of my personal yearning to spend time touching the things of the past before they disappear.

The chapters that follow explore different facets of this subject and attempt to answer some questions: What constitutes domesticity today and how has it evolved? What are the parts of its history we've forgotten? What is the enduring value of homemaking?

I begin in the first chapter by exploring the undying appeal of the objects we keep as material links to our personal history and the different ways we maintain contact with the past, and by discussing the painful conflict many people feel as domesticity becomes devalued.

Chapter 2 explores the ancient strength of women's domestic role, personified by the powerful hearth goddess Hestia in Classical Greece. It examines the relevance of this mythology in restoring dignity to the ongoing work of the home.

As my research showed that domesticity encompasses several main elements—housekeeping, cooking, and work with textiles—the rest of the book treats each in turn.

I come at the subject of keeping house from different perspectives. Chapter 3 explores the largely forgotten history of housework and the people who have performed it, from heroic medieval housewives to Victorian parlor feminists. Chapter 4 looks at home economics as it was shaped by one generation of women and influenced generations to come. In Chapter 5, I attempt to show how the crucial domestic crossroads that came with the 1960s and 1970s—the juncture of traditional homemaking and the women's movement—raised questions that haunt us still about whether homemaking can be seen as a valid cultural contribution.

Food is the topic of the next two chapters. The culinary deskilling of America that is described in Chapter 6 has been prompted partly by the corporate takeover of our home larders and partly by Americans' devastating workload. Chapter 7 addresses the repercussions of the death of home cooking.

The final chapter examines the panoply of spinning, weaving, knitting, crocheting, and sewing that comprises home textile production, traditionally a defining function of womanhood. As hand-worked items find themselves anything but urgently required today from a practical standpoint, especially in America, they continue to fill an invaluable psychic need.

IN EARLIER BOOKS I explored the challenges faced by executive women climbing the corporate ladder and by military women making their way in formerly all-male fields, such as combat aviation, in which being female strikes many people as just plain wrong. In my most recent book, cowritten with my husband, we reported on the benefits of taking away barriers to girls playing sports so that our nation's daughters can derive the gains afforded by physical activity, including a robust sense of self. In all these projects, my objective has been to show why it makes sense to allow the widest possible array of life choices to girls and women.

Focusing on the benefits of domesticity might seem an odd follow-up, yet I believe this is another cause to which the ideals of feminism apply. It is imperative to restore respect for the work of the home, work that is still a primary focus of women rather than men, though that is gradually changing. I hope this book helps answer the social judgment that says the domestic achievements of our mothers and grandmothers were somehow trivial and that women's efforts at hearth and home today are something for which we must apologize, something inherently superficial or at least subordinate to our work in the public sphere.

I wrote this book for selfish reasons, because I myself want to know what it is I'm losing before I throw it away, and what it is that's worth preserving.

Jean Zimmerman
*July 19, 2002*

# Made from
# Scratch

# CHAPTER I

# Heirlooms

MY GRANDMOTHER, born in 1913, was the last of the old-fashioned American homemakers. A farm wife, she lived her whole life in small-town western Tennessee, midway between Memphis and Nashville, near the border of Kentucky. Her family was close-knit. My grandmother was raised next door to her own grandparents, catty-corner from the house in which her future husband grew up, and together my freshly married grandparents settled on that same block, first in the little house where my mother was born and then in a classic sprawling Victorian conveniently situated next door to my grandfather's first business, a filling station.

Not a soft, big, maternal type, my grandmother was bird-small yet not breakable. She was fashionable, never dowdy. Yet despite her stature and her style, my grandmother embraced the heavy labor of farm life. My grandparents planted fields of feed corn and cotton, soybeans, and okra on farmland outside of town. At the farm, coarse-haired hogs rooted in a pen, and up a rutted muddy road grew a vast peach orchard. Summers, my mother and her sisters and brother helped the field hands harvest strawberries, hunching on their hands and knees over the easily damaged fruit. All of the picking was hard: fuzzy okra pricked the fingertips, and cotton sat like a boulder in the canvas bag slung over the shoulder. Standing sentry behind a big wooden table, my grandmother would count the slatted produce carriers as the pickers brought in each harvest.

Hers was a country life, hard and simple, with one foot planted back in the nineteenth century. Even years later, sending my grandparents letters was easy: the only address required was their name and "Greenfield, Tennessee." You could add "Main Street" if you wanted to get fancy, but the information was unnecessary, a letter would get to them without it. When my mother called home after moving away, the town switchboard operator didn't need to hear her name to connect her with her parents' house.

By 1920, the number of Americans living in cities for the first time outweighed those living in the country, down from 95 percent of Americans who lived in farm country in 1776. A wood stove or a spinning wheel had disappeared from almost every American household, and nearly every home had electricity. In rural Tennessee, though, some things that defined the labor of women like my grandmother hadn't changed. Up through the 1940s she kept a horse and a milk cow in the yard under the catalpas and churned butter in a big ceramic crock on the back porch. Apple and damson trees supplied fruit both for eating fresh and for putting up. The family lived a few blocks from the grocery store, but fresh meat wasn't something you bought. In fall a pig from the pen would be slaughtered for its lard and to send to the barbecue pit. My grandmother's job included wringing the neck of the chicken for every platter of fried chicken she put on the table.

My grandmother sewed all the clothes for her children, selecting fabric at E. and J. Brock, the old general store that sold yard goods. Sometimes she would create matching outfits for herself and all three daughters. Walking to town on a Saturday night as teenagers, the girls would model their homemade dresses, stepping across the railroad tracks that sliced through town under the water tower with GREENFIELD in giant block letters on its side.

A woman named Elrina lived with her husband in a small wooden shack in the corner of the back lot behind the house, and she helped out in the kitchen. Mostly, though, my grandmother herself dished up the stewed tomatoes, chicken-fried steak smothered in milk gravy, black-eyed peas, collard greens, and dinner rolls. This was food that was made from scratch, homegrown and in some cases hunted down. One Thanksgiving when I was a child, my grandmother roasted a wild turkey that my grandfather had killed and my mother cracked a tooth on a pellet of buckshot. Opening the refrigerator to find a cold drink on a summer afternoon, I discovered skinned squirrels in Tupperware and was told that Grandpa shot them out of the trees in the backyard.

Through the 1950s and 1960s, as the world around them convulsed with social changes, my grandparents still lived close to the land. Something seemingly eternal, never changing, was the shared assumption that care of the home was a woman's responsibility as well as a source of accomplishment that deserved respect.

My grandmother inherited the mantle of homemaker from her own mother and her mother's mother. I spent afternoons at the house of my great-grandmother, where we drank grape soda and watched Art Linklater on the black-and-white TV. We took a photograph the summer I turned twelve that we called "the four generations": my great-grandmother, grandmother, mother, and myself. The dress I wore, my favorite dress, had strips of lace, factory-made lace, crossed on the moss green front like the ribbon on a present. I didn't know then that Granny herself was a lace maker, that her house was where the real needlework took place, where she spun intricate webs of polished-cotton thread. I knew Granny in her nineties, with a head of old-timey white pin curls and crepey white arms. I didn't know the richness of the craft life she'd led. The exquisite work that came from her hands was already antiquated, not worthy of mention.

The places don't exist anymore, but the material objects that inhabited them are touchstones of my memory that help define an ideal of home: the orderly, shady house of my grandmother with its Dresden figurines and porch glider, its frigid metal drinking cups with drops of condensation down their sides, the crochet hooks of ivory and aluminum and a skein of plain brown wool, the pecan shells crackling underfoot out front. I can smell the tomato vines in the back garden, picture the speedy flight of purple martins at the towering birdhouse my grandfather built, hear the warble of the quails the neighbors kept in a chicken wire hutch. In my own attic now, a dusty cardboard box still shelters some of the most stunning relics of my family's domestic history—the dozens of linens elaborately handworked by my grandmother and my great aunt, my great-grandmother, and her mother before her.

MY MOTHER HASTENED AWAY at age 17 from the swollen heat, the mute burgeoning physicality of small-town Southern life. She had never worn a store-bought dress until she went to college. Now she eagerly created a new identity for herself that would not include home-sewn clothes, hand-picked strawberries, or chickens whose necks were wrung in the backyard. At an East Coast women's college she studied art history and then married an Ivy Leaguer, the prototypical man in the gray flannel suit who commuted every day to a Manhattan advertising firm. At home in our one-step-down-from-Cheever suburb, my mother hosted cocktail parties and traded PTA responsibilities with other women, but most of her time was spent as was her mother's before her—buying, preparing, and serving food, cleaning her house and keeping up her property, and attending to the clothing and other needs of her family. With all her smarts and sophistication, in these responsibilities she hadn't come all that far from the lives of her foremothers. Still, though her daily routine wasn't exactly what she had planned in her studious college days, she saw it as an improvement upon the backwater housewife's role she had escaped. She knew she didn't want a farm life. She had watched her mother and her aunt and grandmother sew, and thought it way too laborious, not to mention dull—all those finishing seams you had to learn, when you could be reading instead.

My mother came from the postwar generation of suburban housewives that Friedan described so well. These highly educated, increasingly frustrated women understood from intense personal experience that change was needed—indeed, that it was already under way. Economic forces were pushing women into the workplace, and the women's movement was providing the political underpinnings for the push. Housewives, however, harbored the piercing fear that as the world around them moved ahead, they might be left behind, stranded between the domestic assumptions of the past and the unknown ways of the future. Women who gave birth to the baby boom generation may have wanted no part of the traditional life of the home, the life lived by women like my grandmother, and yet many of them performed its day-to-day labors to a tee in studied replication of the past, with the anodyne in many cases of Valium or vodka.

My own mother, with her *ikebana* and spotless carpets, obsessing over the cleanliness of our Formica countertops, was likewise trapped (in the unshakable opinion of her adolescent daughter). She had the distaste for home-sewn clothes that comes naturally to anyone who has grown up wearing nothing else. Nonetheless, she was perfectly capable of hemming my school jumpers, her mouth bristling with pins. She maintained a well-ordered sewing box and recognized the importance of darning a sock, positions I gradually came to consider quaintly anachronistic if not downright pathetic.

My family endorsed the recognized hierarchies of the day. My father had the "real" job that took him out of the home. His kitchen skills were limited to boiling an egg and making toast. My mother put dinner on the table for a family of five every day for over twenty years, which effort was within my family certainly not considered a "job" at all but a rote accomplishment, given no more notice than the weather. Good homemade spaghetti sauce and beef-barley soup emerged from my mother's kitchen, and even fudge tunnel cakes and carrot cakes when baking them was fashionable in our community. Her goal, though, was to escape enslavement by a hot stove. She didn't go out of her way to tutor me in the kitchen only because she didn't want me to get stuck there, the way some women will say they refused to learn to type because they never wanted to become secretaries.

My mother rejected the farm life of her mother and of all the small-town matrons who predated her. Yet she wasn't ready to abandon the home. Dust free and immaculate, our house was my mother's clear domain. Though she hired cleaning help when she could afford to, its care was still undeniably her responsibility, and her pride.

As I watched, growing up, my mother tried to cobble together the abyss between the past and the future. Attempting to make sense of her experience, I shaped an apocryphal theory that went like this. Yes, she kept a beautiful home. In so doing, she transferred her intelligence and taste from a possible professional career to the so much more mundane reality of creating a domestic life. This was really a tale of wasted talent, unnecessary "sacrifice."

The story's message was simple and oddly like my mother's before me: *I must get out.*

⤬

WHAT HAS MADE IT possible for the home to be an arena of caring, as in my house growing up, is, of course, the labor of women. In the women's studies courses offered in college in the late 1970s, when I was in school, we learned that women had been "inculcated" to be homemakers and to produce that labor, and that this was a bad thing. At Barnard, our texts were Tillie Olsen and *The Feminine Mystique*; going back further, we read Charlotte Perkins Gilman's *The Yellow Wallpaper*, the nineteenth century novella about a woman driven to despair and madness by her imprisonment in a domestic role. I soaked up Simone de Beauvoir's argument that women's lives, with their mindless daily chores, did not provide for the kind of daring and adventurousness necessary for exploring and creating important innovations in the world. Her stance on homemaking was adamant: "We have seen what poetic veils are thrown over her monotonous burdens of housekeeping and maternity: in exchange for her liberty she has received the false treasure of her 'femininity.'"

The women's movement of the 1970s cleaved the world of work into two parts. One part, the public part, the "male" part, was deemed vital, engaging, and valuable. The other part, the part left behind in the house dust, the work of the home, was meaningless, humdrum, the stuff of subservience. The division of labor between women and men, I came to believe, was inherently unfair. This translated into a devaluation of women's prescribed jobs along with the mandate that women were supposed to get out of the house and plunder a piece of what in the past had been almost exclusively a male domain. Entering the workplace in the early 1980s, I felt the powerful cultural tug of this idea, being employed, as I was, at a nonprofit think tank devoted to helping women climb the corporate ladder.

That men should likewise venture into the domestic world was only vaguely endorsed and articulated, centering on the demand that they do their fair share of the dishes. In 1983, when I was in my mid twenties, *Esquire* published a feature extolling the "vanishing

American housewife," picturing an example of that endangered species on her knees, smiling brightly, cleaning a toilet bowl. I remember feeling that only an idiot (or a sexist pig) would believe that women were doing something important in the home. Home was a place from which women were to be liberated.

The academic style of feminism that nurtured my generation—the baby boomers who are now pushing Maclaren double-strollers through supermarket aisles—did not celebrate the home or the homemaker and did not furnish the theoretical tools for us to grapple with our new roles. That women are drawn to traditional modes of parenting is documented in a recent Yankelovich poll that found 87 percent of women believe women are still the main family nurturers, even in two-paycheck families. Not only that, a majority of women, whether working or not, wish they were better parents. We are, many of us, still left high and dry by our political education.

We are torn in a way that is not only theoretical but intensely personal. At the same time that female public achievers earn accolades, many educated and hardworking professional women are unsure they don't long for a life that more closely approximates that of their homemaker mothers. "Having it all" seems to have been a pipe dream. According to a poll conducted in 2000 for Lifetime Television and the Center for Policy Alternatives, 59 percent of women with children under six said they were finding it harder to balance the demands of work and family than they did four years before, and 30 percent said it was "much harder."

My own inner maelstrom centered for a time on the view out my window of my across-the-street neighbor. The mother of three children under the age of seven, she had temporarily forsaken her career as a psychiatric social worker to raise her kids while her husband, a patent lawyer, worked hours that took him away from home from 7 to 7 every day as well as out of town on frequent business trips.

Sitting at my desk, in front of my computer, I watched her unload her groceries from her car in midmorning, two-year-old in tow, and was surprised by the sharp sense of envy I felt. She did the "mindless" chores I'd once been convinced to despise—put in her petunias on a cool spring afternoon, or sit on the swing in the back-yard as her kids raced around her when school let out. A milk-and-cookies mom, my friend was famous locally for her skill at creating elaborate sugar cookies for holidays, birthdays, block parties, and Super Bowl parties. Here was I, adhering to my professional "career path," spending days trying to produce rather than maintain, mornings at my desk rather than in the sale aisle at Stew Leonard's. Much as I told myself that my friend could choose her path and I could choose mine, I coveted her nest and the license she took to tend that nest.

My jealousy peaked one Indian summer weekday. I watched my perfect neighbor out on the grass, painting a cardboard packing container with red and white stripes to make a popcorn box Halloween costume for her eldest daughter. She stood in the delicious sunshine, performing her labor of love well in advance of the holiday, when I'd likely be scrounging at the last minute for wigs and makeup for my own daughter's costume. What most ate at me was that she had the time and peace of mind to create something memorable, by hand, that would be appreciated by her family—that might even become a perishable but nonetheless important "heirloom," to be reused as costume or fort or any number of other objects as her kids grew up. Bland assurances about "balancing" home and work don't provide much solace in day-to-day situations like this.

It sounds almost foolish today to admire a woman like my neighbor for this kind of effort. Even now, when there is an academic thrust toward teaching the contribution of women to American history, our inclination is to showcase the women who have achieved in the public sphere. We canonize the rare woman scientist or politician of the past or we pay tribute to those women who ventured out courageously to fight for the right to vote. We herald the Second World War's Rosie the Riveter for performing the gritty jobs soldiers left behind. This is all well and good. Little mention is made, however, of the work that ordinary women have always performed in the home, around and about the paid work they've done intermittently—unless you take into account the appreciation of right-wing zealots, who glorify homemakers as long as they remain properly subservient to head-of-household men. If many of us didn't respect our mothers for the worth of their domestic labor, it stands to reason we might lack respect for our sisters who choose to be what is now called a "full-time mom." Women who don't work outside the home often complain that people they meet at social events treat them as if they are invisible. It's discomfort with homemaking that causes the phenomenon: we can't accept that the labor of the home remains vital, even in the twenty-first century.

As a culture, today, we have devalued the work of the home, denied that it was work that ever mattered, and believed erroneously that willing it into nonexistence was possible and that women could take on jobs, whether full-time or part-time, and somehow still get it all done. If you add up all the hours, though, as economist Juliet Schorr does in *The Overworked American,* you see just how many more hours women are putting in than men between housework and paid work.

It's particularly distressing to see women dismiss the domestic arts as unimportant. Hunter College psychologist Virginia Valian has investigated the phenomenon of women's subtle bias against the achievements of women. "In almost every study I've reviewed," she states, "it's not only men who undervalue women. Women also do it." The denigration of the homemaker's role, then, may reflect the internalized sexism that some women have developed under a continual barrage of negativity, prejudice, and discrimination.

Because the work of the home has been deemed insignificant, we've been able, over the past fifty years, to walk away from it with an alacrity that's breathtaking. What is remarkable is how completely we've stripped ourselves of the skills, rituals, and allegiances that have sustained humankind since time immemorial. An age-old female craft tradition is threatened with extinction. Stitching a hem, making pie crust from memory, and countless other "quaint" and "trivial" domestic arts have now largely vanished from the cultural vocabulary. We've "disappeared" them. When we haven't abandoned them altogether, we've commodified them by giving them over to the marketplace, hobbified them in the manner of holiday craft kits, or celebrated their anachronism in "living history" exhibits. The domestic arts involved, which were centuries, sometimes millennia, in the making, are now undergoing their most substantial transformation ever.

Yet we can't seem to walk away from domesticity and feel sanguine about it. Americans' ambivalence toward homemaking and homemakers is captured perfectly in the public's love-hate response to the phenomenon of Martha Stewart. In the early 1980s, when Stewart was simply a successful food professional rather than a lightning rod for domestic angst, I attended a reception she catered. Her knitting-needle-thin steamed asparagus and other veggies spilling out of a boulder-sized hollow bread loaf were the talk of the hors d'oeuvres table, since at the time crudités were still a novelty. Martha was a sprite, dancing around and through her catering staff serfs. Not everyone liked her, but it didn't occur to anyone not to respect her. Since then, she's been dubbed the doyenne of domesticity, but she's equally domesticity's demon.

In her magazine, books, products, and television appearances, Stewart perpetuates an ideal of home that many Americans feel is unattainable, an expectation of homemaking people fear is unachievable. She represents all that we want to shove under the carpet or that we wonder whether we're ready to relinquish. She provokes every uncomfortable conflict we feel about home. I listened over dinner as a group of my peers ridiculed Stewart's recommendations on organizing a linen closet by labeling the shelves to match beds and sheet sets. "In my household, we never even fold our sheets!" said one woman. "Who has time? We just throw them on the shelf. Who does she think she is?"

Critics charge that the problem with Stewart is her hypocrisy, that she's too rich to have to mash her own potatoes, and that assessment may have some validity. America has idolized domestic poseurs before, however. In the 1920s, a company known as Washburn, Crosby and Company, which would eventually become General Mills, looking for a way to promote its then-unpopular bleached wheat flour, created a fictional ace homemaker named Betty Crocker. For years, the woman who performed this part responded to mail, published cookbooks, and hosted radio shows to which she would invite Hollywood stars to share culinary tips. That act never fazed anyone, but today a businesswoman representing domestic ideals is a painful rock of Fleur de Sel in the wound of our discomfort over our own domesticity or lack thereof.

The most venomous anti-Martha sentiment comes not from the elders or the youngers, who feel less conflict over how they approach keeping house. They're glad to get a good holiday gift-wrapping tip or lemonade recipe when they can. Instead, the noisiest Martha-bashers are the baby boomers, the cohort that's insecure, needled by unspoken doubt over whether hanging gingham curtains we've sewn by hand is a worthy investment of the precious few moments of free time we've managed to scrounge. (The average reader age of *Martha Stewart Living* is forty-one, while the average age of the e-customers for Martha by Mail online skews even younger, at thirty.) Easier to conclude domesticity's overrated and Martha's a dimwit or a dupe, and be done with it. The self-doubt lingers, though: *That was the world we left behind, didn't we? We were supposed to escape the home, weren't we? All that's not valuable, anyway. Is it?*

The reality is that Stewart's franchise has shored up crafts that would otherwise be a lot closer to extinction, and offered a vision for a contemporary domestic way of life. She articulated this aspect of her business on a segment of Charlie Rose after the multimillion-dollar initial public stock offering of her company in 1999: "I was serving a desire—not only mine, but every homemaker's desire—to elevate that job of homemaker. It was floundering, I think. And we all wanted to escape it, to get out of the house, to get that high-paying job and pay somebody else to do everything that we didn't think was really worthy of our attention. And all of a sudden I realized: It was terribly worthy of our attention."

It is time to honor and preserve the achievements of the women of the past, our female elders, grandmothers, great-grandmothers, the "Aunties of high repute," to use Harriet Beecher Stowe's beautiful phrase, the repositories of our collective wisdom. To do this, we must break through a cultural silence about homemaking and its value for everyone, including feminists, even today.

The poet Margaret Walker has written:

> My grandmothers are full of memories
> Smelling of soap and onions and wet clay
> With veins rolling roughly over quick hands
> They have many clean words to say,
> My grandmothers were strong.

It is time to celebrate the labor of those people, mainly women but sometimes men as well, who performed these jobs of caring over the centuries, and also to assert the dignity of those who continue in those labors today. This includes unraveling the tangle of guilt we in the baby boom generation feel over performing these tasks, or not performing them, or sharing them with the men in our lives.

I believe revaluing "women's work" is a feminist act. We need to find a way to celebrate the "vanishing housewife" without echoing the patronizing tone of the *Esquire* feature of the 1980s.

THERE IS A REASON beyond their monetary value that we pass heirlooms from one generation to the next. Families save the handcrafted products of their ancestors, along with the humble mass-produced objects (tables, chairs, chests, saucers, and plates) that evoke their day-to-day lives rather than the worldly accomplishments that might appear in an obituary. Endowed with the power to cross the barrier of death, family artifacts speak over a bridge from a distant time, different in so many ways, to the present, and to unite the two in a way that can't be measured or duplicated.

Robert Frost calls home "something you somehow haven't to deserve," a birthright, a gift, a thing with which we all (or almost all) come equipped. Because it is *of* ourselves, it is the place where we can most *be* ourselves. The Latin *lares* and *penates* are beneficent household *gods* but they have also come to refer to household *goods*, the treasured possessions of the home, as if divinity resides in the very chairs and rugs and tables with which we surround ourselves. I know this to be true, since my family eats at the same table around which my great-grandparents took their supper as newly-weds, and I find meaning in that at virtually every meal.

John Steinbeck describes the power of even the humblest family heirlooms in *The Grapes of Wrath* as the women of the Joad family struggle to decide which of their few belongings will fit on their encumbered wagon.

. . . the women sat among the doomed things, turning them over and looking past them and back. "This book, my father had it. He liked a book. *Pilgrim's Progress*. Used to read it. Got his name in it, right here. Why, here's his pipe—it still smells rank. And this picture—an angel. I looked at it before the first three children came—didn't seem to do much good. Think we could get this china dog in? Aunt Sadie brought it from the St. Louis Fair. See—it says right on it. No, I guess we can't take that. Here's a letter my brother wrote the day before he died. Here's an old-time hat. These feathers—I never got to use them. No, there isn't room. . . . How can we live without our lives? How will we know it's us without our past?"

The most beloved objects with which we surround ourselves are unfailingly domestic.

When my maternal grandmother's belongings were dispersed among my extended family, I was given some good furniture, along with mundane items, such as my grandmother's circa-1970s microwave. Perhaps the greatest treasure I inherited is a vintage, curved-glass breakfront that my grandparents purchased when it was already an antique and that holds a series of objects that are talismans of my family history.

Monetarily, an appraiser reported, these items have little worth, as most are chipped, mismatched, or simply not interesting to collectors. Yet these objects possess immeasurable power. On the lowest shelf is a broad china plate painted with pink roses and lilies of the valley on which my great-great-grandmother served cake. Above stands my great-grandmother's cut glass perfume bottle, along with six thumb's-height "fancy" chocolate cups and saucers, in pastels and gilt, that my great aunt won at a party. My grandparents' childhoods are represented, my grandfather's by his childhood marbles, rough and opaque, in a faded green cotton sack tied with common kitchen string, and my grandmother's by her tiny, tarnished silver baby cup. The breakfront stands in my bedroom, and these are the last things I see before falling asleep and the first upon waking each day. They are the sentinels of my past.

Equally remarkable are the stored handworked linens beneath my attic eaves. My great aunt, who produced much of this work, taught me to crochet when I was in grade school, and I held her in awe. Even as, growing up, I questioned the domesticity of my mother and the mothers of my friends, I had intimations that there were strengths inherent in the role of the homemaker, having spent summers in Tennessee with Auntie, who was a high school home economics teacher. Because she was a strong person, and because I watched her teach home economics as a science, in a cavernous lecture hall filled with long slate-topped lab tables, I suspected at some level that the work of the home could be a rigorous and respectable endeavor. The sheer longevity of the textiles impresses me, as does the knowledge that these items signify my family's past.

Historical restorations have become our national curio cabinets. From the isolated cottage maintained by the Daughters of the American Revolution they have evolved in the past half century into an institution that educates and entertains and a major destination along the family tourism trail. Visiting historic sites provides us with an infusion of the tradition we rarely possess today in our own homes, packaged in such a way that we can step in and step out without losing more than a beat in the breakneck pace at which we live. We can stop at the 7–Eleven to buy a Big Gulp and a microwaved hoagie on the way to observe open-hearth cooking techniques demonstrated by docents required to wear contact lenses because their eyeglasses would wreck the illusion of historical accuracy.

One popular historic site is the home of Washington Irving in Sleepy Hollow, New York, a rustic little cottage he called Sunnyside, with impossibly simple, charming rooms. His "snuggery" was as self-consciously constructed a home as a dwelling could be, improved upon continuously by this extremely sophisticated writer over the course of decades. Irving built Sunnyside to last. The imported tendrils of English climbing wisteria he planted at its stucco entrance load it down today practically to buckling, but 200 years after the vine took root it still thrives. When the railroad came through, cutting between his house and the Hudson River, Irving fumed—it ruined his bucolic vision of home. Today, when highways pierce many a historic property, a train seems quaint, but the contrast between past and present grates more harshly than ever.

The business of restorations has boomed in recent years as visitors throng to soak up a different way of life—to touch the objects of the past as I can touch my family's heirloom textiles. Virginia's Colonial Williamsburg, the grandfather of American historic sites, restored and rebuilt with Rockefeller money, admits well over a million visitors each year. Impeccably kept up and earnestly educational, its beautiful gardens may themselves be considered as historically accurate as any architectural restoration. The diarist Frances Trollope recorded her impressions of Virginia when she traveled the country in 1832, describing the profusion of flowers and butterflies she saw in Virginia—one of the few cases where the reality exceeded her expectations—and a semblance of that natural beauty still flourishes at this pristinely preserved village that was in its time essentially a getaway for colonial politicos. Trollope, a housewife turned fancy-goods proprietor, would have loved to shop at the restoration's dozen or so "authentic" stores, doubling as gift shops, as much as tourists do. Taking home a cone of sugar in blue paper or a muslin bonnet satisfies some of the longing to put a piece of this version of the past permanently in one's life once the weekend's over. (Similarly, in Gettysburg, Pennsylvania, recognized more for its battlefields than its fashions, a store called Miller's Bon

Marché furnishes shoppers with period ladies' and children's fashions and accessories. The owner, Beth Miller, uses her expertise in Civil War clothing to teach classes of women to sew ballgowns, cage crinolines, or a custom-fitted corset or quilted petticoat. The women who shop or study at this wonderful bazaar have discovered a way literally to wrap themselves in the past.)

At Williamsburg, interpreters try to pull visitors into the reality of a different time. Among the crowds in line for a lunch table at one of the site's tavern-restaurants, a bewigged, powdered, yellow-crinolined tavern keeper cruised the waiting families. "Are you learning housewifery?" she demanded of a ten-year-old girl with braids and a blue satin bomber jacket that read "West Virginia—Dance-Tap-Jazz." Eyes cast down, the quintessentially twenty-first century child shyly replied that, well, her mother was teaching her to cross-stitch and how to make her bed.

One of Williamsburg's most popular buildings is the Powell House, where schoolchildren participate in cookery at an open hearth or engage in other activities that would have transpired in the large, airy kitchen (though in summer, a Powell House cook-interpreter confided, the room gets uncomfortably toasty, over 150 degrees when the fire is blazing, just as it would have in the olden days). Kids accustomed to the digital manipulation of GameBoys relish pulling the seeds from cotton bolls or kneading bread dough. That a charred, spit-roasted ram's head—a gourmet colonial entrée—graces the middle of the table elegantly set for supper fazes them only a little.

Yet time travelers draw the line at too much reality. The fiery heat and the ram's head represent the limit past which this historic site's domestic "reality" cannot go. "We heard from our visitors constantly that they want to believe they are in the eighteenth century," says Laura Martinsen, a manager in the restoration's School Groups Services Department. "Which kind of makes us chuckle, because if we handed you a chamber pot and said, 'Wash that,' it would become a little too realistic for people. *Sorry, we can't treat that ear infection. Hope you heal, but you might die.* To some extent, people want a romanticized version."

Thus, although the interpreters who do the food preparation for the site also slaughter the animals raised on-site for cooking, they now perform the task behind the scenes. A few years back, a couple wandering the tidy, picturesque eighteenth century streets with their children stumbled upon a hog butchering on the lawn behind one of the taverns, and they didn't stick around for a discussion of how small fry in the olden days clamored for the pig's bladder, which served as an old-fashioned balloon. They filed a complaint asserting that their children were harmed by what they saw. "These days people will bring a lawsuit over anything," the Powell House interpreter told me. Now food historians demonstrate salting, lard rendering, and fresh pork cooking in a sanitized program called Hog to Ham, where the activities start after the hog has already become meat.

Plimoth Plantation, the living history museum in Plymouth, Massachusetts, has always placed a premium on creating "reality," warts and all. The site is up the hill from Plymouth harbor, away from the Styrofoam-packed lobster dinners served on its weathered wharf, away from the schoolteachers and students in a gaggle around the chip of Plymouth Rock that still remains after the plundering of centuries of tourists ("its very dust is shared as a relic," in the words of de Toqueville), up from the Plymouth Wax Museum with its faded dioramas and cheap weather effects, and conceptual light years from the cinnamon potpourri and engraved souvenir teaspoons displayed at the John Alden Gift Shoppe. At Plimoth Plantation, an obsession with authenticity borders on the neurotic, if only because the choice of what to enshrine sometimes appears arbitrary. From its inception in the mid-1960s, the living museum site has been cited for its refreshingly gritty—dirty, in actuality—presentation of the past. One historian wrote approvingly about the first years of the site that unlike other restorations, the staff at Plimoth "did not wear the black clothing often associated with our pilgrim ancestors. Women . . . who slaved over an open hearth, or men who labored in the fields, were not pristine at the end of the day. Rather, they looked, smelled and felt like they had been working hard." Salaried historical interpreters inhabit their roles for the entirety of the warm-weather season, arriving at their replica stone homes in the Pilgrim Village at dawn to take their spots before the hordes arrive. The staff—the Buckingham Guards of pilgrim history—don't break character, much as children try to get them to. John Alden is John Alden, not a college student on his way to the beach and a beer after working hours.

The women of Plimoth cook the family pottage over the sooty, stuffy hearths even in the blazing high noon of summer. Management encourages interpreters to eat what they cook. The blackened eel I saw on the sideboard in one house was someone's unfinished supper. As alien from our time and habits as some of the site appears, visitors find ways to identify with seventeenth century life. I listened to one tourist in shorts and sunglasses at the door of a rough-hewn pilgrim house sound out an aproned, bonneted interpreter on the cultivation of rosemary—"I've had so much trouble getting it to winter over in my perennial border back at home!"—and get some concrete advice, gardening tips transmitted from one century to another.

Philosopher John Locke said that children will retain more if they play themselves into learning. The people who run Plimoth Plantation try to make the place not only authentic but broadly appealing, offering children's birthday parties at which guests can dress like a pilgrim and play seventeenth century games. Many historic sites make efforts to teach children the ways of the past, but spanning the distance between centuries can be a challenge. At one eighteenth century farm restoration in my area, I heard a frustrated-sounding interpreter try to knock some sense of reality into a crowd of suburban elementary schoolchildren distracted by the highly exotic stench and flies of a working barnyard. "Leather is the skin of all these animals!" he yelled as they raced around holding their noses and swatting the backs of the free-ranging sheep. To many of these kids, leather simply materializes as shoes or belts or the seats of cars, and to discover otherwise constitutes a minor revelation.

An extensive foodways program at Plimoth invites adult visitors to dine on specialties re-created from period diaries and receipts by a skilled kitchen staff under the guidance of a culinary historian who explains each course as it is served. At one springtime lunch I attended, two dozen people delightedly chowed down on some rather tough brown bread, asparagus with orange sauce, a green "sallet," a fricassee of fish, and a roasted turkey. It struck me that living history is one of the few popular leisure activities that inherently honor the daily domestic labor—the cookery, sewing, household chores, and gardening—of the past. This dining table and the dusty streets outside harbored the last remaining evidence of our longstanding homeways, protecting them from the encroachment of the present, preserving the old ways as aboriginal tribes have found a way to preserve their culture by going ever deeper into the rain forest. The everyday is presumed here to be worthy of careful maintenance—and precious vacation time.

Americans' taste for historical restorations can be located to a large degree in their dissatisfaction with the current culture of domesticity. Writer Wytold Rybzynski maintains that, "Their nostalgia is not the result of an interest in archaeology, like some Victorian revivals, nor of a sympathy for a particular period, like Jeffersonian classicism. Nor is it a rejection of technology. People appreciate the benefits of central heating and electric lighting, but the rooms of a Colonial country home or a Georgian mansion—which had neither—continue to attract them, for they provide a measure of something that is absent from the modern interior. People turn to the past because they are looking for something that they do not find in the present—comfort and well-being."

Does appropriate nostalgia, nostalgia that is based on real concerns, mean we need to reject the technologies that have already been invented to lighten the domestic workload? Do we need to return to the Little House on the Prairie to find the comfort and well-being we crave? And could we tolerate the concomitant woodchopping, water hauling, and lye rendering? The answer for anyone except the most dedicated back-to-the-landers is probably *no*. More than 5,000 American families lined up to appear on the 2002 PBS series "Frontier House," which immersed its thoroughly modern participants in a careful semblance of the past's harsh realities. As viewers watched the series, though, the resolve of the experiment's "pioneers" wavered. The 1880s living environment was inspiring, but conditions were much more primitive than families had bargained for and way more difficult to adjust to. Somehow there's got to be a way of integrating the microwaves of today and the cornmeal mush of yesterday (actually, there is already, with microwave quick grits that take no more than five minutes, but the texture's lousy). We must discover how to progress without abandoning the richness of our domestic past.

Historical reenactors forge one way of doing this. Women can adopt historic personas in muslin and stays at weekend Civil War conventions, say, then return to their DSL lines and desk jobs on Monday. This approach works for some. To travel back and forth in time wouldn't seem totally satisfactory for the majority of Americans, however, if only because it requires a dedication to the craft and hobby of reenacting on weekends that many people believe have already become full enough, what with watching their kids play softball, running errands or mowing the lawn, or squeezing in a round of golf if they are lucky.

THE IDEA OF women's work, the domestic arts, the act of creating a safe and comfortable home environment, are concepts that today carry extreme intellectual and emotional freight.

Now I find myself in a predicament strangely similar to my mother's, deciding what value to place on the work of my own home, how to integrate that work with the rest of my life and with my personal identity. I need to resolve which homemaking skills, knowledge, and attitudes to hand down to my school-aged daughter. At mid-life, I seem to be the only person who brings home-baked goods to meetings where everyone else relies on store-bought. Somewhat to my chagrin, I recently won the pie-baking contest in my hometown.

Here is the paradox: as the organic tradition of homemaking declines, commercialized homemaking, homemaking as artifice, thrives mightily. The glue-gun craft explosion, the "Antiques Roadshow"–fueled antiques craze, the popularity of bread machines, *Victoria* magazine, Martha Stewart, the dominance of "country style" decorating all indicate there are some essential qualities of the home for which people hunger. The "voluntary simplicity" movement that originated in the early 1990s reflected Americans' concerns about overconsumption and overstress, suggesting the value of a way of life gone by. Pantries, the kind found in many a grandma's house, have once again become an integral part of new-home buyers' dream specs. Stores tout products reminiscent of a more home-oriented past: "nothing short of a spiritual guide" reads a holiday ad for a pot pie cookbook featured alongside Lincoln Logs and vintage martini shakers at Restoration Hardware. Other recent cookbooks have titles like *Back to the Table: The Reunion of Food and Table*, and *Recipes from Home* (whose recipes are based on dishes served at a popular Manhattan restaurant of the same name). Artificial, frozen, freeze-dried, and space-age foods are still multimillion-dollar businesses—from Tang in the 1960s to microwavable "butter-flavor" popcorn in the 1990s—but the hot trend is the return to old favorites. We're seeing a renaissance of such dishes as coleslaw, fried chicken, mashed potatoes, and spaghetti and meatballs. The fashion at restaurants and those home kitchens where cooking still takes place is firmly in the direction of regional cooking, authentic ingredients, and roots foods transformed into gourmet oddities, like a stone-ground grits soufflé with chanterelle and shiitake mushrooms.

Some traditions remain rock-solid: the popularity of the three best-selling women's service magazines—*Better Homes and Gardens, Family Circle,* and *Ladies' Home Journal*—remains as strong as ever, with a combined circulation of 17.1 million, nearly twice the combined circulation of *Time, Newsweek,* and *U.S. News & World Report.* In the bruising magazine market there is even room for the launch of a new magazine devoted to the humble home arts. *Real Simple* astonished industry forecasters by selling double the projected circulation of its debut issue, which featured articles on homemade ice cream, laundry tips, and easier ways to clean the bathroom. The hipper-than-thou *ReadyMade,* a California-based shelter magazine launched in winter 2002 that takes an alternative approach, with articles on how to craft homey accoutrements from everyday objects—a planter out of a shower curtain, a fruit bowl from a vinyl LP, and a meat-cart bed—demonstrates the appeal of domesticity refashioned for the dot-com generation.

Is the return to the home nothing but escapism? Should we celebrate the heroic farm wife who is now virtually extinct? Can we be glad that we have progressed to a mechanized age in which we reap the rewards of the traditional with a dwindling investment in home-making? There is a double bind that many of us endure but feel unable to resolve in a meaningful way: the tension between our public and private lives. We know deep within ourselves that home and hearth are important, but we feel guilty about acting (or not acting) on that knowledge. A stressed-out mother with a demanding job in commercial illustration told me recently with obvious relief that "we don't have to do it all because Martha will do it for us."

PEOPLE SEEM EAGER to relocate the hearth to someplace other than the heart of the home. The television is often described as the contemporary hearth, or the computer, or the workplace. In fact, the hearth can mean anything we feel strongly about. The dancer Maya Plisetskaya, for example, one of the greatest ballerinas of the last century, has described her entrance onto the Bolshoi stage: "I awaited my music, my cue with a shiver of joy, a feeling of incomparable happiness spreading throughout my body. Three more bars. Two more. One more. There. My music. I step out onto my stage. It was a familiar creature, a relative, an intimate partner. I spoke to it, thanked it. Every board, every crack I had mastered and danced on. The stage of the Bolshoi made me feel protected; it was a domestic hearth." If there is no actual hearth on which to base these metaphors, though, I don't know that we can survive. Successive iterations weaken the analogy: if everything can be a hearth, then nothing is.

Restoring respect for the home and its labors is something of a high-wire act, since to praise the homemaker is, for many people, to criticize the career woman. I suspect, though, that the successes of feminism are secure enough that we can begin to enlarge its scope. We have come far enough along the path of change to be able to stop and take stock, and perhaps retrieve a thing of great value that we have nearly left behind. As a feminist, I have no interest in downgrading the accomplishments of women in the worlds of law, science, sport, politics, or literature. In our rush to celebrate pioneers who have broken into worlds long regarded as male turf, however, we have overlooked a rich sphere of human endeavor.

The only way forward is for us as a society to relearn to value work in the home without falling into reactionary traps about "proper" roles for women and men. A new paradigm must rise out of a culture in total transformation, through the prevalence of divorce, two-career families, and a consumer culture dominated by powerful corporations. It's time for a reevaluation of the modern cultural landscape, the monotonous world of strip malls and chain restaurants. In the deracinated America of today it would seem there is, literally, no place like home.

We know something is lacking. We see the domestic void in myriad ways all around us, but we don't recognize what we could do to halt the destruction and hold on to traditions, make domesticity intrinsic to our lives rather than peripheral or fetishized or commodified. Can we establish what elements of homemaking people miss and desire? Can we determine ways we can hold on to these elements without finding ourselves mired once again in 1950s Pleasantville, with all the color leeched out of our lives?

Searching for a revitalized sense of home shouldn't be undertaken because it's good for you, the way it's good for you to eat your broccoli. We owe it to ourselves to live our lives fully, to reap the pleasures that present themselves to us as humans. Washing the kitchen windows might not readily appear to offer psychic fulfillment, but perhaps this is because we have forgotten what it means to live as agents of our own environment. We've given away much of the power over how we live in our most intimate daily life. We've come to believe that minding the hearth is a role of lesser value, and in part this is simply because any embodiment of that power has grown remote, unknown to most of us. We don't learn in school about any primordial strength in homemaking, starting with the domestic phenomenon that made civilization itself possible . . . Hestia's fire.

# CHAPTER 2

# Hestia's Fire

HUMAN BEINGS ARE HOMEBODIES. This remains an essential truth about us, despite the intrepid zeal of our trailblazing, our irremediable wanderlust, and our celebrated voyages of discovery. "Nothing is so sweet," wrote Sophocles over 2,000 years ago, "as to return from the sea and listen to the raindrops on the rooftops of home." What makes a person a pilgrim or voyager rather than a desperate refugee is the certainty that he can go home again.

How we feed ourselves, how we clean and groom ourselves, the ways in which we care for each other in our most intimate moments are all functions of the home. Domesticity is what sustains us in the deepest sense of the word. It remains the touchstone, the mooring ground, the still point around which our lives revolve. Divers have discovered 9,000-year-old hearths along with human bones in once-dry caves in an underground river system on the Yucatán peninsula. Even nomadic Bedouins honored the hearth, carrying their fire with them in camelskin bags. Home "is the place of peace; the shelter, not only from all injury, but from all terror, doubt and division," in the words of the nineteenth century social critic John Ruskin.

In the last half of the twentieth century, however, the realm of the home has undergone a transformation. Much has been written about the rootlessness, lack of community, and increasing isolation of modern life. Relatively unremarked, though, is our alienation from the ancient ideal and historical reality of home.

We have already experienced a fundamental change in all that is closest and, I would argue, most meaningful to us. What are the possibilities for the revival of a dying tradition—the organic tradition of homemaking, one that stretches back thousands of years? Can we stem the decline of the very idea of home and somehow reclaim it to improve our lives?

Part of the answer lies in the distant past, when a goddess protected the hearth and mortal women held the power of fire.

THE GREEK GODDESS HESTIA, guardian of the domestic hearth, was among the most honored of the Olympians. The eldest sister of Zeus, Apollo, Athena, and the others in the Greek pantheon, she is today the least known. It is worthwhile exploring the mystery and power she held for our ancestors, because what she represented for their civilization has bearing for us still.

Every home in Greece featured an altar to Hestia, a fire that burned continuously in the center of the open court in the very middle of the house, on its floor of close-packed dirt. It was here, over these sacred flames, that a family would roast sacrificial goats or lambs or burn their succulent-smelling fat to please the deities.

For the citizens of Greece, such rituals determined their very existence. Over Hestia's fire they staked the hope that their crops would flourish, that loved ones would recover from illness, that they would successfully wage war or woo a lover. The gods, in the ancients' cosmology, were patrons, resembling larger-than-life humans rather than any sort of Holy Father. What they did was make deals: an exchange of gifts in return for favors, a spiritual tit for tat. So as a version of prayer the Grecian people offered sacrifices.

For most deities, such as Apollo or Athena, monthly rituals or celebrations would suffice, but Hestia required them daily. Libations of sweet wine, Homer writes, must be poured to Hestia at the start and end of every meal, and she must receive her sacrificial due even before Zeus, her powerful younger brother.

In accord with her great power, shrines dedicated to her worship were consecrated throughout the city-states. It was the first act of the faithful, whether pledging gifts to the marquee-name Zeus, Apollo, Poseidon, or Athena: offer obeisance at Hestia's unassuming altar, where a hearth fire burned day and night. In a family of fiercely jealous deities she alone contrived to share the smoke of sacrifice with all the others. "Universal reverence is paid Hestia," writes Robert Graves, "not only as the mildest, most upright and most charitable of all the Olympians, but as having invented the art of building houses."

Alongside the Parthenon, records Plato, shoulder to shoulder with the temples of Zeus and of Nike Athene, burned the fire of Hestia. According to law, each new polity must erect the temples of these three Olympians before any others. When migrating to a new city, colonists carried fire from her main altar to light the new prytaneion, and a priestess would be appointed to make sure that the new fire never went cold. Because Hestia was considered the arbiter of social justice, the prytaneion in Athens served as the headquarters of the standing committee of the Senate, and the Senate House contained its own altar to the goddess. Judges pledged scrupulous fairness in her name.

Zeus the great father and Athena the warrior maiden may have seized the popular imagination with their savage and silly exploits, but Hestia alone enjoyed omnipresence. Simply put, every hearth on earth, whether in home or temple, was Hestia's altar. And her power lay simply in her presence—in the existence of the hearth fire. Unlike the other gods, she would engage in no competitions, quarrels, or conquests, take no lovers, and embark on no adventures. From the perspective of her worshippers, Hestia just . . . *was.*

Yet this very ubiquity seemed to work against her. Of all the Olympians she was perhaps the most obscure. Typically, the Temple of Hestia at Hermione in Southeast Argolis featured no image of the fire goddess, only the altar on which her acolytes performed their sacrifices. She was of great ritual importance but, perhaps because her powers of the hearth were so very integral to life, she remained nearly invisible. Brilliant marble likenesses of her sisters and brothers from that time still adorn the halls of the world's great museums, but Hestia was hardly anthropomorphized. From Greece, one of the greatest representational cultures in history, almost no contemporary images of Hestia have come down to us. The few times we see Hestia portrayed in art, her head remains veiled and her breasts modestly covered, while her bearing is stately and austere. The placid expression on her face does little to unravel the mystery of this most enigmatic goddess.

Zeus, wrote Homer, gave Hestia "a high honor instead of marriage, and she holds a place in the middle of the house and the richest share. In all the temples of the gods she has a portion of honor, and among mortals she holds first place among the goddesses." Some historians characterize her as the quintessential old maid, a Grecian virgin queen. Yet without the sacred flame of Hestia, without warmth, without cooking, there could be no continuation of the species itself. In fact, Hestia was the deity of fertility and of hospitality, the protector of orphans and of missing children. One rite to please Hestia required carrying a five-day-old child around the hearth to welcome it into the family. Perhaps Hestia had to remain a virgin to keep the home fires lit and make it possible for the sexual vitality of humans to flourish.

Hestia embodied not only the domestic hearth fire but the fiery center of the earth. The earth-core fire shared the name *omphalos* with the fire of the hearth, meaning embers banked over with soil to control their smoke while allowing heat to radiate. The ancient mythology was, of course, borne out thousands of years later by the scientific discovery that the earth's center is in fact composed of a molten mass. Hestia was deemed the middle of the universe as well, according to social psychologist Ginette Paris, the "central planet around which all the planets of the universe were coordinated."

The elemental power of Hestia has roots in preliterate cultures whose works of art speak silently of the worship of female deities, millennia before the birth of Christ.

From earliest times, fire and female divinity were one. The archaic image of the Great Goddess, common throughout the Eastern Mediterranean, depicts not a human image but again, long predating Hestia, an omphalos, a heap of burning charcoal covered with white ash. Leaf-shaped, heat-warped implements of clay and stone have been dug out of Cretan and Mycenaen shrines; archaeologists surmise they were used for tending the sacred fire. Millennia later, the symbolism of the smoldering charcoal heap remained. At Delphi, in the time of Hestia, an omphalos carved in limestone signified the center of the world and was inscribed with the name of Mother Earth.

Hestia's spiritual heritage also lies in Paleolithic images of charcoal and terra cotta. This goddess was "mistress of the home and hearth, protectress of the domestic fire," writes Z. A. Abramova, who published the official anthology of Upper Paleolithic artwork in the U.S.S.R., as well as "sovereign mistress of animals and especially of game animals."

Feminine power since ancient times clearly derived from fire, specifically the hearth fire that was synonymous with home. A woman's greatest power lay in domesticity, and it was gigantic. Women and men worshipped fire and they worshipped Woman, and the two were one and the same.

Other deities of antiquity seem to have less to do with fire than with sheer female authority. Figures of marble five thousand years old have been discovered on even the wildest, smallest windswept islands of the Aegean, places that are little more than a crag and a beach—smoothly polished sculptures that could be a beach pebble until you see the clearly delineated breasts and waist, improbably, mathematically precise, expertly worked marble sparely evoking the female form, with crossed arms, level shoulders, and a clearly scored pubic triangle. Though grave robbers sold many of these Bronze Age treasures, hundreds remain in perfect condition, revealing a primal elevation of Woman to Goddess, streamlined to those physical features that define the female form—arms, legs, belly, pubis, and breasts, and above the whole a wide-eyed, unflinching face, the face of an all-seeing, all-powerful deity.

Later, the supreme Minoan deities in the region appear to have been female. Deep within the darkened sanctuary of the Temple at Knossos, atop a ritual table, archaeologists uncovered an earthenware Snake Goddess, the household divinity who was long revered as the symbol of bountiful nature. With serpents—a fertility symbol that would reappear at least through the garden of Eden—encircling her outstretched arms, bared breasts, erect nipples, a majestic skirt, and stern countenance, this Lara Croft of goddesses would surely have inspired a somewhat timorous reverence.

By the time of the Trojan War, the Minoans had been decimated by violence and volcanic eruption, and the age of fertility worship had largely passed. Greek invaders sandbagged female divinity by marrying off the local goddesses to their male gods. Ultimately, Zeus—once a lowly weather god—grabbed the glory on Mount Olympus. But the elemental power of the hearth goddess, though less ostentatious than that of the other deities, never ceased. A sacred fire still defined the heart of the home.

The women of Greece maintained an essential tie to the goddess of the hearth, quite simply because the central fire of the home was her specific domain. A Greek burial plot beneath the Athenian Agora holds the skeleton of an 18-year-old woman whose feet are flexed in a manner archeologists believe would come only from squatting before a cooking fire. The hearth of the home—and every one, remember, represented Hestia—was a woman's responsibility, whether she lived in a room or a palace, whether her home had a dirt floor or stone mosaic, whether the walls were rubble and mud or wood, or the roof reeds and branches or curved red ceramic tiles. It was an associative chain, of women to hearth to Hestia, on which female power was based.

In the domestic fire the sacred and utilitarian meshed. Then as now, women cooked for their families, fitting in meal preparation among the jobs of spinning, weaving, and sewing cloth, grinding grain, and fetching water. On feast days, families invited friends over to roast a boar, then offer the smoke to the gods and divide the meat among the participants. The scraps on the altar would be left for the beggars.

The fire wasn't only for burning. In the center of the home's main room, the hearth was the still center around which all daily activity turned. As such, it was the major territory of women, who sat by its side to weave or spin. Even royal women—like Penelope— would weave while entertaining guests, thus enacting another sacred idea, hospitality, represented by Hestia. Here at the hearth-side women performed the crafts for which they were highly esteemed. Wool, a valuable commodity that figured in virtually all the clothing worn in classical Greece, could only exist through the carding, spinning, weaving, and sewing of women.

"It is reasonable that the essence of things be called Hestia," observed Socrates, according to Plato. It is only upon grasping the life-and-death meaning of the hearth in antiquity that Hestia's power comes clear. For subsistence and for religion—and in ancient minds the two were clearly intertwined—fire represented that without which humans could not live. The hearth fire embodied the Grecian godhead, the life force, and it was women who perpetuated it both spiritually and materially. Hestia's holy, nonintrusive essence transformed a house into a home. She was the most intimate and yet the most remote of deities.

Ubiquitous, therefore undervalued. Everywhere, therefore nowhere. Identified with women, therefore lost amid the busy hierarchies of men. Idolized, yet frequently taken for granted. Sound familiar? Hestia is my mother. She is all our mothers, laboring in obscurity while our Olympian fathers did the really important work, striding the world stage. Work in the home and the inherited female craft tradition, the warming hearth and the spirit of home, exist even today in suspended time, caught between accolade and oblivion. Perhaps we will recognize the sacred domestic realm as an absolute human necessity only when it vanishes.

Continues Robert Graves: "Her fire is so sacred, that if ever a hearth goes cold, either by accident or in token of mourning, it is immediately kindled afresh with the aid of a fire-wheel."

Is it too late to rekindle the flame of Hestia in our own time?

WORK IN THE domestic sphere can be a difficult subject to broach in twenty-first century America. Even the language that frames the debate presents problems. Talking about the labor of the home, I have faced objections to the word "homemaker." It's too old-fashioned, runs the typical reaction, too overloaded with negative associations. Yet the word is still widely used throughout middle America (in newspapers, for example, particularly in obituaries) in place of the out-of-favor "housewife" or Roseanne's over-the-top "domestic goddess."

Many baby boomers fall back on the self-description "stay-at-home mom," a term that omits reference to anything but the most socially acceptable aspect of this crucial function of life, caring for children. This is too narrow. There is more to homemaking than minding kids, as energy consuming and valuable as that function might be. Children normally leave the home for school around age five, if not earlier, but mothers continue to shoulder the responsibility for care of the home (and, usually, for the extended family) throughout their lives. Yet the rest of the work of maintaining a family and a home is ignored, minimized, dismissed as trivial, or seen as a series of products and services that can be purchased as needed: in any of these formulations, it is work that constitutes a necessary but unwanted burden.

We've fallen into the habit of viewing the work of our homes in a negative light. In the 1970s and 1980s, in a modern-day *Lysistrata*, women stormed out of the home, boycotting the work of the home until men took part. The work had been so long denigrated and marginalized, however, that men wanted no part of it. Why would anyone, male or female, join in the work of the household when that work is consistently deemed unfulfilling and is undervalued by most of society? And in fact men and women both have fled from housework as from contagion. Men's participation in housework peaked at ten hours per week in 1985 and has dropped slightly since then; women's participation has tumbled from twenty-nine hours per week in 1985 to fifteen hours per week today.

Yet a contradiction exists here: when people "take off work" to do the job of maintaining a family and home, they find something in that activity that is gratifying and important. Witness the numbers of women (and men) who would love to cut their work schedules back to part-time in order to spend more time at home. Surely the work of our homes is as critical to our survival as the work accomplished by any high-priced attorney, corporate mogul, or politician. Yet rarely do we hear this truth acknowledged in the culture at large, because it may sound reactionary, or it may trap women or set them back, or because in our economy we cannot figure out the value of the work of the home in terms of dollars and cents. In this day and age, we're not expected to honor homemaking. All around us, though, are hints that we long for and cherish and want to preserve this part of our cultural life, even to return it to the center of our psychic world as it was in the time of Hestia. The Greek word for hearth means "focus." We have lost our focus, and we yearn to get it back.

NO ADEQUATE TERMINOLOGY exists to describe the intense, imaginative, and varied labor people do in the home, and so it goes unremarked, even by homemakers themselves. "Women have had the power of naming stolen from us," said Mary Daly, the outspoken feminist theologian. "We have not been free to use our own power to name ourselves, the world, or God." Betty Friedan called the phenomenon she wrote about "the problem that has no name," but many of the tasks that comprise homemaking consist of work with no name. "Housework gets noticed only when it's not done," says Gloria Steinem. Too often, work in the home exists in a twilight zone, beyond the pale of language.

Housekeeping. Homemaking. Stay-at-home wife. All these terms are too passive, too narrow. For a time, "the feminine mystique" entered the breach, and it resonated with women of a certain generation and class. It also had an impressive pedigree: Simone de Beauvoir had critiqued the state of the housewife's mind as "a state of distraction and mental vacancy." The housewife, she intoned, "makes nothing, simply perpetuates the present." Before her, nineteenth century suffragist Lucy Stone, purportedly the first American woman to keep her surname after marriage, enunciated a similar idea, declaring, "I know not what you believe of God, but I believe He gave yearnings and longings to be filled, and that He did not mean all our time should be devoted to feeding and clothing the body." We lack a contemporary term that respects rather than disparages the person who keeps house.

Domesticity belongs to "the dimension of human existence known as tacit," as writer Kathryn Allen Rabuzzi puts it in her book *The Sacred and the Feminine: Toward a Theology of Housework*. In other words, it is taken for granted, invisible, although it forms the foundation of everything of value that is explicit. Artists and writers derive inspiration from domesticity; they make the implicit explicit, which is the thrill of art. So we recognize and value the picture poet Donald Hall draws of a woman kneeling to sew—

> *snip snip in the church of scraps,*
> *tissue like moth's wings,*
> *pins in the cushion of her mouth,*
> *basting and hemming*
> *until it stands up like a person*
> *made out of whole cloth*

—even though our day-to-day appreciation of the craft of sewing has significantly dimmed.

Linguist Suzette Haden Elgin has argued that it is precisely because there is no way to talk about housework in everyday discourse that it has become devalued. She asserts that there will never come a time when the work of the home can emerge as a positive concept from the silence surrounding it.

Marjorie DeVault is one of the few sociologists addressing the question of how to capture this elusive role of the home, how to speak of the important tasks of domesticity. In *Feeding the Family: The Social Organization of Caring as Gendered Work*, she talks about the element of caring as "knowledge of the individual," in contrast to the anonymous, mechanized, flattened experience that used to be the punishment of convicts but is now accepted by almost all as the way we must live (aside from "special occasions," such as birthdays and holidays). Caring, says DeVault, is an act of will rather than an expression of morality or virtue.

Historians narrate the public accomplishments, the wars, the larger deeds of the world. The achievement of those who work in the home has not traditionally been described, an indicator of its perceived value. When we assess the value of this work now, however, we can see that although the average homemaker makes no sweeping laws and argues no court cases, she wields inestimable influence within the domestic domain. "There is nothing stronger in the world than gentleness," said the Chinese writer Han Suyin. I was moved by the regretful tone of a man I spoke with as he remembered a woman he had married young and long since divorced: "She was the best wife-cook of her generation." It may be undervalued and uncompensated, but domestic skills are still essential to the quality of our everyday lives.

One way to see homemaking is as a composite of various elements: the tradition of caring for people in the household is one, as is Robert Frost's definition of home as sanctuary—"the place where, when you have to go there,/They have to take you in." Home means maintaining the handmade against corporate encroachment. And, in helping individuals sustain those habits and tastes and traditions that matter the most, homemaking can accurately be described by the evocative phrase of nineteenth century domestic authority Lydia Maria Child as "the art of gathering up the fragments so that nothing is lost." Anthropologists write of the "kinship web," the extended family for which American women, as part of their domestic function, take responsibility for maintaining, sending cards, watering plants, taking care of ill relatives, making, buying, and sending gifts, visiting—staying connected. Women maintain and build relationships, and sometimes salvage them. This is all part of the domestic work that still exists and that strengthens the moral fiber of our world.

For the purposes of this discussion, I propose the term "homeways" to describe those traditions that families or individuals preserve and also the domestic life of a larger clan, culture, or country. Celebrating our homeways may require a vast change in the way we live, a vast shift from traditional roles rather than locking women into the domestic role of the past. Women are working outside the home as well as within it, and this is as it should be. The work of the home continues, though, so we will have to enlarge our idea of who will perform this invaluable labor. If men share a reverence for home and hearth, they may be more likely to tend it.

WHEN TRAGEDY STRIKES, the need for enduring home traditions becomes suddenly obvious. Some experts say the reason we turn to what we term "comfort foods" in difficult times is that they are quick, easy, and something unnecessary to think about, because we need to shut down additional sources of stress, even the question of what to prepare for dinner. It's more than that, however. Upon a death we bring homemade casseroles or soup, not deli potato salad from the supermarket. When we are unhappy personally or worried about world events, we crave slices of homemade apple pie rather than McDonald's apple pie in a cardboard packet, because we need the solace of knowing that we are cared for, and that sensation only comes with home-prepared food—even if we ourselves prepare it. In late November 2001 the American Institute for Cancer Research released study findings that due to "stress, grief and anxiety" after September 11, almost 20 percent of the U.S. population—56 million people—had reverted to eating the comfort foods associated with childhood. That's healthy self-love, self-nurturing, an ability the lack of which sometimes leads to desperate measures. The decline of cooking knowledge and skills doesn't bode well for our survival in future times of need. Asked in an interview with a *New York Times* reporter about the possibility of human life after an apocalypse, Tom Wolfe commented astutely that "only the grand-mas will know how to survive."

Nothing brings back people from the grave. In times of war, want, or social upheaval, however, our homeways console with their immediacy. Uncertainty and fear cause us to crave the foods of our childhood, which fulfill our need for a simple, good thing. Psychologists note also that the family ritual of eating dinner together serves as an important tool for restoring a sense of nor-mality. Making something by hand suddenly surges in appeal: "Peo-ple want to sew, create and get back to basics," said Judi Appel, the owner of a fabric store in Morro Bay, California, who saw an influx of customers in the fall of 2001. Objects that are handmade denote caring as well as physical warmth, which is why, despite the avail-ability of mass-produced blankets, knitters contribute long hours of labor to produce afghans for children with AIDS. It is why, in the rescue effort immediately following the terrorist attack on the World Trade Center, one baker's offer of a dozen servings of apple brown betty seemed to overshadow the breathing masks and other vital supplies being distributed at the same time.

BENEATH ITS BENIGN SURFACE, the decline of domesticity is a subject with complex and significant economic and political impli-cations, a reflection of changing values that are sending our society in a direction we may belatedly discover we don't want to go. Another Greek writer, Euripides, captured the anguish of the pos-sible loss that lies ahead. "No other sorrow," he wrote, "can com-pare with the sorrow of leaving home."

We may already be halfway there. Consider the contention of sociologist Arlie Hochschild in her book *The Time Bind: When Work Becomes Home & Home Becomes Work,* that both men and women are finding an emotional solace at the office that has in the past come from domestic rituals. She argues that parents are increasingly rejecting the uncertainties and quotidian responsibilities of daily child care. The real meaning in people's lives has gradually been relocated to their jobs, where men and women actually interact with people much more frequently than they do at home, where the most common shared activity is watching television. At the office, people are more likely to accomplish work that is assigned meaning and importance by society as a whole.

Hochschild describes a growing new "time industry" that offers goods and services that allow working parents to save time. These offerings are "being developed to extract smaller and smaller bits of time and effort from family life and return them to the family—for a price—as ready-made goods and services." Some of these, she notes, "replace the practical activities of a 1950s housewife."

In some parts of the country, for example, a parent can phone in a dinner order to a child's day care center in the morning and in the evening pick up both the child and the ready-for-the-oven meal. The Homework Club, an after-school program in my community, offers this service, and I've heard people comment what a help it is in their busy lives. One day care center Hochschild visited offers a dry-cleaning service; others arrange transportation to children's swimming lessons.

Proliferating personal service companies will, for a price ($25 or more per hour), bring a child's forgotten homework to school, water houseplants, pick up a cat at the airport, arrange dental appointments, even set up play dates for your child. "Rent-a-Husband" enterprises schedule a handyman to fix a broken toilet or leaky roof. Hochschild writes of a 1-800 telephone service available in some cities called "Grandma Please!" that puts kid callers in touch with "an adult who has time to talk with them, sing to them, or help them with their homework."

At the heart of contemporary domesticity is a paradox. On the one hand, what I call homeways, the organic traditions of home-making, are dying, victims of a social disconnection of truly historic dimensions. As a result, frequently no household domestic author-ity is present to convey the essential teachings of the old traditions. It is a very different thing to learn how to bake bread from your mother rather than learn it in a bread-making class at the local adult education establishment or from a cable television show or a book. We've pushed homemaking as a concept out of our lives. People still undertake the role of homemaker because the work of the home, of course, still exists. Apart from organizing the con-sumption of the home, though, many of us today, women and men both, have only a generalized, amorphous idea of what homemak-ing means.

John Ruskin continued his assessment of home with a warning and a promise. "So far as the anxieties of the outer life penetrate into it, and the inconsistently minded, unknown, unloved or hos-tile society of the outer world is allowed by either husband or wife to cross the threshold it ceases to be a home; it is then only a part of the outer world which you have roofed over and lighted fire in. But so far as it is a sacred place, a vestal temple, a temple of the hearth watched over by the household gods . . . so far it vindicates the name and fulfills the praise of home."

When we dismiss the spirit and the substance from our domes-tic lives, when we admit the commercial to the exclusion of almost any other thing—when we flick a switch to bring up the gas jets in our hearth's imitation woodpile rather than building each fire anew with cut logs and kindling—it may only gradually become clear that something has gone wrong, something has gone missing from our lives. By then, that specific "something," and the means for reclaiming it, may lie too far in our past for us to retrieve. We will have allowed the skills of creating a home to drift away from us, jettisoned in the hectic rush of our lives. We will fail to recognize that the loss of our homeways portends the death of the home itself, and that with the home dies something of the human soul. The danger is that, as a culture, we may wake all too soon to find that home is a place we've inadvertently misplaced.

# CHAPTER 3

# Domestic Saints

MY HOUSE IS A DISASTER AREA. This is one of the most frequent conversational gambits in the contemporary female idiom. I can relate. Housework, in my house, ranks pretty low. Cloudy windows stay smudged, dirty clothes wait to be washed, and clean clothes wait to be folded. Dog hair forms nests in the corners of the living room. Conflicts over domestic priorities eat at me. Should I take out the Dustbuster? Wield the Ty-D-Bol? My ten-year-old is yelling to me—shouldn't my priority be to play with her? Or should I sit down at the computer to do my "real" work? Or start a roast? Or fix the chipped ceramic floor tile in the kitchen? Dilemmas, dilemmas. Usually the will not to clean wins out.

"'House' is being 'cleaned,'" said Emily Dickinson. "I prefer pestilence." Dickinson's century-old complaint still captures the view of most Americans, as housework's popularity plummets. We now spend an average of twelve fewer hours a week on cleaning our homes than we did in 1960, according to the 1999 Americans' Use of Time project at the University of Maryland. Cooking, needlework, and sewing still earn a modicum of respect as domestic arts, but the foulness of housework has become a truism and even a popular symbol for anything Americans despise. A movie a few years back showed a woman seething over a failed romance; as an expression of her rage, she scrubs the toilet with the tee shirt the cad left behind. The gritty, grimy, greasy chores, the ones that blow dust up your nose and shove filth under your fingernails, are universally avoided. We don't want to mop the floor because we don't want to dirty our hands, but also because the act reeks of the menial. We have better things to do, we say, meaning: We *ourselves* are better.

Few people admit they enjoy any aspect of housework, but neither do we like to live like slobs. Too much mess constitutes a marker of degradation. A disordered home can reflect a life gone awry. I remember, years ago, passing the open door of two furiously unhappy brothers who occupied the ground floor apartment of a building where I lived. As I hurried past a stench poured out, along with their accusatory tirades, and I could glimpse inside a hovel, dark and rank, with objects scattered here and there, an environment that seemed perfectly to mirror the minds of these men. Teenagers and geniuses may live in squalor, but for the rest of us, some version of order and cleanliness is the acceptable way of life.

The question, of course, is who will create this sense of order within the home. For centuries, it was presumed that women would act as the guardians of household order, performing the array of jobs we now term housework—cleaning, scrubbing, dusting, sweeping, mopping, and washing. Today, the dignity associated with keeping house since antiquity has all but faded away. Cutting across age, cultural, class, and ethnic lines is the conviction that its undignified labor is something in which no one with any choice in the matter would engage. Though we appreciate the results, a pleasant environment in which to live appears more a trivial grace note than essential to life itself. Memory is short. Only by imagining ourselves in the past can we understand a culture for which the labor of the home had a function so radically different than it does today.

*Eighteenth century New England, ten miles south of Boston. You
wake alone in the November night to hear the wail of your youngest
child. Your husband has gone to trade in the city and won't return for
weeks. The night is black. A chilly rain patters on the leaves outside, and
no moon or stars have come out to brighten the sooty sky. Street lamps
have not yet been invented, and your candle has guttered. When you
hold the crying baby, her flesh burns with fever.*

*You know you must find a cloth and soak it in cold water to bathe her
body and bring down the fever. But to do that, you need light—and the
inside of your house is perfectly dark. Matches don't exist. You grope for
the tinderbox on the floor beside you, strike the steel against the flint. A
tiny spark fizzles. The baby whimpers. Keep doing it while rocking the
cradle with your foot. . . . Finally, a flame . . . hold the burning splinter
ever so carefully, and now you can light the lamp. It's the best you can
afford, a simple teacup half-filled with melted grease and a paper wick,
but casts light enough so you can care for your child through the night.
She'll survive until dawn, when you can go find help.*

Creating light in the pitch black of a cold autumn night wasn't
an amenity, it meant life or death. And it was the job, often, of
women. Today, if my child is feverish at midnight I flick the light
switch to find the Tylenol; at worst I find the number of the pediatrician and place a phone call. Rummaging through drawers to find
safety matches and candle stubs during a blackout means excitement, not terror. A lightless emergency is not without damaging
consequences, but for many people it holds a certain magic, the
way a blizzard raging outside the windows can bind a family in a
snug warm home closer. It creates an intimacy forged out of need
that is not deathly. A lack of light today gives only a taste of what
the world was like before electricity, before gas, before kerosene
lamps, when the world relied upon candles lit by tinderboxes or
fires lit by flint or started, as in Hestia's time, by an ember carefully
transported from a neighbor's hearth.

Through the middle of the nineteenth century a central fire dominated every household, no matter if its occupants were rich or poor, urban or rural, if they lived in the forest or the village, the desert or tundra. Without the hearth, there would be no heat, light, or cooking, no gathering place, no area for drying clothes. Though fire was necessary, a fireplace was not through much of history; in fact, it was invented only in the Middle Ages. Until then the hearth would be laid directly on the floor, in a circle of stones pulled together over a mat of chalk or sand.

Housewives played a crucial role not only in lighting the household fire but in stoking it, orchestrating the fire or fires on the hearth, and adjusting the flames for the light and heat necessary to enable a household to eat and not to freeze, making sure the dwelling wasn't burned down in the process. Over thousands of years, families changed the way they lived in some ways but this is one area that did not change until quite recently: how energy was produced and consumed, and who was responsible for managing it. Until about 1850, the woman of any given household bore the responsibility for making the fire that warmed the family and cooked its food. She brought into being the light that was necessary for emergencies. The housewife's job has always in essence been to keep a household safe, warm, and fed.

Handling fire and fuel, making heat and light, constituted only a few of the everyday responsibilities of the average housewife for thousands of years, until technology advanced enough in the mid-1800s for large companies to produce fuel as an affordable commodity. Until that time, housework was even more crucial than bringing in meat or crops to eat. It was a specialized function, less a series of chores than a skilled enterprise.

Creating light was a part of this. Women stirred the huge vats to render tallow from hogs or deer or moose or bear for candles, then engaged in the time-consuming work of holding sticks hung with wicks over the highly flammable melt before hanging them to cool. In colonial America women held candle-dippings that, like quilting bees, could ease the work with conversation but wouldn't alleviate the tedium of the job, not to mention its odors. Only the wealthy could afford sweet-smelling beeswax. Tallow was the rule, but some households couldn't even afford that and had to make do with firing up turpentine-soaked pine knots or rags soaked in grease.

Providing fodder for the hearth often fell to the housewife as well. Men might cut wood but women would drag it home. If wood was in short supply, as was the case in much of Europe after the Middle Ages, other sources of fuel needed carrying. Households burned whatever was available: peat or heather, straw, thistles, rushes, even seaweed or horse dung. Men would cut and stack the peat, then women would dry blocks in the sun and restack them— and then help haul them home on their backs. Easier to obtain than peat, coal presented different problems, as it was difficult to coax into life and required extensive cleanup of everything it touched. As late as the start of the twentieth century, women in the British Isles toted wood or pine cones on their backs from forests miles from home, with children clinging to their skirts all the while. A traveler described a woman who tied her wood into a barrel-shaped bundle in order to roll it more easily the two miles to her home.

We've come far from women's ancient connection with fire. On camping trips, which revisit centuries-old practices of living closer to nature, we gather around a fire in the darkness and make our own entertainment, singing familiar songs rather than popping in a CD. We eat meat and grain roasted over burning embers—in our case not whole joints and pottage but ground beef and corn on the cob. We might bring our modern idea of home with us when we camp (pillows, air mattresses, sometimes our cars), but we bring an ancient idea of home, too, one whose savor derives from the collective memory of a distant time when life was simpler, fewer ingredients were available, central heating didn't exist, and artificial light had not yet been invented, so the blazing campfire found its reflection in the more vivid light of stars and moon. The intimacy fostered in this setting compensates for the discomfort felt by some modern campers over insects, a hard sleeping surface, no flush toilets or hot water, and the shivery night air.

We've preserved this throwback to antiquity with revisions. One alteration is that women, once the keepers of the hearth, now most often take charge of setting the picnic table rather than building the fire. As many responsibilities as women still shoulder in the kitchen, mastering open flames for cooking is not frequently one of them. The idea in fact is generally accepted that women shrink from even starting up a fire. At backyard cookouts men talk shop around the grill, debating the merits of variously flavored wood chips, how much coal should be put in the funnel, how gray the briquettes should be before you put on the meat, how much and when and whether it's advisable to use lighter fluid. In the meantime, women toss the salad.

It was not until I turned 40 that I approached the grill. I discovered that managing charcoal flames was in some ways easier than following a recipe at the kitchen stove. It required only a match, charcoal, some crumpled newspaper or kindling. There was no special strength required. Even if I scorched a potholder, the job wasn't particularly dangerous. All that had kept me from owning the cooking fire until then had been 150 years of societal habit. And that, when compensated for by the satisfaction of making fire, of reclaiming a skill that was women's from time immemorial, was not at all difficult to break.

☙

AS MUCH AN ART as a science, housewifery through the ages depended on combinations of substances: eight parts of one substance to one of another, say, to blend a paste to polish silver. It took creativity to assemble a pleasant environment from few material possessions. Art plus science produced magic in the cold winter dusk, when social life would end with the setting sun unless someone managed to keep the embers burning. The glow of a fire or lamp or candle reduced human isolation in the little waking time people had outside of work; it allowed for domestic intimacy, for storytelling, singing, games, and conversation.

Even laundry, which today we consider the epitome of mindlessness, required detailed knowledge and imagination. Generations of women fine-tuned its secret formulas and passed them down for thousands of years. Think of keeping fabric clean when the living environment was much dirtier than ours and when cloth was scarce and required costly materials and intensive, complicated labor to produce. Clothes were not easily replaceable. That fact held true not only in some creaky distant dark age but up until the 1800s, for the majority of households. When we imagine homemakers doing the wash, we think of Lucille Ball mugging over a bubbling washing machine, but our memory spans only a fraction of housekeeping history. Cleaning clothes that must last years and remain durable took dedication, hard work, and expertise. The clothes in one English country village at the end of the nineteenth century, according to Flora Thompson, "were worn and altered and dyed and turned and ultimately patched and darned as long as the threads hung together." Today, we breezily purchase laundry soap at the supermarket. In earlier times it could be scarce to buy or require heavy work to produce. Sewing clothes and mending them can also be considered nothing but skilled labor up through the end of the 1800s in most of the United States, even longer in some rural pockets.

The intricate implements of housewifery over the ages put our Rubbermaid tubs and Swiffer WetJet mops to shame. Successful housekeeping required a professional panoply of cleaning products. Of those employed before the twentieth century, we'd recognize few today, with the possible exception of linseed oil and borax. Before Chore Boy, people used sand to scour cooking pots. A trimmed goose wing made an effective duster for reaching into tight corners. The housewife's arsenal at one time included such items as camstone, rottenstone, Spanish whiting, blacklead, sweet oil, ox-gall, Fuller's earth, wood ash, emery cloth, or glass paper. In ensuring cleanliness, she ensured safety, which ensured life itself. Housekeeping equaled safekeeping. To maintain even a minimum standard of cleanliness, housewives had to make heroic efforts. Disease ranked higher among their concerns than comfort, as with cooking and food-borne illness. And all this vital work was performed by hand until the advent of mechanized cleaning aids.

Irons held considerably more importance in pre–drip-dry eras, especially when wash was wrung in the appropriately termed "mangle." They required skill to use, not to mention strength. Flat irons, which drew heat from the stove top, had the shape of those we know but weighed up to fifteen pounds and were known as "sad irons," their name derived from the ancient word for heavy or dense. The array of the tools used reflected the complexity of the task. Box irons were fitted with a heated slug, others hot coals. One type smoothed ribbons, another ruffles. You could thread fabric through a goffering iron and go on to use a crimping, egg, or polishing iron. All of this precision and specificity disappeared with the introduction of the electric iron, as welcome as it was.

That the skill that goes into housework has historically been underestimated makes a certain degree of sense. How can we fully appreciate the components of jobs that are by nature ephemeral?

Mop the floor and the family tracks in mud. Detach the cobwebs from the room's upper corners, the spiders soon return. Wash and dry and iron and fold clothes, and they will inevitably become dirty or stained, and you'll do it all over again.

Sewing or weaving or needlework, cooking and baking and canning earn at least a modicum of glory. Artfully prepared food gives pleasure before it is swallowed, and beautifully woven cloth is admired before it tears. Neither deteriorates so quickly, so invisibly, so forgettably, as the scutwork of the home. Like Hestia, who was worshipped and yet taken for granted, the housewife of ages since has been a powerful phantom. As with ancient Greece, when few myths attended the hearth goddess, in the centuries since we have seen few stories emerge from the work of the home to illuminate that labor or to keep it in our mind's eye as an act worthy of respect.

We feel about housework, the labor of women, something like the way an infant views its mother. The bodily distinction between child and mother is not one the child perceives for some time, primarily because the mother provides so many of the baby's needs, beginning with nourishment and the vital environment of the womb. When the mother breathes, the child breathes. Once in the world, the child doesn't see how essential the mother is to her life, of course. She takes her totally for granted. So it has been over history with the housewife, whose crucial but undocumented labors are so close to us as to be almost totally overlooked.

Housework's basic components remained unchanged for thousands of years. Housewives chopped and hauled wood. They carried water and laid fires. They scrubbed cookware and crockery, swept and dusted, emptied chamberpots. They whitewashed walls. And all these jobs went alongside the cooking, the spinning, working in the fields, tending livestock, caring for children, sewing and mending clothing, and nursing the sick. These jobs remained the same because no labor-saving devices or electricity would develop until late in the nineteenth century, and even then the new amenities extended primarily to the affluent.

Throughout the ages, all over the world, in every sector of society, the day-to-day work of the home has played a central role in how families live and in fact whether family members lived or died. The pivot around which the household turned was the homemaker. The particulars of her job varied from era to era, but the person who performed them was essential.

"A woman has it not in her power to make herself a beauty or a wit; that is the gift of Heaven; but every woman has it in her power to be a good housewife," observed Hannah Robertson in a 1767 British manual called *Young Ladies School of Arts.* Robertson's statement, so foreign to contemporary ears, had a distinctly different flavor when it was written. At that time it was no contradiction to link power and housewifery in the same phrase. In the past half-century, critics have deemed housework degrading and housewives duped. Feminist Kate Millett wrote in her best-selling 1970 polemic *Sexual Politics,* "Many women do not recognize themselves as discriminated against. No better proof could be found of the totality of their conditioning." With perspective, it seems clear that power comes in a kaleidoscope of forms, including that of the archetypal housewife, whose strength sprang from the hearth and who applied her power to a profession that required substantial physical and intellectual prowess.

The current lack of cultural memory regarding women's historic domestic strength has almost certainly colored perceptions about female competence in non-domestic arenas. Perhaps one reason we employ a finite imagination regarding women's capabilities is because we have in our era so infrequently seen women control the elements of fire and water. If it had been recognized how diligently women labored in the home for thousands of years, how inventive, how courageous housewives had to be, not to mention how central their work was to a household's survival, it might not have been so difficult for women to overcome contemporary prejudices in order to break into comparably powerful jobs outside the home. If a woman can keep the all-important home fires burning—keep her people alive and fed and safe—surely she can do anything she sets her mind to.

Only in revisiting the labor of the home throughout past eras can we begin to appreciate its value. What did home look like in the centuries we've forgotten, in times when a woman's strength and power were largely derived from the hearth, whose functions made the difference between life and death? What can we learn from those periods in history when housewives were respected for their ability to carve out a home from the harshest of conditions, when it was woman's particular province to ensure the basics of heat and light and water?

CHILDREN UNDERSTAND the importance of housework from close observation and believe women to be strong as a result of engaging in work that matters—holding them, or feeding them, or keeping the monsters at bay, as well as doing laundry or washing floors or the bathtub. That assessment only changes later, after they see society exclusively validate work outside the home. When as a child I visited my father in his office one afternoon and saw his desk with all the papers and manila folders laid out, a handful of sharpened pencils in the pencil holder, I was mystified. "Where are your broom and mop?" I demanded. I was convinced they were stored in a closet somewhere in the office, waiting for him to take them out and put them to good use. In my cosmology, the only work that existed was the important work of my mother.

Children's perspective is also shaped by exposure to stories, including fairy tales and folktales and those of writers before the twentieth century. Despite the omnipresence of television and movies, most kids still inherit these touchstones of our worldly understanding.

Lenin said, "There are elements of reality in every folktale." The medieval period wasn't a fairy tale, even for the kings and queens who lived in extravagant castles. Yet the stories that originated then say much about the lives of real people in that period. Specifically, in fairy tales as much as the somewhat threadbare history of real women lies the repository of the early housewife's strength. We learn it in stories, then we leave it. But just because we may not recall a time when the woman of the house played a central, crucial part in the life of the culture doesn't mean it never existed. I think we need to relearn these truths to begin to reclaim domesticity and its pleasures.

The fables of the Grimm brothers have had a lasting impact from the time they were told around the fire, through their publication in 1812, to now. Charles Dickens, born the year of their publication, described Little Red Riding Hood as "my first love." Child psychologists like Bruno Bettelheim have interpreted the tales, as have ideologues such as those that led Germany's Third Reich, which propagandized Little Red Riding Hood as a representation of the pure German people saved from a vicious Jewish wolf. Since the 1970s, some critics have even taken the Grimms to task for their purportedly misogynist sensibility.

Out of the tales emerges a portrait of a vastly different world from our own. These were oral narratives passed down in the same way as Homer's *Odyssey;* the Grimms, like Homer, behaved as their scribe. Many date from an ancient French tradition called the *veillée*, about which historian Robert Darnton cites a description dating to 1547: it was "an evening fireside gathering, where men repaired tools and women sewed while listening to stories that would be recorded by folklorists three hundred years later and were already centuries old."

Even the genesis of the first published collection of fairy tales, which introduced Cinderella, Sleeping Beauty, Red Riding Hood, and Puss in Boots to a literate upper class—by Charles Perrault, in 1687 France—bespeaks the social mores of the day. The book was titled simply *Stories* but came to be known as Tales of Mother Goose, and the frontispiece showed an old peasant woman telling stories to a clutch of young children in front of a roaring fire. The name Mother Goose, or *ma mere l'oye*, derived from the name often given elderly peasant women in the typical medieval village who took on chores like tending the geese. Some folklorists have thought there might even be a real woman nicknamed Mother Goose on whom Perrault's title was based, but most agree she was simply a commonplace figure in a largely illiterate society. Sitting around the hearth (women's domain) and spinning (women's "profession") and narrating stories, whether to children or adults or both, was the culturally endorsed role of older women, that society's wise keepers of the myth-making flame. In the Perrault frontispiece, granny plies a spindle to produce flaxen thread as she spins her tales.

There can be no exact parallel between a society's imaginative output and its everyday life. Today, for example, you wouldn't generalize from "Friends" or "The Sopranos" to say that every person in our time parties with their single buddies or that everyone alternates between remorseful self-analysis and cold-blooded killing. Still, elements of the cultural climate of today exist on TV that historians 200 years from now will likely subject to the same type of historical, mythological, and psychoanalytic examination the stories of Grimm and Perrault have received.

We can look through the lens of these works of the imagination to understand much about the daily life of ordinary Europeans during the centuries until Elizabethan times, including the way they kept house. A Grimm heroine earns a fortune in gold, for example, through chores typically performed by that era's women: baking, harvesting, bed making, or spinning flax until her fingers ache. The stories show housewives washing dishes and tending the farmyard animals, laying fires and scrubbing floors, lugging water, plucking chickens, cleaning vegetables, and sweeping ashes. The women of the Grimms' world face hardships that today sound extreme but were then literal, if not commonplace. There actually existed parents who were driven by starvation to expel their children from the home or to abandon them in the uninhabited forest. Infanticide was not unheard of. The wicked stepmother also had some basis in fact, since so many women perished in childbirth, leaving their husbands to remarry women who would raise their offspring. If a woman had trouble delivering a child, a caesarian section was the only chance for the baby's survival; in that period without antiseptic or anesthetic, it would take a miracle for the mother to live.

To grasp the fortitude of the medieval housewife, it's essential to understand the social context of her life. Hardships abounded. Peasants served at the pleasure of the five percent of the population who made up the nobility and spent their days in physical labor until they died, on average under the age of thirty. For roughly a thousand years, from the fall of the Roman Empire in the fifth century through the discovery of America, Western Europeans died young after eking out a hard existence that was rampant with malnourishment, disease, and poverty.

Vast untracked forests of oak and beech covered the face of the European continent, surrounding tiny villages whose residents shivered through icy winters and huddled around the embers after the early sunset. The bounty of acorns and beechnuts in the woods fattened herds of wild boar, which made for good eating but were also vicious. Bears roamed, much more common than we can imagine now and terrifyingly unpredictable. Most frightening were the great packs of wolves that could move hundreds of miles in a few days' time. They infested not only the countryside but the cities, devouring especially the weakest, the oldest, and the youngest inhabitants.

With all these difficulties and dangers, medieval Europe's psychology was to a large degree shaped by its youth. Half the people were under the age of twenty. Boys began working before the age of seven and could actually take on major responsibilities—master craftsman, journeyman, squire, or even king—at the age of thirteen. Girls usually became wives or even widows by age twenty-two. Historian Robert Delort points out a curious emotionality that resulted:

> Hardened warriors burst into tears: they were only 18 or 20 years old, some even less. Their enthusiasm was on a par with their credulity; despair suddenly followed temerity and violence gave way to resignation; one is amazed at their vanity and naiveté. Their feelings ranged from one extreme to the other: love and hate were equally strong. Gambling and games of skill filled an important place in their lives. On the other hand, one must admire the maturity of little girls of 12, mothers of large families at 17, and 14 year old kings.

Youthful though they might have been, housewives then as in every era cleaned and cooked and gardened and hauled water, washed and dried clothing, sewed garments, tended livestock, cared for the sick and the elderly, and nursed the young. The household environment in which they generally worked still holds mysteries, as many implements crafted of wood have not lasted. Low literacy means we have sparse documentation of the typical medieval dwelling. Scholars do know that the typical house of someone neither terribly rich nor miserably poor encompassed a workshop and living space within one ground floor room with a giant, square bed and simple wooden furniture. Archeologists have found pewter andirons and spits, bronze pots and kettles, and earthen vessels for drinking, cooking, and serving. We know that wool was processed at home, and hemp was cut to spin flax and weave cloth of linen.

Housewives baked bread mainly at home under the hearth ashes, even though by the Middle Ages the oven was beginning to appear, introduced by the Romans, who had learned of it in Egypt. Some women brought dough they themselves mixed and kneaded to professional bakers. Fireplaces originated in the eleventh century, yet many families still gathered around braziers, or fires of peat laid directly on a crude floor hearth. Wealthy or not, people dined on trenchers, which were essentially hard-baked plates of bread, spooning meat or porridge and gravy directly on them and eating with their fingers. Since trenchers were needed at virtually every meal, baking was an ongoing responsibility of housewifery.

We know other details about the work of European women through the miniature paintings, stained glass windows, and embroidery that have survived. In the artwork of the time, women not only labor in the home but go out to harvest wheat and carry grain to the water mill. One image shows women alongside men in a carpenter's workshop. In another, they tote baskets of fruit atop their heads while picking apples, with men, in an orchard. Medieval peasant women worked outside the home in textile and beer production as well. Legal and guild records from Germany list women as metalworkers—blacksmiths and coppersmiths, tinsmiths and pewterers. In ninth century Germany, clothmaking, finishing, and dying were done in women's workshops.

Perhaps life's hardships in this era—wolves prowling, hunger pandemic, the Black Death decimating Europe—made too strict a division of labor according to sex a luxury the population could ill afford. The concerns of the majority centered mostly around staying alive. In any case, medieval women's role appears to have been less limited than we generally realize. The domestic arena was ruled by the woman of the house, but if the situation demanded it, if the wheat needed harvesting, she was out there alongside the men in the field, bringing in the crop.

IN OTHER CULTURES over the centuries before the twentieth, the work of the home earned a respect and even a reverence that seems almost exotic now. In seventeenth century Holland, for example, a female presence dominated the home environment, a historical moment rendered luminously visible in paintings by Vermeer, whose interiors glow with domestic harmony. In the room of a typical house, the painter depicts daylight streaming through the windows to glint off a brass candelabra or the grommets on a brown leather chair. In another work he reveals a color-saturated chamber where a blue-aproned housewife ever so simply pours milk into a bowl. Yet another canvas shows domestic appointments that seem to sing in their repose: a hanging wicker basket and brass pot, bread loaves touched with light, carpets draped over tabletops. A woman hunches over a table making lace, a profusion of thread spilling forward. These tranquil, even mystical renderings by so sensitive a social observer reveal the esteem in which the seventeenth century Dutch held their living spaces. Home was more than just a place to hang your hat.

Dutch families even furnished their houses with decorative scale replicas, according to architect Wytold Rybczynski, whose book *Home* describes the evolution of domestic comfort throughout history. These models appeared to be cupboards on the exterior, but once opened "the entire interior was magically revealed, not only the rooms—complete with wall coverings and furnishings—but even paintings, utensils and china figurines." It would surely take passion for one's private dwelling and a sense of unity with one's own personal domesticity to exhibit these lavish miniature monuments.

It stands to reason that a culture that prized its homes to such an extent would esteem the individuals whose energies were devoted to their care. Women's dedicated labor was integral to shaping the well-ordered domesticity we glimpse in Dutch art of the time. In Holland, keeping house was the task of the woman who resided there, no matter how wealthy she was. Housework wasn't seen as a lowly job, the province only of servants. The kitchen, especially, was recognized as the housewife's dignified domain.

It was not her cooking, though, but her insistence on cleanliness that most distinguished the Dutch housewife. It was a highly important job to scour both the exterior of the house and its interior. Visitors to the Netherlands expressed astonishment over the cleanliness of Dutch front stoops. They marveled at the immaculate streets outside and the scrubbed floors inside private homes. Interiors gleamed, whether woodwork or copper, pewter or brass. In Dutch, the word for beauty and purity and for cleanliness is one and the same: *schoon*.

The power of the Dutch domestic sensibility seems destined to last. Paintings made in the 1600s offer solid emotional sustenance to viewers in the twenty-first. An exhibit titled "Art & Home: Dutch Interiors in the Age of Rembrandt" opened in October 2002 at The Newark Museum in New Jersey. Afterward, the museum reported record increases in attendance, voluntary contributions, and shop sales, even as other cultural institutions around the country suffered from drops in attendance over the same period. Mary Sue Sweeney Price, Director of the Museum, attributes the success of the show to a need for "solace, reassurance, and pleasure in these images and objects of domesticity," what she characterizes as "a kind of cultural comfort food."

∞

A FEMALE VISION of transcendent domesticity dominated nineteenth century America. Before 1800, housework had not changed all that much since the stories of the Grimm brothers. Women cleaned and cooked and sewed, cleaned and cooked and sewed again. Making fire and lugging water continued as essential parts of any domestic routine. Gardening and dairying and selling vegetables at the market rounded out the housewife's days. As the nineteenth century progressed, most of these functions remained, but added to them was the responsibility for creating a peaceful refuge from the harshness of the increasingly industrialized world outside.

The home was explicitly exalted in this period. *The American Woman's Home*, published by Catharine Beecher and her sister Harriet Beecher Stowe in 1869, exemplified the treatment of housework as a serious, vital endeavor. Beecher promoted the ideal of the empire of the mother and the home as sacred temple, and helped to convince America that the work of the home had a crucial socializing influence on those who lived in it. Beecher argued for the self-respect of the housewife. "A woman who has charge of a large household," she wrote, "should regard her duties as dignified, important and difficult."

The empire of the mother and the home as temple may strike some as treacly concepts now. Yet perhaps the power of these ideas has lasted longer than we give them credit for, vested as they are in some of the stories we most loved as children and our children most love, which turn on the importance of achieving domestic tranquility. Published in the Victorian era and grounded in the mores of that distant time, the classics of children's literature continue to touch young readers (and adults who read with them) even today. It's lulling background music against the discordant strains of the present.

Wendy in *Peter Pan*, for example, embodies the glory in keeping house. A poignant moment in Neverland comes when the lost boys literally construct a dwelling around Wendy of branches and moss. She sings:

> *"I wish I had a pretty house*
> *the littlest ever seen,*
> *with funny little red walls*
> *and roof of mossy green."*

Of course the boys have their own home under the ground, which consists "of one large room, as all houses should do," with mushrooms for footstools and an enormous fireplace with wash hung across to dry. A home, confirms this story, is as essential for boys as it is for girls.

Author Beatrix Potter, who had a powerful attachment to her ancestral heritage—she presented thousands of acres of her own land in the picturesque Lake District to Britain's National Trust—brought to life in her children's stories the English love of home. Consider Peter Rabbit's family in their sandbank under the root of a fir tree or Mrs. Tiggy Winkle, the hedgehog laundress, who irons in her burrow in "a nice clean kitchen with a flagged floor and wooden beams—just like any other farm kitchen" with "a nice hot singey smell." She wears an apron over her petticoat, an iron in hand, and she works for all the neighborhood, even washing the coats of lambs and mice, and does it all for free, not waiting "either for thanks or for the washing bill!"

One of the most moving passages in Kenneth Grahame's *The Wind in the Willows* occurs as Mole returns with the Rat to his nearly forgotten burrow after visiting his friend's sparkling, cozy home. Mole anxiously enters the dark passageway, frightened of the grubbiness he may find and ashamed to reveal this habitat to his friend. I know I have felt woe similar to that of Mole when he "saw the dust lying thick on everything, saw the cheerless, deserted look of the long-neglected house, and its narrow meager dimensions, its worn and shabby contents—and collapsed again on a hall chair, his nose in his paws." I haven't yet confessed my pain over the mess in my house quite as abjectly as Mole:

> "O, Ratty!" he cried dismally, "why ever did I do it? Why did I bring you to this poor, cold little place, on a night like this, when you might have been at River Bank by this time, toasting your toes before a blazing fire, with all your own nice things about you!"

Mole's consolation is to see his friend bustle about the hole and set a fire, and together they dust and polish until dinnertime, when Rat concocts a banquet out of odds and ends left in the pantry. Mole's home is sacred but must be kept clean to retain its value.

I have received some wonderful presents, but friends' occasional random acts of cleaning have easily matched any other thing I've been given. Once a good friend came over after hearing I was laid up with the flu to tackle the mountain of dishes in my sink. Another time someone drove an hour to my new house the day I moved in, exhausted from hauling boxes. Unasked, my friend started scrubbing the countertops with a rag and some detergent she brought from her own home. She knew it feels better to wake up to a clean kitchen in the morning.

❧

LYDIA MARIA CHILD, the author of "over the river and through the woods, to grandmother's house we go," published *The American*

*Frugal Housewife* in 1832, just as what historians would later term "the cult of domesticity" took hold. It was as a newlywed that she wrote this manual, one of the first of its kind, and its focus on household economy probably derived from close experience: she and her husband were chronically in debt. Not a specialist in the domestic arena, Child addressed far-flung topics in her career as a writer, including children's stories, etiquette books, a history of world religions, a book about women in history, novels, magazine articles, and stories. A crusader for women's rights, against capital punishment, and against slavery, she hid runaway slaves in her home and later wrote a book to teach former slaves to read. *The American Frugal Housewife*, though, was Child's masterpiece. The book went through 29 editions before 1844 and became a cultural icon, not to mention the de rigueur gift for every new bride the way *The Joy of Cooking* is today.

*The American Frugal Housewife* declared its overarching purpose in its subtitle: "Dedicated to Those Who Are Not Ashamed of Economy." Child's notion of thrift and suggestions on how to run a household economically weave together the disparate subjects of the book, which gives a tactile view of the life of women in the mid-nineteenth century.

> The true economy of housekeeping is simply the art of gathering up all the fragments, so that nothing be lost. I mean fragments of *time*, as well as *materials*. Nothing should be thrown away so long as it is possible to make any use of it, however trifling that use may be; and whatever be the size of a family, every member should be employed either in earning or saving money.

The book reads today as more than a little foreign and folksy. Close to two centuries later, her advice sounds far-fetched: to heal a sprain, apply an ointment of ground earthworms; to whiten white kid gloves, use cream of tartar; to preserve eggs, submerge them in a pail of lime-water. Croup? Bathe the throat with bear grease. At this point in the century, Child's readers still made their own soap: her earthy instructions detail making lye from wood ashes, unslaked lye, and grease ("When the soap becomes thick and ropy, carry it down cellar in pails and empty it into a barrel.") Yet in the twenty-first century, we continue to chase down effective methods of housekeeping. The methods differ; the need is the same.

When Catharine Beecher published *A Treatise on Domestic Economy* in 1841, she followed in Child's footsteps but at the same time revolutionized homemaking advice books. In so doing, she became a national household divinity much as Martha Stewart is today. Managing a home was her main focus, and her range of topics was comprehensive. She also treated architecture, focusing on practical designs that would help a house function better, with such innovations as "bedpresses" tucked into alcoves throughout the house, closet and cupboard space. She opposed women's suffrage. If women were going to remain in the domestic realm—which she firmly believed they should—then the home should be improved as an environment for them to occupy, not only as a place of relaxation but also of productive work.

After the publication of the *Treatise*, notes Beecher's biographer, she could venture anywhere in America "and expect to be received as the heroine who had simplified and made understandable the mysterious arts of household maintenance, child rearing, gardening, cooking, cleaning, doctoring, and the dozen other responsibilities middle class women assumed to keep their children and husbands alive and well." The United States was being rocked by the growth of industry, which drew men out of the home, and the greater mobility of families. Just as the expectation for domestic refuge grew, and with it housewives' responsibilities, women resided farther from the mothers and grandmothers who in the past had taught them the domestic skills they required. Beecher's *Treatise* answered this need.

Rather than being opressed by occupying the household role described by Beecher, women were virtually deified. "To American women," she said, "more than to any others on earth, is committed the exalted privilege of extending over the world those blessed influences, which are to renovate degraded man." The function of women in sustaining "a prosperous domestic state," she wrote in the *Treatise*, would be critical to "the building of a glorious temple," an apotheosis of American society. In what Beecher's biographer calls her "ideology of domesticity," the labor of the home and she who performed it were as significant as any other element of nation building.

*The American Woman's Home,* authored by Beecher and Stowe in 1869, in part updated Beecher's previous hit. Some marvelous technical innovations were also included: instead of dirty fireplaces, forced hot air heating; and a water closet on each of two floors. It made perfect sense for Beecher to collaborate with her sister Harriet, since Stowe's writing career had long focused on the subject of how to create a happy home. Her first article for the huge-circulation, influential *Godey's Lady's Book* in 1839 was called "Trials of a Housekeeper." Throughout her life Stowe— thought by many to be the genius of the illustrious Beecher family—worked both as a professional writer and as a housewife struggling alongside her minister husband to make ends meet. Immersed in domestic life, she had what she described as a mystical experience during a church service. When she went home she took up a pencil and the brown paper wrapping in which the morning's groceries had been delivered to set down the first scenes of *Uncle Tom's Cabin,* which would appear in 1852.

And so out of church revelation and grocery paper was born our nation's first mammoth best-seller. America for some time after publication went Uncle Tom-mad, with numerous theatrical adaptations performed and songs popularized. So was the rest of the world, as the book was translated into twenty-three languages. The city of Berlin even renamed a street for the book: "Onkel Tom Strasse."

Cloaked in somewhat sentimental prose, the story nonetheless galvanized public opinion against slavery to such a degree that the book is given credit by many historians as a factor in causing the abolition of slavery. The difference between *Uncle Tom's Cabin* and other antislavery tracts of the time, according to one writer, was that Stowe "provided a mirror in which America could examine itself." A well-worn and possibly apocryphal anecdote has Lincoln receiving Stowe at the White House nine years after the book became a phenomenon with these words, "So you are the little woman who wrote the book that made this big war."

It is fitting that Stowe used the tools of housewifery to start what would become an undertaking of massive public import. As fervent an abolitionist as many of her intellectual peers, she combined her political and social passions with an equally fervent belief in the ultimate dignity of the domestic realm.

A good example of the way her ideal vision of domesticity combined with a political world view lies in a magazine Stowe coedited called *Hearth and Home*, first published in 1868 and intended for an audience of both men and women. The contents included dress patterns and recipes alongside agricultural advice, national and international news, and outspokenly feminist articles on suffrage and cooperative housekeeping. In an era when a miniscule number of women held paying jobs, *Hearth and Home* even ran articles that explored the idea of women working outside the home.

The point isn't only that she held the two positions or dedicated herself to both causes. It was the very rootedness in home and its virtues that made her stand against slavery possible. Stowe, writes historian Glenna Matthews, "used the moral authority of the housewife to justify speaking out against slavery."

While exalting domestic life in literature, Stowe nonetheless suffered its burdens. In the first several years of her marriage she bore four babies, including a set of twins, and went on to have another three children. Orchestrating the household, even with the help of family members and servants, proved difficult for Stowe, whose temperament reportedly went more toward focusing furiously on one thing at a time rather than an attempt at cohesion. Eking out time to produce articles and stories, even as one of the most popular writers of her time, provoked stress. One letter she sent to her husband revealed her frustration with the domesticity she still espoused. "It is a dark, sloppy, rainy, muddy, disagreeable day," she wrote,

> and I have been working hard (for me) all day in the kitchen, washing dishes, looking into closets, and seeing a great deal of that dark side of domestic life which a housekeeper may who will investigate too curiously into minutiae in warm, damp weather. . . .
>
> I am sick of the smell of sour milk, and sour meat, and sour everything, and then the clothes *will* not dry, and no wet thing does, and everything smells mouldy; and altogether I feel as if I never wanted to eat again.

She shared the sometime woes of every housewife in a letter to a friend: "I am but a mere drudge with few ideas beyond babies and housekeeping. As for thoughts, reflections, and sentiments, good lack! Good lack!"

Yet she viewed the nineteenth century parlor culture as incredibly important. Stowe exalts the elders who preserve passed-down female domestic wisdom and asserts that a place should be set aside in heaven for "domestic saints," the women who steadfastly nurture a household's inhabitants.

In many ways she resembled women of today, sometimes harried and anxious, sometimes guilty about whether she was dedicating enough energy to her children. She also felt intense pride and welcomed the accolades she received after the publication of her masterpiece. In a letter to her husband she prefigured Virginia Woolf by decades when she stated: "There is one thing I must suggest. If I am to write, I must have a room to myself, which shall be *my* room."

Other reformers of the day shared Stowe's domestic loyalties. "Come here and I will do what I can to help you with your address, if you will hold the baby and make the puddings," wrote Elizabeth Cady Stanton to Susan B. Anthony upon receiving a letter from Anthony imploring her to help her with a speech ("Now will you load my gun leaving me only to pull the trigger & let fly the powder & ball—"). Susan B. Anthony and Elizabeth Cady Stanton made an odd couple. Anthony stares out of photos thin, set-mouthed, with a schoolmarm's penetrating gaze, the classic spinster, while Stanton poses all chubby face and knowing smiles. The mother of seven, who appreciated the fine clothes and fripperies of the Victorian era, Stanton was the writer of the two, while Anthony provided conceptual brilliance. Though both brought passion to the cause, each lacked force without the other. Without their complementary skills female suffrage would not have passed in 1920. Yet home as an ideal and a reality for nineteenth century women dominated both their lives.

In 1854, Stanton asked Anthony for help with a speech to demand that the New York State Legislature expand the Married Woman's Property Act. She had a baby daughter who was not yet five months old and asked Anthony to come to Seneca Falls to help research the speech, writing, "I have not time to look up statistics." She explained,

> While I am about the house, surrounded by children, washing dishes, baking, sewing, etc. I can think up many points, but I cannot search books, for my hands as well as my brains would be necessary for that work. . . . Men who can, when they wish to write a document, shut themselves up for days with their thoughts and their books, know little of what difficulties a woman must surmount to get off a tolerable production.

The experience seems not to have soured Anthony on domesticity. In an 1887 speech, she advocated the importance of home, especially for women of economic independence. "A home of one's own," she said, "is the want, the necessity of every human being, the one thing above all others longed for, worked for. Whether the humblest cottage or the proudest palace, a home of our own is the soul's dream of rest, the one hope that will not die until we have reached the very portals of the everlasting home."

To view Anthony's Rochester parlor is to see a typical, if somewhat sparsely decorated, room of the period, with cozy fireplace and grate, landscape over the mantel, piano, soft cushions on the chairs, and, perhaps less commonly, thick leather-bound books on a round table—the very table, it is said, on which Anthony, Stanton, and other activists wrote the Declaration of Sentiments in 1848, the document that first asserted the right of American women to full suffrage. To be one of the most radical women of the day didn't obviate the parlor sensibility that dominated the nineteenth century.

In fact, Anthony challenged anyone claiming that suffragists were not just as domestic as their peers who objected to women voting:

Do any of you still cling to the old theory, that single women, women's rights women, professional women, have no home instincts? . . . All this is done from pure love of home; no spurious second-hand domesticity affected for the praise of some man, or conscientiously maintained for the comfort of the one who furnishes the money; nor because she has nothing else to busy herself about, but her one impelling motive is from the true womanly home instinct, unsurpassed by that of any of the women who 'have all the rights they want.'

True, some thinkers of the time denigrated the home as an unworthy focus for women's activities. "Home," intoned George Bernard Shaw, "is the girl's prison and the woman's workhouse." Charlotte Perkins Gilman, the grandniece of Catharine Beecher, believed in shutting down the functions of the individual home. The survivor of a devastating marriage, she suffered a breakdown and went on to chronicle it in her famous novella, *The Yellow Wall-paper*. Gilman saw no value whatsoever in the private home.

Home cooks, Gilman believed, were bad cooks. A system whereby women maintained the home and men worked outside it was inherently unfair. Food would be better prepared in restaurant-style kitchens for groups of people. Collective laundering could easily be conducted at a central station. There was no need for women to behave as "feeders and cleaners." She wasn't the only reformer of the period to advocate collectivizing housework and removing it from the home, but her voice was the most influential.

Observing her parents' unloving marriage and her mother's combination of emotional coldness and passionate domesticity perhaps predisposed Gilman to her view that the home oppressed women. Yet she had also witnessed domestic happiness of family members, including Harriet Beecher Stowe, her great aunt. Ambivalent as she was, Gilman married, then after having a baby had her nervous breakdown. She writes movingly of this period, when with "a charming home; a loving and devoted husband; an exquisite baby, healthy, intelligent and good; a highly competent mother to run things; a wholly satisfactory servant—and I lay on the lounge and cried." Her physician's counsel was to "'live as domestic a life as possible . . . and never touch pen, brush or pencil as long as you live.'"

She left her husband and translated her personal experience into a crusade to erase domesticity entirely. Gilman's *Women and Economics,* which analyzed women's parasitic dependence on men, appeared in 1898 to rave reviews (*The Nation* called it "the most significant utterance about women since *The Subjection of Women* by John Stuart Mill). On the lecture circuit the writer untiringly spoke to suffrage groups, labor unions, and other progressive organizations. She insisted upon the modern, favoring all technological progress and criticizing those who "worshipped backwards."

"There is nothing private and special in the preparation of food," she said. "A more general human necessity does not exist. There must be freedom and personal choice in the food prepared, but it no more has to be cooked for you than the books you love best have to be written for you"—an interesting precursor of Burger King's "Have It Your Way" campaign. Gilman endorsed all prepared and processed food, especially hot cooked meals. She advocated that women follow men out of the home, to "make that world our home at last." She could not see that the culture of the handmade, the culture of personal touch, would disappear along with the dissolution of homemaking.

Gilman never did persuade a wider public of the sense of her ideas, perhaps because the groundswell of public opinion in the Victorian era overwhelmingly favored the home as a crucial foundation for all other good things. She did, however, gather a group of followers to live collectively in Boston for several years, an experiment that was ultimately abandoned. When it came down to it, few Americans seemed eager to prepare meals or do laundry in communal settings with people who weren't family.

As America entered the twentieth century, the connection between women and their homes had been solidly established. One of the most influential interior designers of her day was Elsie de Wolfe, who stripped down the fussy Victorian look and replaced it with sleek, minimal furnishings, often in shades of beige. In 1913 she wrote,

> We take it for granted that every woman is interested in houses— that she either has a house in the course of construction, or dreams of having one, or has had a house long enough to wish it right. And we take it for granted that this American home is always the woman's home: a man may build and decorate a beautiful house, but it remains for a woman to make a home of it for him. It is the personality of the mistress that the house expresses. Men are forever guests in our homes, no matter how much happiness they may find there.

Women were in charge and men were fortunate to occupy a place within their domain. Another expression of this sentiment was the well-known horror of men at spring-cleaning, also dictated by the woman of the house. An illustration from a 1879 issue of *Harper's Bazaar* shows a man fleeing so fast his top hat flies off behind him; in hot pursuit are a mop, broom, bucket, and other cleaning implements. The caption reads, "The Householder's Annual Misery. 'The spring housecleaning days have come,/The saddest of the year.'"

Frances Trollope marvels at the New York City custom of "changing house"—switching from one rented house to another— on the first of May. It resembled, she wrote, "a population flying from the plague, or [ . . .] a town which had surrendered on condition of carrying away all their goods and chattels. Rich furniture and ragged furniture, carts, waggons, and drayment, white, yellow, and black, occupy the streets from east to west, from north to south, on this day."

Edith Wharton wrote in *The House of Mirth*, in 1905:

In Mrs. Peniston's youth, fashion had returned to town in October; therefore on the tenth day of the month the blinds of her Fifth Avenue residence were drawn up, and the eyes of the Dying Gladiator in bronze who occupied the drawing-room window resumed their survey of that deserted thoroughfare.

The first two weeks after her return represented to Mrs. Peniston the domestic equivalent of a religious retreat. She "went through" the linen and blankets in the precise spirit of the penitent exploring the inner folds of conscience; she sought for moths as the stricken soul seeks for lurking infirmities. The topmost shelf of every closet was made to yield up its secret, cellar and coal-bin were probed to their darkest depths and, as a final stage in the lustral rites, the entire house was swathed in penitential white and deluged with expiatory soapsuds.

A generation gap separates Peniston and her niece Lily, to whom her aunt's house, "in its state of unnatural immaculateness and order, was as dreary as a tomb," and who "felt as though she were buried alive in the stifling limits of Mrs. Peniston's existence." Lily, brilliant as she is, "did not know one end of a crochet-needle from the other" and "resented the smell of bees-wax and brown soap, and behaved as though she thought a house ought to keep clean of itself, without extraneous assistance."

Wharton, herself a house fanatic and talented interior designer, portrayed Mrs. Peniston as somewhat dotty, but new-woman Lily

Bart winds up broken and lost, a tragic figure, made so partly by her rush into modern independence and away from the old ways—including perhaps those of hearth and home, even the "expiatory soapsuds."

Women of this era wanted to launch themselves into a more modern way of life. The problem was, progress had to remain within traditional restrictions. The solution: housewifery itself would become a profession. Its practitioners, the home economists, would take a little less from the ideal of a glorious temple and a little more from the model of the factory floor.

CHAPTER 4

# Home Ec 101

IN THE SHADOWY BASEMENT of the junior high, along a dim hall-way remote from the math and biology and English classrooms where we spent most of our days, the home economics lab seemed suspended in the amber of forgotten tradition. It's not as if we were folding linens at right angles—it was alien enough that we were learning to cook and sew in school. Rushing through the recipe to finish by the end of class, we fried bacon and shredded Gruyère to bake quiche lorraine. Why we were spending academic time preparing food never came clear; the whole experience seemed a weird cultural throwback, but as a way to get through the school day it ranked higher than algebra—and we got to eat what we cooked—so we willingly went to class.

To our teacher we must have appeared equally alien, psyche-delic-era adolescent ragamuffins who were distressingly apathetic about domestic matters. Bringing in an apron from home was a course requirement and one that we viewed as hilarious. Mine was a familiar, well-used garment of my mother's, thick cotton with a piece of white molded plastic for a waistband, with styling that enhanced the fustily anachronistic quality of the whole experience.

In the early 1970s, a time saturated with sex and drugs and rock and roll, home ec appeared to be more a gut course mandated by school fuddy-duddies than preparation for any meaningful life experience. Perhaps the most eye-opening aspect of the course was its exclusion of boys, which for me, with my somewhat naive thirteen-year-old's expectation of equity in all of life, just about discredited it completely. While we girls baked banana bread and stitched blouses, our male peers hammered together napkin holders in wood shop. That one boy goofed on the school administration by insisting on enrolling in our home ec class just put the gender divide in higher relief.

Something colored our attitude about the experience: we knew nothing of the history of domestic science or in fact of the work of the home in a larger sense. The way we saw it, our mothers were engaged in cooking or cleaning or sewing for one reason only, because they had no choice. With our adolescent certainty, we knew we wouldn't grow into their aprons. All we wanted to cook, really, was . . . fudge. And that we could easily manage ourselves, at home, on sleepovers with our friends.

If you went to high school between 1930 and 1985, your home economics education most likely had some similarity to mine, though your attitude toward the experience may not have been so sour. Nearly everyone of my generation has a vivid home ec memory. One friend who grew up on Long Island enrolled in semesters of both cooking and sewing against her wishes, through a glitch in the school's new computer system. Beneficiaries of her baking class, her family ate homemade challah every Friday night until she graduated from high school (her husband, jokes my friend, started dating her "because of the bread"). Then her grandmother gave her a sewing machine, and she developed a specialty in patching people's jeans "with extra denim and a strong zigzag stitch." Since adulthood her sewing has been limited to buttons and camp name labels, but she dreams of buying a new machine. My friend confesses today that these courses were the most useful of her early academic career.

Another friend recalls the open layout of the home ec room, "like a sprawling commercial kitchen in some 1970s ranch home." The teacher resembled Julia Child, with soft folds under her chin, penciled eyebrows, coarse brown hair, and a white apron. The class covered weights and measures, table etiquette and thrift, cheese fondue and the bread to dip it in. Having grown up on Wonder Bread and frozen vegetables, she suddenly was making spinach lasagna and baked Alaska. The class also sewed stuffed toys, yellow Easter chicks or black and white pandas out of synthetic fur. By the early 1980s in her school district, boys and girls alike were required to study both home ec and shop, and most students crafted plaques and bookends as well as coffee cake and cocoa.

It was Ellen Swallow Richards, a nineteenth century reformer, who vowed to make keeping house a science. The first home econ-omist in America, she had an indelible impact on all those rooms full of stove tops and sewing machines, felt and yeast.

Richards, a science prodigy who was one of the first Vassar graduates, set her sights on studying graduate chemistry at MIT. She was allowed to attend as a "special" student, on the stipula-tion that she work in a lab separate from her male classmates, and that the only degree the school would confer was a second BA. After receiving her bachelor of science at MIT and a master of arts from Vassar, in 1873, she accepted MIT's invitation to become an instructor in sanitary chemistry, and it was there she crafted the idea of applying scientific principles to managing the home.

Richards' plan for what she at first called the "home life educa-tion movement" sprang from the same philosophical tradition as that of Harriet Beecher Stowe, Catharine Beecher, and Lydia Maria Child, centered in the restorative value of the home and the dignity and worth of women whose job it was to manage it. There her view-point diverged, however: the writers of the early nineteenth century advised women on economy, health, comfort, and spirituality, but Ellen Richards made her focus the weights and measures and the right angles of housekeeping. The functioning of the household, believed Richards and her followers, could be streamlined. Domestic science was meant to offer training that would enable housewives to organize their households most effectively.

Richards grew to be friends with Melville Dewey, creator of the decimal system; he suggested "home economics" instead of domestic science as the name for a new hybrid field that would combine the social and natural sciences. The American Home Economics Association found its name and its mission in Lake Placid, New York, in 1899. Eleven scholars at the conference brought credentials in chemistry and biology, physics, bacteriology, psychology, and sanitary science. Dewey also served as president of the New York Efficiency Society and, it has been said, even shortened his name in the interest of efficiency, first to Melvil Dewey and then to Melvil Dui.

The American Home Economics Association was founded in 1909. Even before that, a handful of agricultural colleges offered courses in domestic science. The Morrill Land Grant Act of 1862 had provided for the development of home-oriented programs at midwestern and western state colleges. Private women's colleges in the Northeast thumbed their collective nose at home ec—according to the president of Bryn Mawr, there were "not enough elements of intellectual growth in cooking or housekeeping to furnish a very serious or profound course of training for really intelligent women." The more elite state schools, such as Cornell, and large coed universities, like the University of Chicago, likewise weren't offering many choices in "household technology" or "sanitary chemistry." Still, by 1916 there were 17,778 home economics college students, most wanting to teach home economics, compared with 213 in 1905. By 1916–1917, twenty percent of public high schools had home ec classes.

The exclusion of boys from the study of home economics—the policy I was to chafe at in my high school half a century later—was set early on by the agricultural colleges where these teachers were trained. The founder of Kansas State Agricultural College wrote:

> When the boys learn to grow wheat, the girls learn to make it into bread! When the boys raise apples, the girls give them pie! And so both sides of the house shall be trained, until the perfect home shall be attained, and every community will bless those women who are experts in the line of domestic science.

As women went to college and graduated with degrees in domestic science, they flooded the job market and soon were sought after by appliance manufacturers. Companies recognized the power of advertising and professional endorsement in soliciting women's patronage. In 1916, when the American Hoover Suction Sweeper Company set up shop, famous efficiency expert Christine Frederick demonstrated that using a vacuum cleaner did a much more thorough job than old-fashioned carpet beating. By this time she was consulting with many domestic appliance companies, advising them on how best to sell their products. In 1927 she told the British electrical goods industry "to stress their hygienic qualities and to use the familiar anxiety-inducing arguments to drive the message home."

"Our greatest enemy is the woman with the career," wrote Christine Frederick in the *Journal of Home Economics*. The labor of the home, she insisted, should provide women with sufficient creative satisfaction. After all, homemaking included everything from cooking, to care of children, to nutrition, to home decor. Domestic work is not drudgery, she continued, but just as engaging as "any of the fields in which women are running with eager feet because it expresses their wonderful individuality."

Scientific household management and advertisement meshed

perfectly. For example, the J. R. Watkins Company teamed up in 1941 with Elaine Allen, "the Author of the World's Most Popular Cook Book" (the *Watkins Cook Book*) to produce a compendium called *Watkins Household Hints*. Allen, Director of Home Economics for the company, assured readers, "I have used the name Watkins, This is because I have personally tested, and can fully recommend, Watkins Quality Products—household necessities for over seventy years." Watkins Soap Flakes, Watkins Pure Ground Cinnamon, Watkins Insecticide, Watkins Corn Pads, Watkins Moth Crystals, Watkins Sewing Machine Oil . . . all receive their due in this handy volume.

Some company-produced domestic advice pamphlets were more blatantly self-promotional than others. "The Housewife's Year Book of Health and Homemaking," out of Battle Creek, Michigan, alternated bran muffin recipes and farmers' almanac entries with essays on the evils of constipation, on "bulk," and "rules for safe reducing," all featuring Kellogg's All-Bran, naturally.

According to historian Susan Strasser, home economists "defined new tasks in mothering and in consumption, tasks to be overseen by experts who claimed to combine the rationality of science with the efficiency of business, replacing love, common sense, and old-fashioned ways as guides for housework."

The changing domestic philosophy reveals itself in two advice books of different periods. *Home Cook Book*, published first back in 1874, before the crest of the domestic science movement and often reissued in subsequent years, was dedicated to the idea that "no matter how talented a woman may be, or how useful in the church or society, if she is an indifferent housekeeper it is fatal to her influence, a foil to her brilliancy and a blemish in her garments." The book makes the point that housekeeping ought *not* to be taught in classes and by professors. Instead,

There is no earthly reason why girls, from eight to eighteen, should not learn and practice the whole round of housekeeping, from the first beating of eggs to laying of carpets and presiding at a dinner party, at the same time that they go on with music, languages and philosophy. The lessons would be all the better learned if, instead of sitting down at once out of school hours, the girl was taught to take pride in keeping her room nice, or in helping about such work as canning fruit for the season, hanging clean curtains, or dusting every day.

Professional accomplishment, emphasizes the *Home Cook Book*, can easily coexist with domestic skill. "One of the valued contributors to the New York press is a woman who reads Horace in Latin, and Bastiat's political economy, makes point-lace and embroiders beautifully, who at the gold mines with her husband [sic], built the chimney to her house, and finished most of the interior with her own hands." Moreover, it is a crucial job: "the whole family system depends on you."

The book details rules for etiquette at the table and marketing hints that ring of an era that now sounds archaic—lamb, if fresh killed, should have bluish rather than greenish veins in the neck, and the feet and bills of old geese are red while those of young geese are yellow. Cotton rag carpets can be dyed blue when boiled with copperas, prussiate of potash, and oil of vitriol. Slices of raw onion will soothe a bee sting. Recipes call for "a half spoon of butter" or "a piece of butter the size of an egg." Rather than martinet exactitude, the book advocates cherishing the "home feeling, the attachment that grows for the pleasant enduring objects of daily use."

By the time the home ec curriculum found its niche in the country's public secondary school system, it had been established as a progressive, modern approach to domesticity. This being the Progressive Era, educators wanted to reform old-fashioned home traditions by replacing them with efficient, "scientific" practices.

Recently I looked through the carefully preserved, crumbling paper textbook and class notes of one middle-school girl who studied home ec in a New York City public school in 1924. Her delicate cursive, its ink now faded to brown, enumerates the steps for Excellent Steamed Carrots:

> Amount for one girl
>
> 1. Boil water in the bottom of double boiler
> 2. Put on uniforms wash hands [sic]
> 3. Wash carrot
> 4. Scrape carrot
> 5. Empty garbage and wash carrot
> 6. Cut carrot in half, quarters, eighths, sixteenths, thirtysecondths
> 7. Place in strainer. Cover and cook until tender. Serve in a heated vegetable dish

Photographs in the *Handbook of Directions for Home Making Activities* issued at that time by the New York Board of Education show groups of white-capped, white-aproned, ethereal girls, resembling Red Cross nurses in *A Farewell to Arms* more than junior high students, washing dishes in a high-ceilinged class kitchen and hand sewing in a "home making apartment."

Unlike the 1874 *Home Cook Book*, the *Handbook of Directions* opens with tables of abbreviations, from a pound down to a few drops (f.d.) and a few grains (f.g.). In the progressive ideal of home, no measurement was left to the judgment of the individual cook or housekeeper. Under the heading "Bed" we learn that "Metal beds are more sanitary than wooden ones. Single beds are more healthful than double ones" and "The bed should appear square and box-like when made." In washing dishes, it is important to wash in the following order: glass, silver, china, cutlery, and cooking utensils.

Even garbage cans require detailed instructions: scrub pail, dry, keep covered, and on Friday specifically, sterilize and air in the sun.

The authors of the Victorian era *Home Cook Book* specifically disapproved of girls learning in school the lessons they could get in their own homes. After the turn of the century this approach changed completely and often caused rifts between girls who had learned the "correct" way to keep house in school and their old-fashioned or old-world mothers.

Friction between generations may have been inevitable, considering the magnitude of technological advances between 1890 and 1920, which revolutionized so many aspects of housework. Suddenly there were gas, electricity, ready-made clothes, factory-made furniture, bakery bread, processed food, refrigeration, and new, easier ways of doing laundry. Women continued to bear the responsibility for the labor of the home, but the means of performing that labor had drastically changed.

It began with oil. In 1783 a Swiss physicist named Aimé Argand had developed a lamp that drew up oil through a meshed wick and allowed a flickering light that revolutionized how people spent their time at night. Where before there had only been candles, now a burning lamp could be used to read by, talk by, work by. Different oils followed. Europe used Colza oil, which had been extracted from the seeds of a turnip. The superiority of whale oil in brightness and clarity created a booming industry in New England.

These oils took a back seat to kerosene once an amateur geologist from Canada discovered in the mid-1880s that it was possible to extract the flammable oil from asphalt. Kerosene proved cheaper than whale oil and cleaner as well. By the 1880s, most American families had one oil or kerosene lamp.

Gaslight came to the big cities of London, Baltimore, and Paris in the early 1800s, but Americans rejected gas in their homes until after the Civil War. More household labor ensued with coal gas, which dirtied walls, curtains, and upholstery. People didn't use gas or electric ranges for some time, but woodstoves had by the end of the nineteenth century almost completely replaced open-hearth cookery, and fire still heated the house.

Suddenly the dynamic of homemaking shifted, as the ability and power to generate energy reverted to giant companies that distributed new fuels, such as kerosene and natural gas. Still, the broad availability of gaslight did not mean that every household wanted or could afford it. Technology was slow to change the lifestyles of even the wealthiest individuals in part because people don't often embrace change if it means a loss of beauty or comfort. In London, for example, gas could be piped in to light Buckingham Palace as early as 1850, but Prince Albert chose to illuminate the cavernous passageways and staterooms with hundreds of wax candles instead.

Then came electricity. By the late 1920s over three-quarters of American homes were electrified. Twenty years before, Westinghouse had introduced the electric iron, which beat out hot plates, toasters, and coffee percolators as the most popular household appliance. Electric ironing meant no longer sweating next to a hot stove! The spread of electricity was so rapid in America that in 1927 the number of homes with electricity was equal to that in the rest of the world combined. More than half of these households owned a vacuum cleaner.

New products powered by electricity required less persuasion to buy. Sewing machines, available since the 1860s, saved some of the labor of hand sewing. Electric refrigerators replaced iceboxes, the tin-lined wooden boxes that sat atop a cut block of ice, and butteries, cool rooms used to keep dairy products fresh.

The labor of the home continued, of course. Lamp cleaning, when kerosene came in, was a dirty and constant job—wiping the chimney, trimming the wick, washing the shade—along with cleaning up after the smoke from both lamps and wood fires. In fact, the latter was impossible to accomplish thoroughly during winter, there was just so much soot and dirt and dust. Hence spring cleaning.

Once the energy moguls established themselves, members of urban households at least no longer had to chop wood or haul coal. Municipal water systems provided water at the turn of a spigot: running water meant no more lugging water. Vacuum cleaners replaced carpet beating.

So when advances arrived, did the housewife's job scale back to nothing? The answer is complicated. When sewing machines hit the market, their popularity was immediate, but that didn't mean that women stopped sewing their family's clothing. Running water lightened the chores of laundry and dish cleaning and scrubbing floors. But though most Americans had running water by the time of the Depression, in the late 1920s only three-quarters of urban households surveyed and less than a third of rural families had bathrooms. Not only were housewives still hauling water from the pump into the kitchen, they were carrying out slops, both food and human waste. Frontier women and farm wives had especially heavy duties. They confronted hardships that dwarfed beautifying the home or making it a comfortable sanctuary for their families. Modernization of laundry and fuel production lagged in remote areas. Though new technologies afforded more freedom for some women, the net result for most was a diminished sense of authority.

A home economist of the era noted that appliances tended to create more labor: the "invention of the washing machine has meant more washing, of the vacuum cleaner more cleaning, or new fuels and cooking equipment, more courses and more elaborately cooked food." Household chores may have lightened, but they were still arduous. New labor-saving devices saved effort, not time.

What the new fuels and appliances did change was the role of women in the home and the perception of housework. The challenges taken on by housewives every day were increasingly viewed as simple, easy, and rote, taking no time or effort to perform. Mechanization and the introduction of new fuel sources lessened the respect traditionally given to housewives, a change especially striking after the home-centered nineteenth century. The power that had accrued to housewives now went to machines. Woman's strength as energy generator—literally the keeper of the flame—had been co-opted by powerful industries that were already tamping down the age-old domestic functions.

Home economics at its most successful concerned how most effectively to manage—and dignify—the home. Its proponents were motivated by the conviction that housework is important enough to merit a discussion of specific functions. Was all this instruction necessary, when increasingly there were machines to do what women did with blood and sweat? Yes, because labor-saving devices were unaffordable for many, and even rejected by some. Electrical lines and water pipes for a long time did not reach to the far corners of the country. The result until the mid-twentieth century is that many households lived much as they would have before industrialization.

True, the vast majority of women no longer had to make soap, grind wheat, or render fat for candles. But the cleaning and cooking and washing were all there for someone to do, somehow. And as extended families continued to break apart and move long distances away, the younger generation needed a way to learn about domestic activities.

Perhaps their female elders stressed the grounding legacy of domesticity in this new century because as decade tumbled after decade, they felt something in the air, a longing on the part of young women for independence from the old roles. It's visible in the works of the flapper era, in the heroines of F. Scott Fitzgerald and Hemingway who couldn't be bothered with keeping house. In one novel, *The Flirt*, published in 1913 by Booth Tarkington, the central struggle concerns sisters Cora and Laura and Cora's attempts to defy convention and resist the suitor her family expects her to marry. It's interesting to see what in particular agonizes her about the prospect of marriage with one suitor:

> "Oh!" she cried. "It's a horrible thing to ask a girl to do: to settle down—just housekeeping, housekeeping, housekeeping forever in this stupid, stupid town! It's so unfair! Men are just possessive; they think it's loving you to want to possess you themselves. A beautiful 'love'! It's so mean! Men!" She sprang up and threw out both arms in a vehement gesture of revolt. "Damn 'em, I wish they'd let me alone!"

Equally interesting is a short story published by popular writer Sarah Orne Jewett in the February 1882 *Atlantic Monthly*. "Tom's Husband" concerns the role reversal of a young married couple; when Tom, who is a stamp-collecting dreamer, inherits a mill, Mary itches to run it.

> "Do you know, Tom," she said, with amazing seriousness, "that I believe I should like nothing in the world so much as to be the head of a large business? I hate keeping house,—I always did, and I never did so much of it in all my life put together as I have since I have been married. I suppose it isn't womanly to say so, but if I could escape from the whole thing I believe I should be perfectly happy."

Mary takes over the mill and Tom runs their home, and for a time all goes well. Finally, though, Tom

> lost his interest in things outside the house and grounds; he felt himself fast growing rusty and behind the times, and to have somehow missed a great deal in life; he felt that he was a failure. One day

the thought rushed over him that his had been almost exactly the experience of most women, and he wondered if it really was any more disappointing and ignominious to him than it was to women themselves.

The story could have been dreamed up by Simone de Beauvoir. One line even predates one of the catchier feminist statements of the 1970s: "Why I Need a Wife," by Judy Syfer, a cri de coeur that appeared in the first edition of *Ms.*:

> I want a wife who will take care of my physical needs. I want a wife who will keep my house clean. A wife who will pick up after me. I want a wife who will keep my clothes clean, ironed, mended, and who will see to it that my personal things are kept in their proper place so that I can find what I need the minute I need it. I want a wife who cooks the meals, a wife who is a good cook. I want a wife who will plan the menus, does the necessary grocery shopping, pre-pares the meals, serves them pleasantly, and then does the cleaning up while I do my studying. . . .

Sarah Orne Jewett, ninety years earlier, writes of Mary, "She was too independent and self-reliant for a wife; it would seem at first thought that she needed a wife more herself than she did a hus-band."

Not surprisingly, this Victorian marriage founders on the shoals of home-front gender bending. Tom grows too "fussy" about house-hold matters, while Mary flourishes as manager of the business. Finally, Tom feels the role reversal is just too degrading and steps forward manfully to insist that they go to Europe: "And three weeks later they sailed."

The 1928 textbook *Foods and Home Making* features a crossing of the two lines, the technical and the spiritual. The author, a home economist named Carlotta C. Greer, begins by extolling the homemaking skills of some of America's "great women": Alice Freeman Palmer, president of Wellesley College, Mary Lyon, founder of Mount Holyoke, reformer Jane Addams. "Service to their homes," she writes, "helped to prepare them for large service in the world." She talks of following in the path of Ellen Richards, who opened up so many occupations that had to do with home-making: social worker, interior decorator, magazine editor, director of home ec at a food manufacturer—or manager of a tearoom.

This revised edition of the 1928 advice book was published thirteen years after the New York schoolgirl's notes, and it reveals how much about home economics had changed in the interim. Here the photos depict scientific comparisons of rats fed on con-trasting diets, and sprayed and unsprayed Rome Beauty apples ("No insects were allowed to grow on the apples shown at left. This accounts for the finely developed fruit."). Line drawings diagram the water, starch, sugar, cellulose, fat, protein, and ash in a grain of wheat or one cooked oat. The text instructs on how to clean and trim the wick of a kerosene stove. In recipes, technique is foremost and flavor secondary. It surely empowered women to know the components of the household's coal-burning range, as well as much of the other information conveyed in these pages. Men, advises Greer, can take part in homemaking. Illustrations inside the cover show an ideal kitchen: a woman washing dishes in front of a frilly curtained kitchen window, a modern unit of drawers and countertop with plants and fruit on it—and her husband smiling beside her, drying dishes (two tennis rackets lean against the cor-ner, and he models a sporty pair of knickers).

There seems something cold and overtechnical, though, about the model of homemaking advocated here, a bit of the staunch cru-sade for perfection in an arena that by nature can't and shouldn't be perfect. One diagram, for example, shows a woman putting a bowl on a table labeled 28 inches with the caption: "A stooped body is like a kinked hose." Its companion depicts a 33-inch table, the woman ramrod straight. "The stoop she conquered!" it reads. That's in a chapter titled "Efficiency and Charm," which about sums up the approach of the author.

Engineer Frank Gilbreth and his wife Lillian, a psychologist, and their twelve children—profiled in the engaging memoir *Cheaper by the Dozen*—personified the concept of "scientific management" pioneered by Lillian and other "efficiency engineers." *The Home Maker and Her Job* was one of Lillian Gilbreth's books. Christine Frederick, the home economist mouthpiece for the appliance manufacturers, measured and timed and snapped photos of women at work to develop easier modes of doing housework. Then she published books that diagrammed how to make more efficient different aspects of keeping house. Housewives were asked to make schedules, keep notes, and take inventory of household and pantry supplies.

The work of the domestic scientists sounds somewhat silly now, fussy and overly strict. We should remember, though, as we grind coffee beans with an easy twist of a compact electric mill or maneuver the DustBuster under the bed, that it was the professional home economists who helped transform the environments we live in and the way we keep them clean so that they would become eminently practical as well as comfortable. They recognized that our domestic spaces are a locus of work as well as relaxation and that the labor conducted there—mainly, now as then, by women—ought to be optimally simple, efficient, and dignified.

The aims of the movement's leaders were broad. Consider the example of educator Francis Willard, who said, grandly, "If I were asked the mission of the ideal woman, I would say it is to make the whole world *homelike*." One president of Wellesley College actually resigned her post to become a full-time homemaker, issuing this pronouncement as her parting cry: "There is nothing better than the making of a true home."

The late 1930s also saw the publication of a domestic advice manual called *The Household Searchlight Homemaking Guide*, the product of *The Household Magazine* in Topeka, Kansas. Perhaps its lasting popularity—it was reprinted for over a dozen years—came as a result of the sheer breadth of its contents. In his foreword, the magazine's editor-in-chief promised that the book would deal "in an intelligible and usable way with a wide range of homemaking problems, including etiquette, weddings, menus, quantity cookery, health, beauty, home furnishings and equipment, dyeing, stain removal, insect extermination, the care of the lawn, entertainment, club activities, and the mental health of children."

The manual's stiff orange cover was embossed with a cozy cottage framed by two tall shade trees, an artifact of a dreamily distant time. Like Lydia Maria Child's *American Frugal Housewife*, the *Searchlight Guide* offers dictums concerning monogrammed table linens (dimensions of folding, size of monogram to the quarter inch) abutting advice on how to shift a bedridden patient, scrape glue from wood furniture, and care for a newborn. Dated though it is (it offers alternative recipes for homemade starch at a time when starch was widely commercially available), it still encompasses an amazing trove of useful information.

We now envision home economics as an antiquated high school geek subject, with aprons and crocheted pot holders the feminine equivalent of pocket protectors and horn-rims. The grand aspiration of the field's inventors, however, was to increase women's power in the realm that was then their obvious primary domain. As time went on, domestic science furnished many women with a passport to higher learning in the hard sciences and, for graduates, a rewarding career in teaching or even in industry or manufacturing. Home economics grew somewhat less relevant to the life of the American everywoman as she began to move outside the home, taking part increasingly in the political process or entering jobs that previously were held exclusively by men. Its influence persisted, however, particularly in rural areas, where cash was short, new appliances less available, and housework nearly as hard as it had ever been, and it helped reinforce the importance of the home and thus of those who labor within it.

The real purpose of home ec shines through a one-page advice column called "The Country Gentlewoman" that appeared regularly in *The Country Gentleman*, a magazine published between 1912 and 1916. Author Nellie Kedzie Jones's purpose was to share basic skills with farm women who didn't possess the conveniences of city life, whose work routines were much the same as those of farm women fifty years earlier. The column mainly focused on ameliorating the conditions of the farm wife's work rather than making use of the newest advances in technology—vacuum cleaners, say—that more affluent urban women might have. Jones wanted to help shape what she called "The new home on the old farm."

A strong woman, Jones served as the Kansas State College of Agriculture's first female professor. She became a first-time mother at 48 when she adopted a daughter from a local minister and his wife. With her husband and daughter, she moved to Smoky Hill Farm near Auburndale, Wisconsin, in 1911 and put her domestic principles into practice. Besides farm work Jones continued to pursue her home economics calling, writing, teaching, and riding the circuit of five midwestern colleges every winter to produce an event called Farm and Home Week, and lecturing as far away as Florida. As she poured herself into making housewifery easier for other women, her own husband rallied to the cause, in her frequent absences from the farm taking on household labors usually assigned to the woman of the house.

Jones's column was written in the form of letters directed to a fictional niece, a farm bride named Janet, who has just moved with her husband Ben to an old-style farmhouse. The advice reflects the needs of housewives at the time and demonstrates the value of wisdom an older experienced domestic teacher can impart.

She urges Janet to refit her kitchen for convenience and ease of use. The advice is specific: get a six-hole range for the stove, a wide and deep firebox, a stove pipe with a damper, and a range on legs and with a large reservoir:

> In cold weather, with chicken mashes to make, calf feed to prepare, and dairy utensils to wash and scald, you can't have too much hot water. Get a range as plain as possible. Much nickeling, curliques, scrolls and gingerbread work generally are a pest to keep clean and are often, from an artistic standpoint, atrocities. A plain surface is easier to black and to clean.

Realistically, Jones can't give advice on running water, as such a system was so unlikely on any farm of this period. A sink, though, is a necessity, and she recommends that Janet must "never lug any water yourself, but wait till you can catch Ben or one of the men." Still, she talks of a refrigerator and a telephone. A storeroom, she insists, must be situated upstairs near the kitchen rather than down in the basement, "since that is where hundred-pound sacks of sugar and flour and oatmeal and calf meal or baby chick food will be stored." They should be anyplace but the cellar when women must lug a load. "It is heartbreaking," she writes, "to see the way some farm women, who have neither store room nor ice box, must climb up and down cellar stairs, with one or both hands loaded. It is cruelly unnecessary."

In this case, the home economics specialist lived under conditions similar to those she advised. The Jones farmstead, for example, also lacked a waterworks system, because she and her husband were too much in debt to buy one. Other domestic scientists touted vacuum cleaner brands, but Jones hawked the wares of no particular manufacturer. She confined her role to lessening the crushing workload of rural women.

On the division of labor in farm work, Jones's practicality won out over sexist ideas of the time. One column read:

"Tomboys" make strong women. Never shame a girl for romping and scuffling with her brothers. Our New England mothers and grandmothers had prudish notions about what was proper for a girl. She did not have a fair chance; she was kept in the house and put at sewing, housework or dolls. Dolls are good on a rainy day for little girls, and boys, too, for that matter, but when the weather permits get the girls out for real athletics. Housework is not very good for the health of a growing girl.

I know this last statement will be disputed, but I want to repeat it in spite of the men who never did housework, but who constantly affirm that housework is the best thing in the world for a girl. They forget that it shuts her away from sun and air; that sweeping fills her lungs with dust; that the hot stove overheats her; that dishwashing makes her stoop-shouldered; that a few of her muscles are over-strained while most of them are undeveloped; and above all there is the monotony of it which so many children hate. Give the girls a chance at some of the outdoor work, and make the boys do some of the inside work. If the girl feeds the hens and hunts the eggs let her brother help her do the dishes."

Jones' daughter apparently lived by her mother's philosophy. In a letter to a friend Jones described her daughter at the age of five jumping over the fence to play bucking bronco with a muddy hog.

THE PROFESSIONAL home economists strengthened domestic traditions, but in some ways they simultaneously undermined them. When they streamlined the procedures of the home, encouraging the use of machinery and rigid, preset steps, domestic scientists helped to undermine the craft tradition that was a historic foundation of domesticity and cut into some of the creativity of homemaking. Corporations descended to pick the bones of the home by beginning to commodify some of domesticity's most cherished features. Earlier, when a mother sewed a gown for her daughter, the dress was more precious for having been made by her hands. Mass production diminished that emotional value. To sell products, company advertising began to use copy that scoffed at grandma's penchant for living in the past. In advocating throwing out the old and bringing in the new, home economists broadcast new values that stood in opposition to the domestic values of the past.

The goals of the domestic scientists seem not to have included preserving the domestic arts so that we would benefit from them well into the future. Their aims addressed themselves instead to the present, to improving the functioning of the contemporary home. Some of the ideas to achieve a better working household now seem awkward, rote, even silly. Unintentionally, however, the home economics movement achieved something more important, in keeping alive a current of knowledge that would otherwise have gone dead.

For my generation, old-fashioned school-taught home economics succeeded in passing on some small assortment of homemaking skills (despite the smirks of the students). We can see the impoverishment of domestic skills that has followed the decline of classroom home ec. Conversance in sewing along with the other domestic arts is fast becoming exotic, in large part because the abilities acquired in the school system are no longer judged worthy of academe. Children growing up now won't learn a slipstich at school or at home, even if they'd like to. In the Girl Scout troop I lead, nine year olds are eager to learn to sew. Few know how to thread a needle. Neither do their parents. Badges Scouts earn today are often stapled rather than sewn on their uniforms.

My mother-in-law, who lives in the Midwest, has for forty years attended the monthly meetings of her local chapter of the Homemakers Club, a statewide organization in Wisconsin. Membership fosters a strong sense of identity based in important lessons of "making do" learned during the Depression. The club's stated goal has always been to teach skills that will help farm wives lessen their workload and offer more nutritious meals to their families. Club membership, she reports, is "dying on the vine," with virtually no young people joining. Still, even as times changed, Homemakers stuck to its mission. Only recently has the group capitulated, in a gesture toward contemporaneity, with a more gender-neutral name, the Association for Home and Community Education.

The name may change, but habits formed during the heyday of home economics are more lasting. We're currently in flux. Go to a potluck in rural Wisconsin, and past the tabbouleh salad and the baked brie you'll find vintage washtub-size slow-roaster crockpots next to a dozen glistening molded gelatin salads. I have a Knox pamphlet from a half century ago that extols "Gel-Cookery" with the unmistakable patois of home-ec-ese: "Each batch of Knox, made under rigidly controlled conditions, is tested for clarity, freedom from impurities, proper setting time and strength of gel. The content of each envelope is scientifically measured to congeal one pint of liquid."

Today, traditions fostered by the home economics movement make tempting targets. In *Perfection Salad: Women and Cooking at the Turn of the Century*, author Laura Shapiro lampoons a world of fancy white sauces and gelatin salads. "Containing and controlling food, draining it of taste and texture, packaging it, tucking the raisins deep inside the marshmallows, decorating it—these were some of the culinary themes of the domestic-science movement," she writes.

Gelatin, however, was not simply a froufrou of a food, it was the product of a hard-knocks economy that stretched a dollar as far as it could. Jell-O, my husband tells me, is how his grandmother managed to feed a family of eight—and this was well past the Great Depression, in the Fabulous Fifties. In a paradox not readily comprehensible today, jiggly Jell-O assumed an importance both cultural and culinary it could not claim in millennial America, when vast amounts of food are readily, bountifully available.

Some of the post–home ec generation believe the discipline to be a victim of changing trends worth resuscitating. A college student in my community, for example, discovered a classic home economics text called *A Thousand Ways to Please a Husband* at a tag sale when she was twelve years old. At her private high school she decided to start an extracurricular Domestic Science Club. During the summer she organized a day camp at her home in which she and a fellow counselor taught old-fashioned cooking skills to younger kids, in one project making both marshmallows and graham crackers from scratch in order to create homemade s'mores. Early lessons in the work of the home, as in anything, have a considerable impact.

When I was a child I saw first hand the authenticity and power of the home economics profession through the example of my great aunt. Auntie and her husband lived in a converted potato storage barn on the two-lane highway out of Greenfield because they couldn't afford a real house. She inherited the property from her father, and with few resources besides ingenuity she and Uncle Bob fixed it up. In front they planted crowder peas, and down in back of the house, in fields surrounding a weedy lake, they grew okra, corn, and cotton. Near the red wood-sided house stood a barn with horses and cows and a few barking bird dogs in a wire pen.

Auntie lived the life of a country homemaker, not poor, but never well-to-do. Uncle Bob, a charming former minor league pitcher, was something of a ne'er-do-well and preferred lying on the sofa listening to the ball game on the radio or talking politics with the men at the filling station in town to working the farm. Until the 1950s their home had no indoor plumbing, distressing their parents, who thought it old-fashioned and downscale to have to use a privy and lug water from town.

The house, narrow and cool, seemed the perfect place to spend summer afternoons, eating salted watermelon, luring kittens out from beneath the sloping front porch, and then as evening came on eating boiled corn dripping butter from a plastic corn holder on the high counter of Auntie's tiny kitchen. It was a small house. Still, an entire room was designated a sewing room and held nothing but fabric and worsted yarn, knitting needles, crochet hooks, and box upon box of tissue-paper sewing patterns.

What lifted Auntie's life above the ordinary was her vocation as a teacher of home economics. This is how she changed the lives of others. A graduate of the University of Tennessee at Knoxville, she graduated in home economics around 1930. A photo of her class shows girls in white jumpers and white headbands, and of course Auntie is the prettiest (she always was—a romantic oval portrait captures her beauty, with dark eyes and long dark hair held back in a puffy white bow). She went straight to teaching high school in Bolivar, a town whose claim to fame was as the location of the local insane asylum. Eventually she taught in Dresden, a fifteen-mile drive from Greenfield.

Auntie taught from a state-mandated curriculum, adhering to the textbooks of the day. Students in lecture halls took notes as she detailed the properties of egg whites and the chemistry of cleansers.

At that time, home economics constituted a rigorous educational requirement. Every girl who graduated from high school in Tennessee had to take two full years of home ec—one year of sewing and one year of cooking. Sewing machines lined the counters, and girls learned to cut paper patterns, pin them to cloth, and produce a dress as a final project. Cooking dealt with the scientific, practical aspects of the subject rather than gourmet—how safely to sterilize canned goods. Participation in Future Farmers of America and Future Homemakers of America created as much enthusiasm as glee club. Auntie had no children of her own, but her students adored her.

At home, too, she taught. All the neighborhood kids and her nieces and grandnieces learned from Auntie how to knit and purl. For herself, she liked to crochet, and she tried without success to teach my mother to tat, patiently bringing along the delicate openwork lace by looping and knotting the thread on a shuttle. Auntie, my grandmother, and my great-grandmother seem to have all plied these needles in a friendly competition for who could produce the most handsomely intricate work. Auntie's facility was legendary, though: "she could go to a movie and knit!" recalls my mother.

She was anything but a little old lady. Tall and rangy, she conferred dignity upon her profession. It's easy to laugh at ads from the 1940s and 1950s that depict women gaily posing beside their shiny new kitchen stoves. Look through the photographs of Auntie at work, though, and you see her resting her hand on a white enamel oven range, pressure cooker at the ready, or gazing frankly toward the photographer as she runs fabric through a sewing machine. Or standing at a wooden podium with a sign behind her that reads "home economics—something to crow about" (illustrated, of course, by a lively rooster). This was a woman, and a profession, that must be reckoned with.

The serious flavor of home economics remains today in some

regions of the country. In the rural Midwest, the vestiges of domestic science held the line through the turbulent end of the twentieth century, maintaining the value and dignity of American housewives. It's no longer sewing and cooking alone, however. In Wausau, my mother-in-law's town, the schools offer "Family and Consumer Education." Seventh graders study nutrition, use a sewing machine, and bake biscuits, and eighth graders move on to electives including Foods and Jobs and a sewing/interior design class. Ellen Swallow Richards' spirit lives on in the guise of the American Association of Family and Consumer Sciences, the name her group adopted when it very scientifically made the decision in 1993 that the American Home Economics Association would have to change; the new name would "more accurately reflect the breadth and scope of the profession," according to the association's literature.

It's not overreaching to conclude that domestic traditions filled a psychic purpose as well as one of necessity after the industrial revolution replaced a significant part of the manual labor of the home with washing machines, vacuums, stove tops, small electric appliances, and all the other labor-saving equipment we take for granted. Just as the home was being transformed, society found itself traumatized by the Great War, the Great Depression, the Second World War, the Holocaust, Korea, the Cold War, and Vietnam, as well as all kinds of smaller-scale flameouts and threats to civilized existence. The effort to pass down homemaking skills from one generation to the next, formalized in the endeavor of domestic science, served as a counterpoint to these devastating events. It may not have offered salvation, but it provided a means of holding on to human values from one conflagration to the next. Teaching the traditions of the home served a political function, signifying a belief in the sanctity of our domestic existence—which is life at its most fundamental—even as the world spun like a tornado around the home.

Auntie's converted potato barn no longer exists, the victim of rising real estate prices in even such a backwater as Greenfield, Tennessee. In its place stands a contemporary barn-style pile
ornamented by white Colonial columns. The pond remains, now a
decorative feature with ducks. Progress has also had its way with my
great-grandmother's house, which after 150 years is now only a memory for the very oldest residents of the town. Its site has been covered
over by a stretch of asphalt belonging to a giant, three-bay gas station, the kind where people dash in and out of the attached convenience store for a pack of smokes before hopping onto the four-lane
highway that now cuts through town. No more leisurely debates
about politics at the filling station. No more rooms filled with yarn
and tissue-paper patterns.

The Luddite in me would love to see no "improvements" in the
American way of life. I cannot help but mourn the loss of homemaking skills, and home economics itself, as a force in the way we
experience our days, in the tactile pleasure we take in life. When
there is no one to teach us to crochet, we lose something of our
sense of touch. Now more than ever we need all the grannies and
nonnas and aunties we can find to pass along their wisdom about
matters of the hearth.

Girls of my generation grew up learning the basics of cooking
and sewing, if not at home then in the classroom. Once we grew up,
though, we found that the real world had no need for those skills.
A rift yawned between the home ec curriculum and the teachings
of the culture at large. Why bake banana bread at home when you
can buy three loaves for five bucks at Sam's Club?

# CHAPTER 5

# A Broom of One's Own

THE I HATE TO HOUSEKEEP BOOK had gone missing from my local library. The card catalog told me that Peg Bracken's 1962 guide to "when and how to keep house without losing your mind," could be found at any number of locations in the county. Going from one to the next I found it wasn't on any library's shelf.

Finally I thought I'd borrow another Bracken book instead. *The I Hate to Cook Book,* her first and more famous, which features quick-and-dirty dishes like Hurry Curry or Spuds O'Grotten. That would do. Or maybe I'd check out *A Window Over the Sink,* a memoir in which the author relates how standing in the kitchen doing dishes allows a woman to commune with herself and reflect on her past.

The problem was the same: all, apparently, had been swiped.

When eventually I found *Housekeep,* called up from the dusty basement archive of the one local library that still housed it, I noticed that it had last been checked out in January 1970.

From this saga I drew two conclusions. One, it had been a while since Bracken's best-sellers had been read. Second, however, Bracken's works were compelling enough at some point to cause them to be lifted off the shelves of libraries, which probably had to replace them as frequently as they do the most popular authors of our own decade. Her world view, a tongue-in-cheek analysis of all that comprised housewifery, was one that hundreds of thousands of readers could relate to.

The tone of *The I Hate to Housekeep Book* is sensible, coolly ironic, even sardonic. Illustrations by the ultimate sophisticate Hilary Knight are in perfect keeping with the tone of the text. Chapters covered "Stains, Spots, Blots, Scars, and Dueling Wounds" and "The Hostess With the Leastest," which advised women how to put together spur-of-the-moment dinner parties when there is nothing in the pantry. Bracken proposed changing the rules of housewifery so that wives and mothers could have an easier time keeping house. Therefore, as she suggests about moths: "Don't do anything about them unless you're sure they're around. Otherwise you'll waste many a bright afternoon which would be better spent seeing your friends or practicing your judo." She advocates not taking housewifery seriously, to do what's entailed at the least cost to oneself.

The usual advice book stance on stain removal is absurd, she writes. Professional stain removal types recommend prompt action, advocating whisking away the stained object, determining the composition of the spot, and getting to work on it with your chemistry kit.

> Well, in many instances this is hard to do. If you are having guests, you can hardly turn to the gentleman on your right and say, "Pardon me, Mr. Fulmeister, but was that a puddle of French dressing or thermidor sauce you just spilled?" Even if he told you, it would be impolite to start treating the stain right then. The perfect hostess would see to it that she spilled a similar puddle herself, in order to put her guest at ease.

She twists the rules of domesticity, adapting them to the perspective of the early 1960s homemaker. While scrapping (some) conventions, and crucifying (some) standards, mainly for a laugh, a more philosophical, even existential subtext enlivens the book's more practical contents, particularly in one chapter: "How to Be Happy When You're Miserable." As you might suspect, the chapter illuminates some of the day-to-day conditions that led Betty Friedan a year later to assert that "vacuuming the living room floor—with or without makeup—is not work that takes enough thought or energy to challenge any woman's full capacity."

The misery of housewifery resounds (to less comic effect) throughout the popular magazines of the time. One writer, Nora Johnson, writes in a piece titled "The Captivity of Marriage," in the June 1961 *Atlantic Monthly*, that the typical wife

> vaguely feels that she is frittering away her days and that a half-defined but important part of her ability is going about unused; she is guilty about her feeling of futility because of her belief in the magic medicine of love. This is the housewife's syndrome, the vicious circle, the feeling of emptiness in the gap between what she thought marriage was going to be like and what it is really like.

Bracken takes a different approach to this subject:

> Life being the daily affair it is, full of jobs that are done only to be done all over again, the random housewife often feels a bit like Theophilus Thistle, the unsuccessful thistle-sifter who thrust three thousand thistles through the thick of his thumb. There is no end to the thistles, nor to the loose ends.
>
> Worse still—if she be young or youngish—the random housewife is often prone to Torschlusspanik, or fear of being locked in the park at night, after the gates are closed.

As a curative, she advises learning to water-ski, writing a cheerful letter, cleaning out the coat closet, even vacuuming in the buff. What she doesn't propose is abandoning housewifery itself.

*The I Hate to Housekeep Book* is an apologia—a funny, ironic one—for the labor of the home, which may be challenging or boring, but is in any case, according to this highly engaging writer, inescapable. In her foreword, Bracken describes housekeeping as the Eighth Lively Art, but says it is lively "in the same way sand-hogging is. They both take courage, muscle, and endurance. The main difference between a sand hog and a housewife is that he has a nice clean tunnel later to show for his efforts, and it stays put, while she has it all to do over again the next day. She must simply keep tunneling."

IN AN ANTHOLOGY of articles published as *Feminist Revolution* by Redstockings in 1975, an artist named Shirley Boccacio, with the pseudonym Virtue Hathaway, tells the story of what she calls the Great Poster Rip-off. Her saga starts in the fall of 1970, "when the underground women's movement was at its height." The story ends three years later, when a Federal judge in Los Angeles refuses to hear her complaint.

The "Fuck Housework" poster, at the center of the dispute, Hathaway describes as "a drawing of a young woman breaking a broom in two, with a smile of commitment and unshakable determination on her face. That poster was born out of the anger and frustration of Women; I was the artistic medium." After designing the poster and getting it printed, she had it copyrighted with the Library of Congress in 1971. At the time she designed the poster the artist had three small children and no husband and made ends meet on $320 per month. The family wore hand-me-down clothes.

Then, incredibly, the poster turned into a cult hit, and Hathaway had a "release from the prison of poverty." Bicycles for the kids, new shoes, "a rug for the bare wood floor." She'd found a way to provide for herself and her family so that eventually she could pursue her goal of writing children's books.

Throughout her story is the redundancy of housework: dishes, laundry, cooking. When a big poster company steals her design, making plates from one of her posters and distributing its own product to stores all over town, Virtue takes action and hires a lawyer. The day of the hearing, she's home caring for a sick child. Problem is, she discovers later, the judge took a look at the poster, threw it up in the air with horror, and refused to hear the case, saying the poster was "patently obscene." She calls her lawyer, who tells her the judge charged that "the poster was against public policy and does nothing but demean our society."

Hathaway is outraged:

"Oh, really," I answered with a note of sarcasm in my voice, "I wonder if Judge Ponte would find it demeaning to be a young Mother who does nothing but clean, cook and care for children 14 hours a day, 7 days a week, year after year. I wonder if the good judge would find it demeaning to have served as a dutiful and faithful housewife for all of one's life and then find oneself living in abject poverty as an old woman, the labor of a lifetime, extolled by society, counting for almost nothing in one's old age. I wonder if our stern Judge would find the mental, emotional and physical fatigue of unrelenting, unpaid housework demeaning if he found himself as a woman in that occupation. You know, Will," I continued, "it was not the word fuck that Judge Ponte objected to; rather it was obscene to him that women are revolting against their assigned place in the kitchen. And, of course, he is right, the poster IS an expression of outrage against public policy, the public policy of exploiting women!"

Ultimately her lawyers cheat her too, and she is thrown back into poverty with her children, a sad example of the paternalistic evils of the same system that had inspired her poster. Hers is a tale that is emblematic not only of the disrespect paid a single mother by a casually sexist court system, but of new, radically transformed attitudes of women toward the housework that had until recently rarely been questioned in public. Current events had begun to undermine a version of domesticity that was already less organic, more mechanical, causing a change in cultural attitudes whose effects we still feel today.

TOWARD MIDCENTURY, the home closed in on American women. Upon the soldiers' return from Europe after World War II some uncertainty prevailed about how to reintegrate men into a society in which women had grown economically self-sufficient. If women went on working, ran the psychobabble of the day, men's egos might go *pffft*.

Freudian psychiatry urged a return to the home of yore. Cooking, preserving, cleaning, and decorating would constitute an effective treatment for the "pathological" condition of feminism. Only through a return to domesticity, with the home "a social extension of the mother's womb," could women's "inner balance" be reclaimed. Popular books and magazines portrayed women as listless dilettantes or vipers, who to prove their femininity should cater to their men in every respect. That women should care for the home was nothing new, but a significant difference separated this era from those that came before: the law was laid down that women could do nothing more than be housewives. That restriction was one that galled after many women's increased experience in paid work during the war.

Yet for many American women and men, clear postwar domestic roles represented a welcome change after the trauma, loneliness, and uncertainty of the war years. The idea of home was itself transformed, as G.I.-bill couples could suddenly afford single-family housing. Levittown, built for returning soldiers and their families, signaled the awakening of a new hunger for a way of life that included all the modern amenities—from car to lawn to television to all the major appliances—while brushing away some of the mustier conventions of the past, such as regular contact with extended family or even grandma living at home.

As the generations broke apart, there evolved new methods of educating young wives about the homemaking skills they would earlier have absorbed through daily contact with their mothers and other female elders—information that was all the more important now that management of the home had become women's primary culturally sanctioned job. In the nonfiction bestseller lists of the 1950s and 1960s we can see the cresting emphasis on house and home. Throughout the early 1950s, cookbooks and home books—*Betty Crocker's Picture Cook Book*, *Betty Crocker's Good and Easy Cook Book*, *Better Homes and Gardens Garden Book*, *Better Homes and Gardens Handyman's Book*—make intermittent appearances. The *Better Homes and Gardens Barbecue Book* and the *Better Homes and Gardens Decorating Book* take their place alongside *The Mandarins* by Simone de Beauvoir in 1956. Turning the page to the 1960s, an explosion of domestic books dominates. In 1960 are *The General Foods Kitchens Cookbook*, *Better Homes and Gardens Dessert Book*, and *Better Homes and Gardens Decorating Ideas*; the 1961 list includes the *Better Homes and Gardens Sewing Book*, the *Casserole Cook Book*, *Better Homes and Gardens Nutrition for Your Family*, and a new edition of *Betty Crocker's New Picture Cook Book*. Through 1963, what we would today call "shelter books" thrive.

Then, after the Kennedy assassination, the pattern veers from home to weightier matters. The only remotely domestic subjects through the 1970s are diet manuals, with the exception of the TV-offshoot *Galloping Gourmet*. Just as the 1940s best-sellers had included no home-related volumes whatsoever, neither did the 1970s. Instead, starting with *The Sensuous Woman* in 1970 and continuing every year throughout the decade, sex books grabbed the American literary dollar.

Before *The Sensuous Woman* and *The Hite Report*, as suburban housewives planted their rock gardens and layered their casseroles, the media pundits' prevailing view was that today's homemaker was an incredibly fortunate creature. *Newsweek* ran a special science report in 1960 that enumerated her advantages:

> Who could ask for anything more? The educated American woman has her brains, her good looks, her car, her freedom . . . freedom to choose a straight-from-Paris dress (original or copy), or to attend a class in ceramics or calculus; freedom to determine the timing of her next baby or who shall be the next President of the United States.

In the 1950s, a loaf of bread cost only fourteen cents, but there was a skyrocketing psychic toll of all this freedom paired with inadequate work opportunities and the devaluation of the labor of the home.

By the late 1950s, the cleaning and cooking and traditional domestic crafts of housewifery had acquired a severely negative connotation, at least among some observers. Most famously, Betty Friedan, herself a suburban homemaker, lambasted housewifery as a meaningless ruse for holding women back. *The Feminine Mystique*'s contention that the housewife role degraded women, as stinging and eloquent as it appears even to this day, constituted one well-turned argument in a series of similar briefs that had been expressed by some—but by no means all—feminist writers over the course of the past one hundred years. These works along with Friedan's were now pored over by women whose lives were changing.

Twenty-five years ago, when I first discovered *The Second Sex* as a college student, Simone de Beauvoir represented everything I aspired to as a woman. De Beauvoir was not only fiercely intelligent, she was visionary, uncompromisingly direct—and she debated philosophy in smoky Parisian cafes with Jean-Paul Sartre. When she asserted that the two sexes had never been equal—"This has always been a man's world"—it rang as a patent truth. Two decades before my college years, in the Stepford Wives–flavored early 1950s, when *The Second Sex* hit American bookstores, both the idea and the manner in which it was rendered appeared totally original and shocking. The swath it cut was enormous, from biology to the entire history of women, to mythology, sexuality and "variants"—prostitutes, narcissists, mystics, and other aberrations. She condemned the societal features that oppressed the female gender; however, her encyclopedia of women's subjugation largely emphasized women's complicity in their own fate.

De Beauvoir lavished some of her most snarling derision on the housewife. The "wife-servant," she wrote, was trapped in the work of the home, "a vague and meaningless rearrangement of disorder."

Few tasks are more like the torture of Sisyphus than housework, with its endless repetition: the clean becomes soiled, the soiled is made clean, over and over, day after day. The housewife wears herself out marking time: she makes nothing, simply perpetuates the present. She never senses conquest of a positive Good, but rather indefinite struggle against negative Evil. A young pupil writes in her essay: 'I shall never have house-cleaning day'; she thinks of the future as constant progress toward some unknown summit; but one day, as her mother washes the dishes, it comes over her that both of them will be bound to such rites until death. Eating, sleeping, cleaning—the years no longer rise up toward heaven, they lie spread out ahead, gray and identical. The battle against dust and dirt is never done.

The housewife, insisted de Beauvoir, collaborates in her oppression.

> It is a sad fate to be required without respite to repel an enemy instead of working toward positive ends, and very often the house-keeper submits to it in a kind of madness that may verge on perversion, a kind of sado-masochism. The maniac housekeeper wages her furious war against dirt, blaming life itself for the rubbish all living growth entails. When any living being enters her house, her eye gleams with a wicked light: 'Wipe your feet, don't tear the place apart, leave that alone!' She wishes those of her household would hardly breathe; everything means more thankless work for her. Severe, preoccupied, always on the watch, she loses joie de vivre, she becomes overprudent and avaricious. She shuts out the sunlight, for along with that come insects, germs, and dust, and besides, the sun ruins silk hangings and fades upholstery; she scatters naphthalene, which scents the air. She becomes bitter and disagreeable and hostile to all that lives: the end is sometimes murder.

This is the kind of judgment inherited by the second-wave feminists that reinforced our eagerness to reject the housewife role of the generation that preceded us—and, equally, to reject housewives themselves as somehow deluded, less evolved creatures than those women who had "freed" themselves from the confines of the home. My view of those women of my mother's generation fell in line with de Beauvoir's colorful take on joylessly tidy housewives, though some of the details of their obsessions had changed with the times. The housewife of the 1970s employed Mr. Clean rather than mothballs, sucked dust from shag rugs instead of silk hangings. In essence, though, her condition stayed the same. She enjoyed no autonomy, no productive work, no dignity; thus, she was "inessential." To wit, according to de Beauvoir: "However respected she may be, she is subordinate, secondary, parasitic."

I didn't see it at the time, but as brilliant as some of de Beauvoir's observations might be, as a whole these passages embody female self-loathing in its clearest manifestation. It is true, as she writes, that the old inegalitarian ways must die and that women as well as men need novelty, risk, and challenges outside the home. But her writings linked this emphasis on finding a new equality with a conviction that the work of the home is in and of itself beneath the attention of independent, healthy human beings. She never suggests men taking on some of the work of the home, instead of women providing housework as a "service."

When I read de Beauvoir in college, what excited me perhaps even more than *The Second Sex* was her autobiography, *Memoirs of a Dutiful Daughter*, which recounts her upbringing and graduation to young adulthood in contrast with that of her two best friends, Jacques and Zaza. I was fascinated especially by the fate of her beloved Zaza, whose life de Beauvoir depicts as a failed struggle to attain selfhood. The tormented Zaza attempts to escape but is unable to resist the clutches of a bourgeois, traditionally feminine existence and so, as is symbolically drawn in the book, suffocates from a lack of the oxygen of liberation. De Beauvoir ends the book at the moment Zaza dies and doesn't describe specifically how she herself grew into the grand dame of feminism. For me, though, the primary message of de Beauvoir's life was a powerful one: stay mired in the traditions of the past, especially domestic tradition, and you die; only if you escape domesticity will you flourish.

The women's movement of the late 1960s and early 1970s burst from the same impulse. For many young feminists, observing the lives of their mothers had revealed no strength or dignity in domestic roles. For some, their social and political experiences in the early 1960s strengthened their blanket rejection of all things domestic.

Sara Evans, a writer who chronicled the battle for civil rights and the formative days of the women's movement, reflected in 1979 that the perspective of many of the early "women's libbers" in the late 1960s took shape from their experiences as college-age newlyweds:

> Most of these marriages were serious attempts to form "democratic" relationships and several have lasted more than a decade. But marriage, however democratically inclined the partners might be, brought with it the cultural burden of certain expectations for both "wives" and "husbands." To discard such roles, it turned out, was no mere act of will or ideological adjustment. Indeed, such changes required a final confrontation with that part of one's identity that was labeled "housewife," and then further called for the strength to deal with the subtle expectations of one's well-intentioned but nonetheless well-socialized mate.

When the student movement exploded in 1968, women did not enjoy sexual equality, she notes, but instead experienced "the reassertion of oppressive sex roles, more strongly than ever." At Columbia University in the spring of 1968, 300 students seized classroom and administrative buildings to protest the school's policies as a neighborhood slumlord. For days, women lived alongside their male peers in the captured buildings, hanging posters out the windows, disrupting furniture in the offices of campus staff, singing in the hallways, and bunking down at night. But a difference separated the male and female strikers: the women were expected to cook the entire group's three daily meals ("in a kitchen the size of a phone booth," according to Evans) and to perform all the other housekeeping chores.

Rejection of domesticity established itself as a constant refrain of the era. In August 1968, a demonstration in Atlantic City protested the Miss America pageant. Into a "freedom trashcan," along with bras, girdles, and curlers, demonstrators tossed copies of that icon of homemaking, *Ladies' Home Journal*. That same day, an effigy of Miss America was auctioned off by one of the organizers of the demonstration. "Gentlemen," she said, "I offer you the 1969 model. She's better every year. She walks. She talks. She smiles on cue. *And* she does housework." In the battle for the liberation of women, housework was the sworn enemy.

The young feminists of the late 1960s and early 1970s wanted to be anything but that model housewife. Historian Ruth Rosen makes the point that they had grown up observing the feminine mystique firsthand in the person of their mothers or in the icon of the "ordinary housewife" all around them, in ads, in literature, or on TV. According to Rosen, the women's liberationists were living with a specter. "The ghost haunting these young women," she writes, "wore an apron and lived vicariously through the lives of a husband and children."

It's an image with history. Nathaniel Hawthorne, in *Mosses from an Old Manse*, wrote of "a ghostly servant-maid, who used to be heard in the kitchen, at deepest midnight, grinding coffee, cooking, ironing—performing, in short, all kinds of domestic labor—although no traces of anything accomplished could be detected, the next morning." To free themselves from this frantically busy yet peculiarly nonproductive ghost, many contemporary feminists have felt they must cut her off at the knees, diminish her power by diminishing, if not erasing, the long history of women's role in the home.

A manifesto called "Liberation of Women," published in *New Left Notes* on July 10, 1967, offered a wish list for women's place in the ideal society. It called for all programs which will free women from their traditional roles in order that we may participate with all of our resources and energies in meaningful and creative activity. The family unit perpetuates the traditional role of women and the autocratic and paternalistic role of men. Therefore we must seek new forms that will allow children to develop in an environment which is democratic and where the relationships between people are those of equal human beings.

To this end was advocated creation of communal child care centers, better dissemination of birth control, and availability of abortion.

The third program dealt with housework:

Ultimately technology and automation will eliminate work which is necessary for the maintenance of the home. Until this occurs every adult person living in the household will have to assume an equal share of the work.

In such pronouncements, the work of the home was flatly viewed as nothing more than inescapable scutwork. The 1970 "Women's Strike for Equality" had women marching in the streets in one of the largest feminist demonstrations in American history. Unsurprisingly, refusal to engage in housework was a central theme. Popular posters read, "Don't Iron While the Strike Is Hot," and "Don't Cook Dinner—Starve a Rat Today." Members of consciousness-raising groups found commonality in the complaint that they were, as de Beauvoir had conceptualized it, nothing but servants within their homes.

One article in particular seemed to provoke a sense of "eureka, I'm not the only one ever to have experienced this"—what women had already begun to call a "click" moment. In an early issue of Ms. magazine, a piece by Pat Mainardi titled "The Politics of Housework" made the distinction between "liberated women," who men believe will bestow favors, and women's liberation, which means sharing housework. If the issue sounds trivial, she writes, it is anything but. The present, she writes, is a moment of change:

> We women have been brainwashed more than even we can imagine. Probably too many years of seeing television women in ecstasy over their shiny waxed floors or breaking down over their dirty shirt collars. Men have no such conditioning. They recognize the essential fact of housework right from the beginning. Which is that it stinks.

The author's husband, when backed into a corner and asked to take on the garbage, dirty dishes, brooms, and mops, is determined not to clean house but crafty enough to come up with unobjectionable ways of saying so. Mainardi gives examples.

> "I don't mind sharing the work, but you'll have to show me how to do it."
>
> *Meaning:* I ask a lot of questions and you'll have to show me everything everytime I do it because I don't remember so good. Also don't try to sit down and read while I'm doing my jobs because I'm going to annoy hell out of you until it's easier to do them yourself.

Understand, concludes the story, that women are an oppressed people, that men are the exploiters and women servants who have always taken "care of this bottom strata of life while they have confined their efforts to the rarefied upper regions." There is a solution, however: draft time sheets assigning jobs, and police your man to make sure he is in fact cleaning the oven.

The message was beginning to take on a life of its own. The cover of the very first issue of Ms. had depicted an American Kali, weeping and pregnant, holding an iron, a feather duster, a frying pan, and a mirror along with a telephone, typewriter, and steering wheel. Its contents underscored the magazine's editorial outrage over the daily injustices suffered by women at home with Jane O'Reilly's article, "Click! The Housewife's Moment of Truth."

Fueled by such images and writings, the conventional wisdom grew to be that American women were trapped in an obsolete domestic role from which they could be freed only by the women's liberation movement. It was as if the America of the late 1960s were an extended episode of the "I Dream of Jeannie" TV show. Women could clean up the mess so that it would disappear—with a blink of the eye or a twitch of the nose—but the cost was to have to treat your partner as "Master," stay at home, and go around in crepe harem pants and a bare midriff. Jeannie held the power to put an elephant in the bedroom or spirit Tony back in time, only that power was veiled by her subservience. In a time of the fast, disposable, and cheaply miraculous—paper dresses and freeze-dried ice cream—women wanted a quick fix for all the injustices done to them in the past. It was a rush to the easiest solution: *You won't share? I'm out of here!* The logical next step from the idea that women were subordinated in the home seemed to be that that environment was lesser and the "real world" more important. Thus women denigrated the work of their foremothers and short-changed themselves in the process. Because what self-respecting man would want to share in work "that stinks"?

My friend Sandra, who struggles to alternate cooking and shopping schedules with her husband, recently reflected, "What the feminists didn't take into account is that men wouldn't end up doing any of this stuff." Her comment echoes that of comic farmwife Ma Kettle when she announced in one of her many movies, "I can't make Pa change and be neat, so I'll have to change and be dirty. Been peace in this house ever since." The fact is that men never responded to feminists' demand that they do half the household chores. Instead of sharing, both adults for the most part abandoned the work of the home. Sociologists analyzing how men and women have divided the work of the home over the last twenty years have found that housework is in fact becoming more equal, not because men are doing more but because women are doing less.

Because homemaking itself appeared unworthy of respect, scholarship focusing on the complexities of housewifery has come slowly. The academy has turned insufficient attention to the culture of the home either sociologically or psychologically. Dolores Hayden makes an astute observation in *The Grand Domestic Revolution,* her study of American feminists' designs for homes, neighborhoods, and cities:

> Members of other academic disciplines have looked down on the pragmatic, applied field of home economics but none have dealt with household questions with marked success in the past century. Anthropologists have produced fascinating studies of the forms of dwellings and their cultural significance and have rightly insisted that no society can be adequately understood without giving home life a weight equal to public affairs. Yet the skills of anthropologists have often been directed at the domestic customs of remote peoples, although the position of a woman charged with housekeeping in a Mongolian tent or serving a meal to her husband in "the Lord's corner" of a Swiss farmhouse may have more in common with a housewife living in a New Jersey suburb than the scholar may be prepared to admit.

When social commentators do turn their attention to the labor of the home, there seems to be a predisposition toward praising those aspects of domestic life that are visibly "productive," or in which women have taken part alongside men over the ages, coupled with a regret that the industrial revolution left no jobs of "value" in the home. One recent history of advice manuals raises the question of homemaking's essential purpose with the disappearance of older domestic craft traditions. "The pre-industrial rural home," the authors write, "was a tiny manufacturing center, demanding of its female workers a wide variety of skills and an endless capacity for hard work." Back then, they enthuse, there was little time for housework as we'd recognize it today. This analysis makes a somewhat simplistic distinction between "making bread, butter, cloth, clothing, soap, candles, medicines, and other things essential to their families' survival" and "just making apple pies and samplers." In fact there is sustenance for families and for the culture as a whole in pies and samplers, and there has never been a time when cleaning house wasn't a necessity.

The question has to be asked: Were women in the women's movement of the 1960s and 1970s rebelling against the oppression of sex roles that had existed in perpetuity? Or were they reacting to the consumerism, built-in obsolescence, and finite suburban roles of the 1950s postwar Suzy-homemaker housewife, which was only a small part of the population of American women?

In any case, feminists of the 1970s and 1980s focused not on creating a more equitable environment within the home or on increasing respect for those who continued to labor within it, but instead on the ERA and abortion rights. The goal of the women's movement was to bring housewives into the mainstream workforce and out of the home. Developing new support systems that would help people balance home and work more effectively was not the primary focus.

Phyllis Schlafly's dominance in the vanguard of the right wing and her association with highly visible housewifery (one tactic she favored was wearing aprons to protests) further widened the gulf between the women's movement and domesticity. Most women who considered themselves feminists thought Schlafly had been hoodwinked, brainwashed. That Schlafly was seen as antithetical to the goals of feminism *and* that she personified old-fashioned values of the home suggested there was little way for a progressive person to maintain an involvement in homemaking.

For many in the movement, becoming liberated meant disavowing housework. Women wanted careers, and not only because of the inherent interest and independence and income work provides. By this time almost any job, but especially those typically held by men, had begun to hold obvious cachet, and the scutwork of the home seemed undeniably puny and contemptible.

I HATE TO HOUSEKEEP and the "Fuck Housework" poster represented two responses to the state of keeping house as of the mid-twentieth century. As the decades have passed, the tension between the two has continued to hold us.

The counterculture swung toward rustic domesticity with its 1971 advice book *Living on the Earth* by Alicia Bay Laurel, a twenty-year-old hippie who lived on a commune in northern California. I nearly wore out my copy at the age of 14, learning how to quilt, embroider, sew a smock, and weave baskets. I didn't build a home out of lashed branches and canvas, because I was living under my parents' roof at the time. Still, the creative excitement of the handmade, conveyed in her whimsical line drawings, felt utterly different from my mother's vacuumed and floor-waxed house—as well as from home ec class—and I wanted to be a part of it. My friend and I even took inspiration and instruction from *Living on the Earth* to weave full-size rope hammocks during school gym class . . . such were the times that we somehow persuaded the school authorities to give us academic credit for the project. Some of Bay Laurel's comments have an ancient cast: "The kitchen is the center of the home. The fire is the center of the kitchen." Back to the land is also back to the eighteenth century, as readers learn to gauge temperature in a woodstove to bake their bread, build an ice chest, make lye soap, and do laundry by hand.

Joan Didion gave a more acerbic interpretation to the emerging "earth mother" persona when she chronicled Haight-Ashbury in 1968 in *Slouching Towards Bethlehem* and saw young women there who were holding fast in the kitchen. One of Didion's subjects, Barbara, offers up macrobiotic apple pie along with her views of what she calls "the woman's thing," which she first discovered when she and her boyfriend "went to live with the Indians." Didion observes:

> Barbara is on what is called the woman's trip to the exclusion of almost everything else. When she and Tom and Max and Sharon need money, Barbara will take a part-time job, modeling or teaching kindergarten, but she dislikes earning more than ten or twenty dollars a week. Most of the time she keeps house and bakes. "Doing something that shows your love that way," she says, "is just about the most beautiful thing I know."

Didion's somewhat snide portrayal of Barbara reflects the tension at that time between rejecting or embracing domesticity. Alongside the more vocal rejection of homemaking that dominated the media in the 1960s and 1970s grew a countercultural dedication to homeways. Granted, this alternative viewpoint, which flourished mainly in agrarian hippie communes, also dismissed the homemaking style of the previous generation. As some in the women's movement marched and debated, however, other people were learning from domestic traditions of a more distant past—growing vegetables, weaving baskets, cooking, and laundering with nonchemical cleansers.

Equally significant, they embraced these activities deliberately. Back-to-the-landers chose to perpetuate the homegrown and the homemade, which corporations wanted to replace with a dizzying increase in domestic products. As the 1960s evolved into the 1970s, a trend accelerated that would ultimately threaten the integrity of the domestic arts more than any other. It began, ironically, with the home economics movement. As stricter rules and constructs of homemaking developed, the organic, individual traditions of the home began to fade. The field opened for heavily advertised corporate goods—especially processed foods, some of which, like Spam, found popularity during World War II as troop rations, and by 1959 had sold a billion cans stateside. Other synthetic products replaced rationed items, such as butter, sugar, meat, and other household items. Who would balk at buying these goods? If a well-known home economist advised that nourishing gravy should be prepared with certain ingredients in certain proportions and endorsed a particular brand of canned gravy in a magazine ad, a homemaker just might abandon the recipe she learned from old Aunt Gladys. Celebrities began to advocate for the taste and efficiency of processed foods—none other than domestic icon Donna Reed, for example, served as spokesperson for Campbell's Soup in her 1950s heyday. The classroom teachings of home economics still conveyed the importance of hearth and home, but domestic bliss was to be achieved with products bought rather than made.

By the 1950s, the role of homemaker had been so devalued that when Betty Friedan issued her blistering critique in 1963, women clamored to dump the labor that for thousands of years had been not only crucial to survival but a source of personal strength and dignity. This was not evil or even wrong so much as shortsighted. By dismissing the work of the home as trivial and promoting the flight of women from the home, the women's movement of the

1970s inadvertantly led to greater reliance on corporate goods and services.

Though not mainstream, those who made their own clothes, grew their own food, and provided their own energy held the line against the commodification of traditional home arts that would swamp us in the following decades with the Gap and Applebee's on every block. There was a further radical element to countercultural domesticity: housework to some degree engaged men as well as women. At the beginning it may have been women dipping the candles and minding the babies, but gradually, toward the mid-1970s, and inspired in large part by the phenomenon of the *Whole Earth Catalog*, men around the country began to grind wheat berries, braid leather for belts, and sew shirts or shifts. Sex roles didn't become interchangeable, but these men shared more domestic tasks with their mates than their fathers had.

Slowly and almost invisibly, the way a flower appears the same unless you see its growth through a stop-motion camera, women and men have changed their approach to the work of the home. Housework by women has declined from 30 hours per week in 1965 to 17.5 in 1995, according to a July 1999 study by the University of Maryland. Men's contribution reached 9 hours a week in 1995. This slow crawl toward equality in housework isn't likely to speed up soon. In sociologist William Beer's view, "Men who do housework are crossing one of the deepest and longest standing barriers in human society."

The instructional element of home economics, the strain that told housewives what to buy as well as how to stand and the angle at which bedsheets must be folded, has shifted to a more ecumenical, gender-blind approach. *Consumer Reports*, which originated in 1926 as a club of engineers distributing mimeographed lists of products has evolved into a magazine with a circulation of five million and a Web site. Along the way, in addition to evaluations of cars, radios, and cigarettes, *Consumer Reports* tackled the subjects that the home economists had marked out as their territory. Instant pudding, for example, got the thumbs down in 1945, because though mixes "enable the busy housewife to whip together a more-or-less tasty dessert in a very few minutes," the flavor of the red dessert "is equally likely to be called cherry, raspberry, or strawberry." The photo that ran with the review depicted three blindfolded women putting pudding to the test. Steam irons received equally rigorous treatment in a 1951 article whose accompanying photo showed the soleplate of one model melting down as improbably as a Dali watch. Magazines and books published since then attend to classic homemaking concerns: stain removal, eliminating bathroom germs, storing cleaning products, and tackling rust. The difference, of course, is that without advertising and beholden to no manufacturer, *Consumer Reports*, with its fifty labs and staff of crack engineers, can purport to be the "scientific" source of data. If you page through a cleaning advice volume put out recently by *Consumer Reports*, the contents are much the same as those in 1937's *Searchlight Guide*: stain removal and the surefire system for cleaning a toilet bowl receive their due. This is one legacy of the home economics movement. All the book lacks is the earlier manuals' detailed instruction on posture.

Over the years, despite de Beauvoir, Friedan, and the rising second wave of feminism, some women continued to clean house, enlarge their laundry rooms, take pride in shining silver for the holidays, and consult the experts for advice. Keeping house has spawned a lasting publishing phenomenon as a result.

Reading *Heloise's Household Hints* now is to immerse oneself in the luxuriousness of cheap romance novels: edition after edition, year after year, promise salvation and serenity through cleanliness and order. "If today is your washday . . . let's make that chore fun!" writes Heloise. "To take dents out of ping-pong balls, you can drop them in boiling water, turn them occasionally, and in a few minutes they will be good as new!" Other grime-busting gurus, like Mary Ellen Pinkham, or Don Aslett, who has published twenty-six books specializing in making housework faster and more fun, or best-selling author Linda Cobb (*Talking Dirty with the Queen of Clean:* "tea—the wood cleaner you can drink!") have equally avid followings. Even romance novelist Barbara Taylor Bradford launched her career in 1968 with *The Complete Encyclopedia of Homemaking Ideas.* These advice books, however, offer the practical tips with most of the domestic glory dropped out. They don't offer suggestions on how to approach your life, the way Catharine Beecher did in the nineteenth century, because the idea of home as a locus of spiritual as well as material comfort has by now been so thoroughly devalued.

There are a few exceptions, at least in tone. Upscale readers purchased *Home Comforts*—at a cover price of $35—the 1999 encyclopedic manual by Cheryl Mendelsohn that makes keeping house a craft worthy of a medieval guild. "Homekeeping" is the term Martha Stewart uses to describe everything from "the basics your grandma knew to the domestic arts that may have eluded your mother." Each issue of *Martha Stewart Living* gives such tips as getting red wine off linens or motor oil off jeans—"guidance you can really trust," according to a promotional mailing for the magazine. Stewart's success proves that the hunger for advice in making a home is stronger than ever.

American women today shoulder the twin legacy of home economics, which suggested they weren't doing housework right, and the women's movement, which insisted they shouldn't be doing it at all. As a result, many of us feel acute discomfort about the whole subject, a nagging sense of guilt concocted of equal parts fervor for domestic perfection and aversion to the work required to maintain it. Companies, as they have since the turn of the twentieth century, have launched efforts to capitalize on this angst. Impracticality reigns, with couture housedresses for women who want only to play at being a housewife. One designer sells seductively sheer black halter-necked aprons. In 2002, *Good Morning America* launched a weeklong series focusing on spring-cleaning, an event whose audience, according to futurist Faith Popcorn, is comprised of "homemaking voyeurs," those who want the thrill of a clean house without getting their hands dirty. Laundry soap companies are investing heavily in research and development, hoping that niche products will help them grab more of the six-billion-dollar detergent market. Handy Wipes sell in three flavors. The Swiffer WetJet Mop, which never needs to be wrung (look, Mom, no rubber gloves) has seen skyrocketing sales. Gourmet laundry items now include green tea patchouli ironing water at $10 a bottle. A survey by the National Association of Home Builders found that home buyers ranked a separate laundry room as the most coveted of eighty-eight possible features they'd like in their dream house— this at a time when 98 percent of the world still does its laundry by hand, in a bucket or on the banks of a river. Having cut his teeth on tea kettles, architect Michael Graves has moved on to a product even more basic: the toilet plunger.

For some kitchen builders a Viking Stove will always be the ne plus ultra status symbol. Other homeowners now want the look of the past with state-of-the-art trimmings. Elmira Stoveworks offers a range for home kitchens that looks exactly like an antique wood-burning unit that was first produced around 1850, but this one has an electric oven; commercial-strength high-flame gas burners, self-cleaning, electronic oven controls; and delayed-start, electronic clock/timer—and is priced at $5,000. Nesting means buying for the home more than being in it.

Implements of housecleaning that defined our grandmothers' workdays remain as tchotchkes, design accessories, collectors' items. The last washboard company in America was sold to a new owner in 1999, just before liquidation. Now, using vintage equipment, Columbus Washboards, in Logan, Ohio, manufactures a product using not only the traditional white pine but now the more decorative but less durable poplar. Consumers of the company's washboards include musicians, who now no longer have to haunt junk stores, and craft artists who transform them into furniture, planters, or trash containers.

Feeling both the adamant resistance to housework and the urge to keep up appearances has resulted in a boom in maid services; hiring a housekeeper allows a person to keep her own hands out of the wash pail and her home clean at least to some degree. It may not be such a great deal for the maid, however. The author Barbara Ehrenreich spent time in 1999 working for a service called The Maids and chronicled it in a magazine story that detailed the view of those whose work hours are spent largely on their knees:

> Here you find elaborate dust structures held together by a scaffolding of dog hair; dried bits of pasta glued to the floor by their sauce; the congealed remains of gravies, jellies, contraceptive creams, vomit, and urine.

If dealing in the grosser detritus of daily living isn't bad enough, what's more dispiriting is the relationship between client and employee. Not only do homeowners degrade their "cleaning ladies," so do the maid services, which underpay their workers, give them ten minutes for lunch, and rebuke them for the most minor infractions. The article focuses on the exploitation of those who perform intimate household chores for strangers, but a subtheme is that the work itself is disgusting and contemptible, that the labor of the home is work in which no one with any choice would engage.

It's a conflict that resonates today with so unpredictable an economy. Some families, concerned about falling income or lost jobs, can no longer afford the cleaning help they've depended on but lack the knowledge or inclination to do it themselves. In 2000, according to the Opinion Research Corporation, one-third of 1,000 Americans surveyed said they had given up on ironing, one-fourth had stopped scrubbing floors, and one-fifth said they don't wash windows.

For those of us who came of age in the 1970s amid angry finger-pointing over who's exploiting whom, the fractured bones of our confusion over keeping house have never knit. In my mid-twenties I worked as a researcher for an employer with a home office. As I and the rest of her small staff went about our business, scattering papers and books and magazines all over the place in the process, she would sit at her desk in the corner and every once in a while chirrup, "Neatness counts!" while wagging her finger at us. It seemed ludicrous: of course, neatness didn't really count.

And that brings us to where we stand now. We're damned if we do, damned if we don't. We hate housework. We'd rather be doing anything else. Not only that, but to like any part of housework is socially unacceptable. I have two articles and two books on my desk at the moment, each confessing the writer's guilty obsession with domesticity. One, from a midwestern city newspaper's home section, leads off, "I have a confession to make. I am a closet home-maker. There's something exhilarating about a freshly vacuumed carpet, a hot steamy soup and the thank yous received from relatives unwrapping a hand-sewn cross stitch creation." The headline of the next, from *The New York Times Magazine*, reads "Confessions of a Closet Homemaker: Slaving over a hot stove is my greatest delight, and my deepest shame." The book *Confessions of an Orga-nized Homemaker* purports to offer peace of mind, confidence, and control through efficiency; author Deniece Schofield says that only after she conquered her own chronic messiness could she relax without feeling guilty. Even Cheryl Mendelson, hailed by *People Magazine* as "the doyenne of dustbusters," apparently feels some shame over it all. "I am a working woman with a secret life: I keep house," she begins. It turns out that until publishing *Home Comforts*, the Oxford Encyclopedia of domestic advice manuals, Mendelson had "almost entirely concealed this passion for domesticity [ . . .] without thinking much about it, I knew I would not want this information about me to get around."

More than ever it is something of a heresy to admit one is a housewife. Chances are slim the statement will earn respect. No wonder we feel so little pride about our role in this crucial part of making a home, when so little dignity is afforded it by the world at large. Domesticity is just not assumed to be a thing of value. "Having it all" never, of course, included housework.

AND YET . . . perhaps it is those thousands of years behind us . . . perhaps it is the teachings of our foremothers . . . maybe it comes from growing up in an organized household, or from observing one up close, where the floors are smooth and clean, the furniture polished, the cushions soft or the carpet vacuumed—not necessarily an affluent household, but one that embodies a pleasurable sense of order . . . but somehow, the desire for a well-kept home holds on. Such an environment is not necessarily a formative experience you would consciously register. As Barbara Kingsolver has written, "It's surprising how much of memory is built around things unnoticed at the time."

It's hard not to be torn between the desire for work and money and "free" time and the longing for an environment that glows with what could be called "intention." According to the *Home Cook Book* of 1874, the ideal home "looks as if whole people lived in it, with live sensibilities and intelligence."

In some sense housekeeping is making the most of life, bringing taste and variety into it, compassing difficult ends with invention. Those who dismiss it lower themselves.

It's an assessment as true today as the moment 130 years ago when it was written.

If the twenty-first century sounds the death knell for the home-cooked and the handmade, it won't be as an exclusive result of either the home economics or the women's movement. The truth, as always, is more complex.

Domestic scientists asserted the value of the handmade over the assembly line until they fell under the sway of corporations that wanted to commodify the work of the home so that women would consume their products. As for second-generation feminists, their achievement was immense: they insisted upon women's right to have a life outside the home, one whose value did not depend on her domestic role. Between these forces, however, something was lost: a home life that is authentic and personal and minimally touched by business, and also the possibility of its work being honorable and dignified and shared with women by men.

I am not an apologist for a past that can no longer exist. Yet I think it's possible to speak frankly about the corporations and work pressures and ideologies that necessarily devalue the home in order to free women.

In one of the Grimm brothers' fairy tales, a story called "The Three Little Men in the Forest," a young girl is given an impossible order by her cruel stepmother: she must go out into the frozen woods to bring back a basket of strawberries. Only after she takes a broom in hand to sweep away the snow behind a cottage occupied by magic elves does she find the ripe fruit and see her life transformed—with beauty, riches, love, and a kingdom. Her stepsister counterpart refuses to sweep, and her life takes a turn for the (very much) worse.

Brooms figure mightily in the mythology of setting one's psychic house in order. "I believe I'll dust my broom" sang blues great Robert Johnson, a lyric that seems to suggest setting his love life straight. I visited a woman at a peaceful midwestern lakeside vacation cottage who leaned her broom against the jamb of the simple screen door into her kitchen. A home economics teacher, she would spend vacations at the cottage putting up dozens of pint jars of strawberry preserves. She told me she kept her broom at the ready, saying she swept her small neat kitchen at least three or four times a day. "I guess I'm just a sweeper," she said. It's a housekeeping tool with an ancient pedigree: an early version of a broom in England was the besom, a rough bunch of twigs or dried roots or stalks of the golden maidenhair plant, bound to a sturdy stick. Long ago broom making was one craft in the homemaker's repertoire, today it's a specialist's art available to those who can afford it. In Arkansas, Grassy Creek Brooms are created out of broomcorn and carved "spirit face" sassafras handles and based on Appalachian traditions; Jerry and Judy Lovenstein shape each broom individually.

Even Virginia Woolf, who deplored the waste of women's talent in household chores, reflected in *A Room of One's Own* that the rigors of domesticity have inevitably shaped women's creativity.

> The rooms differ so completely; they are calm or thunderous; open on to the sea, or, on the contrary, give on to a prison yard; are hung with washing; or alive with opals and silks; are hard as horsehair or soft as feathers—one has only to go into any room in any street for the whole of that extremely complex force of femininity to fly in one's face. How should it be otherwise? For women have sat indoors all these millions of years, so that by this time the very walls are permeated by their creative force, which has, indeed, so overcharged the capacity of bricks and mortar that it must needs harness itself to

pens and brushes and business and politics. But this creative power differs greatly from the creative power of men. And one must conclude that it would be a thousand pities if it were hindered or wasted, for it was won by centuries of the most drastic discipline, and there is nothing to take its place.

The tremendous responsibility of what we have come to consider the lowly job of housewifery is what Woolf calls a "most drastic discipline," necessary to foment women's creative power. This is another way of talking about the intentionality of domesticity. She cites it to support her argument that women should leave the home and use that energy elsewhere. When women burst the bonds of the bricks and mortar, though, what will happen to the institution that gave them the discipline to create in other areas?

"The domestic joys, the daily housework or business, the building of houses—they are not phantasms . . . they have weight and form and location," wrote Walt Whitman, himself a wanderer who longed to find a place to make a home. The work of the home is anything but trivial. In fact, the order of domesticity makes possible the groundedness out of which serenity is born. In the addiction recovery movement, for example, newly sober people search desperately for what to do with the time and energy they'd formerly put into procuring and using illicit substances. Common advice: *Clean your house,* which makes all the more sense because one symptom of the addict's sickness is his disorderly living quarters. "Good Orderly Direction" is a euphemism also used by recovering addicts, a way of describing God—another example of the value placed on serenity through order. Mother Teresa raised the idea to a political level, saying, "There should be less talk; a preaching point is not a meeting point. What do you do then? Take a broom and clean someone's house. That says enough."

It might be a measure of a fall from psychic grace that we no longer scrub or scour the way we once did. We might be sacrificing spiritual growth. There is a famous Zen koan:

> A monk came to the Zen master Chao-Chou saying, "Teach me."
> The monk said, "Have you eaten your gruel?"
> "Yes," said the monk, "I have."
> "Wash your bowl," said the Zen master.
> At that moment, the monk understood the truth.

"The average home is a horribly dull place," wrote F. Scott Fitzgerald in a 1923 article for *Ladies' Home Journal*. Keeping house is indeed hopelessly boring in the minds of many people. "I have too many fantasies to be a housewife," said Marilyn Monroe, who could have been a Fitzgerald tragic jazz baby. I remember hearing a man of about 60 talk about the pleasure of the dreamy trance state he fell into while washing dishes; the other people in the room found what he said hilarious. Growing up, my mother would allow no one else to clean her room, with its lilac print wallpaper and lustrous dark wood bedstead. The dullness of housework deceives. Marlene Dietrich scrubbed her hotel room from floor to ceiling wherever she traveled. Simplicity and importance are not mutually exclusive. "Become simple and live simply, not only within yourself but also in your everyday dealings," wrote the Dutch lawyer Etty Hillesum, a Holocaust victim. "Don't make ripples all around you, don't try to be interesting, keep your distance, be honest, fight the desire to be thought fascinating by the outside world."

A message of Cheryl Mendelson's *Home Comforts* is that "the way you experience life in your home is determined by how you do your housekeeping." She writes,

> We should [ . . .] understand [ . . .] that we can permit ourselves to seek better than just "good enough" when it comes to our homes. It

is just as important for us now as it was for people in 1800, 1900, and 1950. Dusting standards may have changed since the 1950s, but our homes still have to be to us what our grandfathers' homes were to them. Our homes are the center of our lives, and we should allow time and resources to make the most of them that we can, and to care for them in a way that consolidates and elaborates their meaning for each of us. At a minimum, we should avoid thinking that time spent on our homes is wasted time, or that our goal should always be to reduce the time and effort we spend on them.

She expresses the idea that housework is "among the most thoroughly pleasant, significant, and least alienated forms of work" that anyone can engage in today, with a description that suggests a state of focus or concentration akin to what others have described as being "in the zone."

Chief Seattle's exaltation of cleanliness in the nineteenth century was apocalyptic: "Man did not weave the web of life, he is merely a strand in it. Whatever he does to the web, he does to himself. Contaminate your bed and you will one night suffocate in your own waste."

Housework should not be only the province of women. Sweeping, mopping, dusting, and laundry can easily be shared—not only by men but by children, who will learn better not to throw trash on the street if they understand the priority of cleanliness at home. When we refuse to undertake the job of cleaning up our own waste, it's an indication that our priorities have shifted in a way that ultimately harms ourselves and others.

It's healthy for children to grow up in a clean house. The Institute for Social Research at the University of Michigan conducted a long-term study to correlate academic achievement and household cleanliness. Researchers assessed cleanliness in 1,351 homes every year from 1968 to 1972, then social workers followed up twenty-five years later with these findings: young adults who grew up in homes rated clean to very clean completed 13.6 years of school and earned wages averaging $14.17 per hour, compared with 12 years of school and wages of $12.60 for those from dirtier homes.

Heaping the dirty work on a "lower" class creates false divisions and keeps one group of people at a "menial" labor that's artificially contrived. It's hubristic nonsense to put trading stocks, say, above scrubbing the floor. We're buying into a way of life whose values are reversed, for example working twelve-hour days for a huge law firm or microchip plant or Home Depot rather than caring for our domestic selves. When we scorn keeping house we teach the next generation that taking responsibility for themselves and this earth is beneath their dignity. When we avoid housework we forego the animal satisfaction of maintaining a clean dwelling.

Peg Bracken's books, dog-eared, gravy-stained, and tattered, vanished from public sight because they once were coveted but are no longer fashionable. The discourse of keeping house went the opposite way. She advocated what was practical, what made sense, and while her books' intent was to save household labor, she didn't necessarily consider all "modern" developments warranted. In her memoir, A *Window Over the Sink,* she laments the loss of kitchens of the past:

> Kitchens were different then, too—not only what came out of them, but their smells and sounds. A hot pie cooling smells different from a frozen pie thawing. Oilcloth and linoleum and apples in an open bowl and ruffled rubber aprons make a different aromatic mix from Formica and ceramic tile and mangoes in an acrylic fruit ripener and plastic-coated aprons printed with "Who invited all these tacky people?" And the kitchen sounds. I am not sure that today's kitchen is noisier. But the noises are different. Today you get the song of the food processor and the blender, the intermittent

hum of the reefer and the freezer, the buzz-slosh-and-grunt of the dishwasher, the violently audible digestive processes of the waste disposal in the sink. Then it was the whir and clatter of the hand-powered eggbeater, the thunk-thunk-thunk of somebody mashing potatoes, or, in green-pea season, the crisp pop of pea pod and the rattle-rattle-rattle of peas into the pan.

That old-fashioned kitchen is a setting in which I somehow feel Virtue Hathaway might feel comfortable even as her "Fuck Housework" poster defined a moment by disappearing from the stores.

These two housewife/writers crafted intelligent responses to their condition pre- and post-Friedan. Between the time of the book and the poster, few sophisticated women could believe wholeheartedly that the work of the home filled an important role for women or in society. Its function had been degraded.

Since that time, the two ideas have stumbled forward, entwined together as if in a three-legged race. The ghost in an apron never has gone away, though it would be easier if it were banished, only a memory—but as William Faulkner wrote, "The past is never dead. It's not even past." That is the nature of ghosts, to be eternally present, and to haunt with an uncomfortable sense of what was and what still could be. Virginia Woolf painted an ambiguous portrait of just such a ghost—an image as terrifying as it is soothing—in her novel *The Waves:* "I shall be like my mother, silent in a blue apron locking up the cupboards."

Will the mildly smiling, long-tressed woman on the poster—the perfect princess from an old-fashioned fairy tale—find that breaking her broom leads to freedom or brings disaster down upon her head? We are still waiting to see.

# CHAPTER 6

# The New Mom

ONE RECENT MORNING I pressed the snooze button one time too many, my daughter was late for band, the dogs whined to be walked, the milk waited to be brought in and the trash to be put out. Suddenly there was no time to pack the all-important school lunch—and anyway, we had no bread in the house. The solution seemed obvious: my husband rushed off to the supermarket to bring back a Lunchable.

While I drank my coffee and my daughter ate her cereal I conducted an unscientific survey. "Do all the kids in your class like Lunchables?" I asked. "I guess," she said with fourth grade reticence, nose in the comics. "Well, how many of your classmates bring Lunchables to school once in a while?" I said. "Everyone," she said. "Are there any kids who don't *ever* bring them?" I said. She thought. "Melanie," she said.

Perfect Melanie. That was my daughter's name for this little girl when she first got to know her. Melanie's parents are nothing if not careful and protective of their children. Melanie participates only in the best, most wholesome activities—French lessons outside of school, circus camp in the summer. Her mother brings carrot sticks and orange sections as a snack to rec basketball practices. Melanie and her siblings have flourished. Her parents appear perfect, too.

There is always a family that throws a large shadow over all of us imperfect types. I am not perfect. Neither are the vast majority of parents. We begin with such grand aspirations when our kids are babies—no television, no synthetic fabrics, no plastic toys, even. By elementary school, only the strong survive. The rest are easy prey for the superprocessed, supersized, supersimple, supersweet, kid-enticing products available right down the street in the local supermarket's refrigerator case.

Kids have gone nuts over Lunchables, a fact that has made perfection a whole lot more achievable—if not nutritionally, than at least in streamlining the school lunch packing ritual of harried families. I recently spotted a boy in Sam's Club of about five, riding in his mother's grocery cart, clutching a four-pack of "lunch kits" as though it were his best friend. Oscar Mayer sold 1.6 billion boxes in the ten years after Lunchables were introduced in 1988, with a 15 percent increase in sales each year. In 1998 alone the product's total sales equaled about $530 million. The Lunchable itself has grown, from a simple ham and cheese and cracker picnic to a feast that includes a "pizza" you build, a drink, and a dessert. The line has proved so popular that the company has extended it numerous times, most recently creating a Mega Pack with forty percent more food than the original.

The dominance of Lunchables and other prewrapped processed take-alongs isn't the first step the lunch bucket has taken toward oblivion. Back at the turn of the century, a young woman named Elizabeth Stern described a remarkably similar situation in an utterly different time and place. In Stern's detailed memoir of growing up a first-generation American in an Eastern European family in a midwestern urban ghetto, she tells of her household's Old World habits and more specifically the generational transformation of its homeways. A skilled seamstress, the author's mother Sarah "eked out the family income by making aprons—by hand!" while bearing eleven children, seven of whom died before age two, in a cramped windowless basement. The family is so poor that Sarah must gradually cut up the voluminous stiff white silk wedding gown she had worn in Russia in order to sew dresses for her daughters here in the U.S. "I can never remember my mother in my childhood in any other than one of two positions," writes Stern, "standing at the stove cooking, or sitting in the corner; her foot rocking the cradle, and her hands stitching, stitching."

There is no time for school. Instead, Stern's mother entrusts her with scrubbing the house for the Sabbath, a meticulous and important job of which she is proud. A volume of *Little Women* she discovers in a heap of old torn papers at the rag man's shop serves as her only textbook until she enters high school. Then the girl's life is transformed. Stern describes her experience of touching, for the first time, in biology class, the golden petals of a nasturtium—she had never seen a living flower in all her childhood. Equally transformative for her is coming up against the lifestyles of her fellow students, rich girls whose families had long since abandoned the ways of their native countries.

Lunch hour becomes the great divide, the moment Elizabeth makes the crucial break with the culinary practices of her family that will lead to her eventual assimilation as a "modern" American. To me, this is the heart of the book, and the incident that prefigures the transition of our own turn-of-the-century children's lunchboxes from homemade peanut butter and jelly to depersonalized plastic-encased "lunch kits."

> What an embarrassing moment was that one when I opened my first lunch-parcel! I noticed with misgivings that the others had brought boxes. I brought a newspaper package which mother had prepared for me while I hastily brushed Fanny's hair and rocked the baby for her. I saw that the boxes of the other girls held dainty squares of paper, white cloths; I could not understand. I opened my

newspaper. In it there lay a mass of fried potatoes, crushed tomato, huge, irregular slices of bread, and a chunk of filleted fish. Mother had risen at daybreak to cook some fish for my first meal at school. There was a gasp of sympathy from the girls. I must confess that I myself would not at that time have been greatly shocked—had it not been for the other girls.

"Oh, it got crushed. What is it?" asked one.

"Of course you must throw it away," commiserated another.

I threw it away.

There were offers of sandwiches, fruits, pie. I had never eaten a sandwich before. They seemed very meager fare to me. I was hungry for my mother's bread and fish. Thereafter, though, I threw all the lunches which mother gave me into the trash can outside the school building.

Over time, Stern grows eager to scrap the ways of her mother. Her youthful home, she comes to believe, "had not been American." In college, a "new and clear ideal of the American home came to grow in my heart."

By the time Elizabeth marries and has a son, she has proudly dispensed with the ways of her forebears, instead creating a "modern," antiseptic, whitewashed living environment. Having begged her mother for the family copper fish pot, she installs it in her immaculate living room and fills it with decorative autumn leaves. Then Sarah, Stern's mother, comes to visit. With dull eyes and trembling lips, she looks upon the scene, seeing there is no place for her here.

The sandwich/fried fish dilemma was one salvo in the battle between the old and the new, a battle the modern American home ultimately wins. Despite the writer's comfort in her assimilation, however, it seems clear she is replacing what was time-honored and rich with a more barren interpretation of keeping house. Her tale is permeated by a profound sadness that resonates a century later as we face many of these same conflicts.

Ultimately, our approach to food can't be extricated from our relationships with people in a broader sense. Adult Elizabeth prepares meals the way she learned to away from home, in a white kitchen that is used for nothing other than cooking. Sarah cannot touch the food, is not allowed by her daughter to help, and feels alien in this new-style kitchen. "So mother went out to the porch, and she looked out upon the tree-shaded street," writes Stern. "And an infinite loneliness was hers, a loneliness at the thought of the crowded homely ghetto street, where every one goes about in shirt sleeves, or apron or kimono, where every one knows his neighbor, where every one speaks mother's speech."

Oscar Mayer, the producer of Lunchables, is owned by Kraft, the processed food queen that manufactures among other brands Breakstone's, Miracle Whip, Tombstone Pizza, Tang, Oreo, Kool Aid, Velveeta, and Capri Sun. Kraft products can be found in 99.6 percent of all American households. The company leverages its different holdings when it can by combining products—Lunchables is a good example, its plastic compartments filled with Kraft processed cheese and luncheon meat, Capri Sun, and a candy bar. On its Web site Kraft offers a recipe for bacon snack bars that incorporates sugar, corn syrup, peanut butter, and three of its products: Oscar Mayer Real Bacon Pieces, Tang, and Honey Bunches of Oats breakfast cereal. The treat is ready to serve up in fifteen minutes. Lunchables eschew bacon snack bars for less exotic components that will appeal to children: ham, cheese, soda crackers, pepperoni, mozzarella, and tomato sauce.

The line continues to expand beyond cold cuts. Hamburger Lunchables has as its centerpiece twin shrink-wrapped, tiny, smooth hamburger buns like miniature Claes Oldenburg sculptures alongside shrink-wrapped shriveled wafers of ground beef that make a Big Mac look gourmet. Would a child actually eat these "burgers" cold at school lunchtime? Who cares? There are no food cops in kindergarten, and besides there's a really cool Scooby Doo thingamajig for kids to play with while drinking their Capri Sun flavored sugar water.

The popularity of Lunchables spawned a breakfast version that lets kids dip cold "waffle sticks" in syrup or decorate them with icing. "Saturday morning traditions," reads the promotional material, "now available any day of the week."

Lunchables have critics. According to the Center for Science in the Public Interest, versions that include a candy and a drink get fully two-thirds of their calories from fat and sugar. In a study by the Medical College of Wisconsin, rats that ate ham-and-cheese Lunchables had a 20 percent increase in blood pressure compared with those that consumed regular rat chow. Bonnie Liebman of CSPI told the *Washington Post*, "It's not rocket science to know that sugar, white flour, cheese and meat is not the healthiest lunch to serve your child." Dr. Clarence Grim, a high blood pressure specialist who conducted the rat study, reported that some Lunchables contain nearly three-fourths of the recommended daily salt allowance. Nonetheless, some schools feature Lunchables on the cafeteria menu. Sleepy Hollow Elementary School in Amarillo, Texas, sells Turkey & Cheese and Nacho Cheese Lunchables every day of the week at a bargain price of $2.25.

Other companies continually try to muscle in on Oscar Mayer's lunch-kit fiefdom, with some improbable results. Smuckers, for example, launched "Uncrustables," frozen crustless sandwiches that have crimped edges to seal in oozing peanut butter and jelly once they defrost. Time-pressed moms supposedly feel even more terrific tossing an Uncrustable into Junior's lunch tote knowing that "with a name like Smucker's, it has to be good." It's a long way from 1897 Orrsville, Ohio, where company scion Jerome Smucker supposedly hand-pressed his own apple butter, signing the lid of each crock he produced.

Lunchables are only a small crag of the mountain of processed food beneath which home cooking may one day be crushed. In any American grade school cafeteria, kids are devouring Go-gurt, mozzarella sticks, squeezable Jell-O, Yoo-hoo in boxes, Ritz Bits—everything wrapped in plastic, totally disposable, and emphatically not made from scratch. "Fruit" snacks, such as "roll-ups" or "gushers," which didn't exist a few years back, take in over a billion dollars annually.

Not that processed food can be called a new phenomenon. Kraft began producing processed cheese in 1914 to ship to U.S. troops overseas. Miracle Whip was introduced at Chicago's 1933 Century of Progress World's Fair. Kraft Macaroni and Cheese Dinners hit grocery shelves in 1937 with the slogan, "Make a meal for 4 in 9 minutes." Cheez Whiz celebrates its fiftieth anniversary in 2003. Tang was launched in 1957, Shake 'n' Bake in 1965, and, in 1966, Cool Whip, the revolutionary nondairy whipped topping.

Folgers coffee, the first beans that Americans didn't have to roast and grind at home, was marketed to miners during the Gold Rush, and the instant variety was introduced a century ago at the 1901 Pan American Expo in Buffalo, New York. In 1909, George Hellman moved condiment preparation out of the home kitchen by packaging his wife's recipe for mayonnaise. Instant oatmeal wasn't the recent invention you'd imagine but one dreamed up by Quaker Oats back in 1916. In 1929, Clarence Birdseye jump-started the frozen food business—now a 20-billion-dollar-a-year industry—with "frosted" fish filets and spring peas preserved miraculously out of season (a precursor was Sir Francis Bacon, who attempted to freeze chickens by stuffing them with snow). Wonder Bread turns out not to be a product of the processing-mad 1950s but of the year the stock market crashed. Integral to its success was the innovation of the pop-up toaster, which needed regularly sliced pieces of bread to work properly. Instant mashed potatoes also hit the stores in 1929.

The previous year, one writer in a popular magazine had warned, "In another generation the woman who knows how to make bread or an apple pie will be as extinct as a dodo." As convenience foods exploded in popularity and in profitability, however, few observers felt overly concerned over what would happen to the culinary heritage of the home.

A landmark in the production of prepared food was the debut of the ninety-eight-cent Swanson frozen TV dinner in 1954. That original TV dinner tray is now on display at the Smithsonian Institution in Washington, D.C. The Distinguished Order of Zerocrats, an organization whose purpose is to advance the frozen food business, established the Frozen Food Hall of Fame in 1990 to honor those whose dedication and hard work have ensured the industry's success. Each spring, the Zerocrats vote on the newest inductees. The TV dinner's inventor, who has been inducted into the Hall of Fame, remembers at the beginning "getting hate mail from men who wanted their wives to cook from scratch like their mothers did." For the most part, passions over precooked frozen entrées long ago died away. Now, TV dinners seem nostalgic icons in their own right, and we can barely recall a time when fixing a meal from the freezer was anything but a matter-of-fact, uncontroversial experience.

∽

CULINARY AUTHORITY James Beard called American cooking "anything you eat at home." Beard didn't live long enough to experience the phenomenon of "home meal replacement," however, which is current food industry jargon for the familiar idea of takeout dinners to serve within one's own abode. In a situation that sums up our deeply ambivalent feelings about the home, most of the meals prepared in America today are *cooked* by restaurants, but people don't necessarily want to *eat* in restaurants. According to a 1999 National Restaurant Association Survey, more than three-quarters of Americans dine on takeout every month. Over half of all restaurant meals in the year 2000 were consumed off the premises.

Many of these meals were purchased at the drive-in window— fast-food franchises accounted for more than 80 percent of the growth in restaurant meals in the last five years. "Restaurants would seem to be lurching back to the era of the French Revolution," writes Molly O'Neill in *The New York Times*, "when having lost their personal cooks to a populist revolt, the aristocracy began to rely on public eateries to prepare dishes they could carry away and enjoy in the privacy of their beleaguered palais." In our beleaguered suburban palaces, we have a nagging sense that a crucial component of "home" is missing—the scent of a home-cooked meal. According to a 1999 National Eating Trends Report produced by NPD, half of all meals are now prepared outside the home. In the 1970s, 80 percent or more women prepared at least one meal a day in their home kitchens, but in the 1980s the number of home cooks had dropped to 74 percent, and in 1998 fell to 68 percent. Even when we do prepare our meals in our own kitchens, what we're doing is more often assembling prepackaged ingredients—only 56 percent of all meals made in North American homes include one or more homemade items. "Much better than your own mom could make," brags Mama's Food Shop, a take-out service in New York City. It's an indication of how far we've slipped culturally that these are not fighting words.

In spring 2000 Outback Steakhouse, one of the country's most successful chains, introduced what they called "curbside takeaway," whereby diners phone in orders along with descriptions of their cars, then drive to a designated spot outside the building where the food is delivered. Nancy Schnied, the marketing head of Outback, attributes the success of the program to the fact that, "We definitely know people aren't cooking." She adds, "It doesn't matter whether there's a working woman in the household or not, they're still not cooking."

What cannot be replaced, of course, is the culture of caring that produced the home-cooked meals we used to eat. "My grand-daughter will remember that my wife did this thing called 'cooking,' the way my wife remembers that her grandmother did this thing called 'sewing,'" predicts Harry Balzer of the of the National Public Diary project, which tracks American eating habits.

Advertising for consumer products boasts of their ability to replace the homemade. Marketers promise the taste of the home-made dinner without the effort it takes to prepare it, and whole prepared meals from supermarket freezers are outpacing individual packaged goods. "We've eliminated the middlemom," crows an ad for Kellogg's Rice Krispies Treats, the marshmallow squares that are associated with Donna Reed–style homemaking. The assumed premise is that women are happy to have the troublesome task of preparing food "eliminated" from their lives. A spokesperson for Stouffer's told USA Today that the company launched its Oven Sensations line of dinners "because studies showed consumers wanted to use the oven but just didn't have time to do it." To fix dinner, the cook has only to pour the meal out of a bag into a baking dish, pop it in to bake, and set it on the table.

In place of home cooking we now have "homestyle." The box for "Homestyle Bakes" by Banquet, which needs no refrigeration, boasts a "complete dinner—chicken included!" for four to five diners. Its ingredients, marked boldly on the box, include "country chicken, mashed potatoes and biscuits" and, in smaller lettering, "100% white meat chicken & gravy in a can, potato mix & biscuit

topping mix." Busy consumers are promised "easy 5 min preparation," and are assured they can relax: "One dish oven-baked real
dinners made easy." If you aren't sold yet, read the back: "Now you
can give your family a truly complete, delicious, real homestyle dinner with less effort. Everything you need is in the box, including
delicious all-white meat chicken in hearty gravy, a creamy mashed
potato base and a flaky biscuit topping."

As hearty and creamy and flaky as the homestyle bake might
be, some of the ingredients don't sound very homelike—maltodex-
trin, modified rice starch, xanthan gum, MSG, sodium stearoyl
lactylate, datem, isolated soy protein, mono- and diglycerides, "flavor," sodium phosphate, partially hydrogenated soybean and/or
cottonseed oils, dipotassium phosphate, natural and artificial flavors, calcium stearoyl lactylate, sodium acid pyrophosphate. The
box does indeed contain chicken, flour, and dried Idaho potatoes,
but on the whole this dinner qualifies as mystery meat in the guise
of home cooking and tastes of nothing so much as salt and chemicals. On the other hand, at $4.19 for five servings, it's a dinnertime
bargain.

Banquet isn't the only company on the homestyle bandwagon.
Stouffer's offers a line of frozen "Homestyle Dinners," including a
version with roast turkey and all the fixings. "Nothing Comes
Closer to Home," reads the box copy, "End your day on a good note
with a good meal." And in dramatic type across the package:
"Make dinners as successful as the rest of your day!" Campbell's
promotes its Supper Bakes, "all-in-one meal kits that actually taste
like homemade meals," with a glamour shot of gravy-drenched
meat and pasta and the legend: "You know those people who spend
hours in the kitchen, slaving away until their sauce is perfectly seasoned? That's us."

In the rush to offer a semblance of tradition, product ads advocate against genuine tradition. A television spot for Buitoni asserts,

"Traditional Italian mamas just ain't what they used to be" to hawk prepackaged fresh pasta in plastic. "Create your own tradition," it urges. The ad campaign that has been most direct in dismissing home cooking traditions—and in disrespecting those who worked to preserve them—is the one for Kraft Stovetop Classics. In one, two grandmother types in aprons and frumpy hats demand, in a huff, "What's next, Thanksgiving in a box?!" Below it reads, "It's like Sunday dinner at Grandma's. No wonder they're miffed." In another ad the same two women ask, "Know what you can do with your potatoes?" The copy concludes, "One-dish, oven-baked chicken dinners—*their* dinners—no wonder they're miffed."

It's not only entrées that get the home-style presentation. Companies also have launched instant homestyle sweets. Jell-O offers cheesecake that takes only fifteen minutes to assemble: "Who doesn't have time for that?" The pectin maker SURE-JELL advertises its product with a recipe taking "30 Minutes to Homemade" and the lines, "All of the love. None of the labor." From Mrs. Smith's we hear these comforting words: "Mrs. Smith's wants you to spend more time with the family . . . and less time in the kitchen." The company's solution is for customers to bake its frozen pie and top each slice with a dollop of Extra Creamy nondairy Cool Whip. Duncan Hines produces cans of "Creamy Home-Style Cream Cheese Premium Frosting," the kind all the mothers in my town buy to ice the cupcakes at school or birthday parties. It may be homestyle, but it contains no ingredients from the home larder. With no cream cheese and no butter, the frosting instead contains an amalgam of partially hydrogenated oils and sugars and an appetite-suppressing array of obscure preservatives, food dyes, and one of the food industry's most closely guarded secrets—"natural and artificial flavors." In *Fast Food Nation*, Eric Schlosser investigates the complex artificial flavors found in just one product, a Burger King strawberry milk shake, and discovers no fewer than forty-nine chemicals.

"Meals made from scratch are the exception," according to Tom Van Aman, the executive vice president for Retail Measurement Product Management at Information Resources, Inc. in Chicago. He told the audience at Pack Expo 98 that meal preparation time dropped from three hours per day in 1960 to twenty minutes in 1998. Consumers have largely given up cooking, he asserted, saying they'd just as well quit grocery shopping, too, but they still want to eat well.

According to the food-trend-tracking NPD Group, the number of people owning even the most basic kitchen equipment continues to drop. The number of households with frying pans dropped to 94 percent in 1999 from 99 percent in 1993, the number of homes with mixers fell to 81 percent from 91 percent, and just 57 percent of households owned a roasting pan compared with 67 percent six years before. Just over half of Americans now use their stove daily, down from almost 70 percent in 1985. "And when they do bother to cook something," NPD Group's Henry Balzer has told *The Wall Street Journal*, "it's most likely a frozen dinner (sales are up 22 percent since 1996) or a one-pot meal (the number of side dishes prepared fell 14 percent in the last decade)." A pediatrician described how her medical practice has suffered as a consequence of parents' unfamiliarity with basic kitchen measures. "I tell them to give the child a teaspoon of medicine," she told me, "and they don't know what a teaspoon is. They've never cooked with one."

In response to customers' lack of familiarity with kitchen equipment as well as their lack of time, food companies communicate that their products are both easy and fast. It's hard to tell who is more fixated on speed of preparation, always rushed consumers or manufacturers who are desperate to distinguish their product from that of the next company. The boxes of hot cereal stretch along the supermarket shelf, across the aisle from the sugared cereals in their bright silly boxes that embody a distinctly different marketing strategy. What can a company possibly say about its farina? Every hot cereal is old, wholesome, bland. Perhaps advertising preparation time will pull the shopper eyeball back from the Oreo Bites next door. "Cooks in ten minutes!" reads one box. "Five minutes!" shouts another. "Two minutes!" "One minute!" "Instant!" Saving prep time makes some sense, perhaps, in the morning—although the difference between two minutes and five when you're stirring oatmeal seems fairly negligible. But when we spend five minutes preparing dinner from a box rather than twenty minutes making it fresh, the question has to arise of just what we're rushing off to. Both kids and adults now eagerly devote hours each day to PlayStation and hundreds of Internet game sites, for example. Dispatching the pleasures of cooking good food in order to slay dragons on EverQuest.com seems not that rewarding a trade-off.

What do we want to do if we "don't have time" to cook? We apparently don't want to produce anything. As has been well established, what Americans most want is to consume: consume dinners out; consume movies in movieplexes and giant tubs of popcorn and supersize sodas as we're watching; consume products, cruising shopping malls for pleasure rather than creating entertainment at home.

Still, older values remain compelling, a fact of which food manufacturers are well aware. Many packaged goods capitalize on the iconography of home. Some bread marketers rely upon traditional images of wheat and on bread as the staff of life:

> Arnold Country White is a bread that all the family will enjoy. It has the soft texture of a moist, newly baked home-made loaf. And a fresh, rich flavor that reminds you of the country. Only unbleached flour is used—slow baked to bring out the flavor.

Arnold's "Wheat Design," an almost Biblical sheaf image, is actually trademarked by Arnold Foods Company, Inc. The picture above the product name shows a red barn and silo with a butter-yellow roof, surrounded by ribbed fields of green and brown. These loaves are obviously not homemade—in addition to old-fashioned ingredients such as wheat and malted barley flour, milk, yeast, butter, honey, and salt, each loaf also contains calcium propionate, monoglycerides, and soy lecithin—but most consumers have probably forgotten the taste of home-baked bread, so what matters most is the idea conveyed on the package.

Today, we expect the bread we buy in the store to contain artificial ingredients. Sometimes, though, confronting the reality of the bread "product" can be startling. Wonder Bread, for example, continues its tenure as the cheapest, plainest, most texture-free loaf on the grocery shelf. The company's Web site is worth a visit. One page shows Stonehenge built with hefty slices of Wonder Bread—an apt image considering the longevity of the ancient towering slabs. A loaf of Wonder Bread, too, could probably last millennia. In fact, my daughter's elementary-school class conducted a science project in which the students attempted to grow mold on bread, sealing slices brought from home with drops of water in plastic bags. The Wonder Bread contributed by one child was the marvel of the experiment, because it was the only piece on which not one mold spore grew. It was a completely sterile host. When the Wonder Bread brand was born, marketers promoted its hygienic properties as well as the idea that unlike homemade bread, factory bread had no pesky holes through which sandwich fillings could leak.

Consumers suffer a little-acknowledged psychic loss now that most bread is purchased in stores. Writing about the alternative, M. F. K. Fisher said:

> It does not cost much. It is pleasant: one of those almost hypnotic businesses, like a dance from some ancient ceremony. It leaves you

filled with peace and the house filled with one of the world's sweet-
est smells. But it takes a lot of time. If you can find that, the rest is
easy. And if you cannot rightly find the time, make it, for probably
there is no chiropractic treatment, no Yoga exercise, no hour of
meditation in a music-throbbing chapel, that will leave you emptier
of bad thoughts than this homely ceremony of making bread.

We may not take the time to bake bread, yet Americans long for
rustic simplicity in their food, and that holds especially true for
food that incorporates grains. Think of the warm bread loaf set
before diners at some restaurants and how quickly it disappears!
Again, food marketers know this. A two-page magazine spread
advertising Post Cereals employs the headline: "Not everything
that goes into Post Selects fits in the box." Below is a rural-feeling
backdrop replete with red barn siding and seven smiling workers,
framing a wood sign with the company logo and product name.
The opposite page offers an arrangement of wholesome foods atop
a time-burnished board. A rustic whole-grain loaf of bread with its
first few hand-hewn slices toppling forward joins piles of walnuts,
including some still in the shell, and almonds and pecans, cranberries and blueberries and dates. An old, hand-carved wooden scoop
holds some of the cereal itself. The image reads harvest, bounty,
health. Another Post ad shows a bowl of Cranberry Almond
Crunch juxtaposed against a colander brimming with just-rinsed
cranberries. A quote reads, "You can see the tangy sweet cranberries and sliced almonds. What you can't see are the hours Beth
spent in our kitchen to get the combination just right." Perhaps
Beth is the sole cook at the factory, but more likely she stands as an
icon of the healthy homemade, sounding for all the world like the
resident mom or grandma at the Post corporation, stirring and baking and tasting the ingredients just in from the fields. You can
almost hear her cracking the walnuts.

Of course the truth is nowhere near the illusion. Post operates highly sophisticated test kitchens in which food technicians perfect that natural, old-timey flavor and texture. It's a version of the marbles in the shaving cream, the long outlawed food-styling techniques that led the way to truth in advertising. Now the images in ads adhere to strict regulations and there mustn't be a whiff of falsehood, but no one will criticize an advertiser for preying on desires for the old-fashioned values of home and hearth. That's simply the coin of the realm. And it works. For people who cannot find the time to cook or bake but who are starving for the homemade, for an out-of-reach way of life and style of eating, this may be the closest they can get. In this devil's pact, the prepared food corporations sell us an illusion of home cooking and with it we buy an illusion of taste, an illusion of satisfaction, an illusion of comfort, an illusion of nutrition and health.

I brought home a package of iced oatmeal cookies loaded with artificial ingredients to see how they tasted and my husband tore into them. My daughter, too: "They're good!" she said. We've trained our taste buds to savor fat and salt and chemical additives, synthetic flavors concocted in factories. Vanillin takes the place of vanilla because the genuine extract is "too expensive" in the judgment of the manufacturer. But how do you judge expense? In terms of the monetary cost to the producer, or the more qualitative cost to the consumer, for whom an authentic taste experience has vanished, and who misses out on the primal pleasure of handling food and the satisfaction of creating something good to eat?

Scanning food industry periodicals means stepping into a world of culinary mirrors. Food professionals assert that their business serves a vital purpose. "The generation after the Baby Boomers simply doesn't know how to cook, so there's really a need there," says Jeff Sandore, vice president of retail marketing for Tyson Foods. But producing ready-made home-style food in vast quantities requires techniques grandma never could have imagined. The argot industry leaders employ among each other to describe the food they place in consumer cupboards and home freezers—dense with phrases like "flavor profile" and "formulation technology" and "mouthfeel"—never finds its way into the ads or packaging that help us make decisions about what we eat.

Theirs is a business obsessed with lab breakthroughs no one ever thought they needed and concepts of which hungry Americans are blissfully unaware as they dig into their homestyle "meal solutions." The industry congratulates itself over such discoveries as these: carbon dioxide or nitrogen pumped into a packaged meal can extend its shelf life, and cultured dairy solids injected into chicken breasts work beautifully as preservatives. What's profitable for food companies is putting out a product such as chicken that is "perceived-fresh" though it's been marinated, coated with preservatives, and prefrozen. The overriding objective is to capitalize on the consumer's need for speed. In dried soups, vegetables are freeze-dried, spray-dried, puff-dried, drum-dried, air-dried, or air freeze-dried. "Here, dear, have some puff-dried minestrone." As "mouthfeel" constitutes one holy grail for prepared food scientists, so does artificial flavor that convinces the mouth it's real. The "toolboxes" of flavor that scientists provide for food manufacturers have to evolve to keep pace in a hugely competitive market, and that means developing chemical tastes that are ever more complex and realistic, increasingly what the industry terms "complete"— just like the real thing, if anyone had time to cook the real thing. Beef flavor additive, for example, now breaks down more specifically into "roasted" beef and beef "roasted with pan drippings," according to Stephen Williams, Ph.D., who is section manager of flavor technology for an ingredient supplier. "Savory flavors," he explains, "are designed to provide authenticity, intensity and complexity." Supplying processed meals with savory flavors has grown critical because the large-scale manufacturing process that makes them so easy to cook fast drains foods of their genuine tastes. So scientists like Williams develop flavor additives that simulate actual forms of cooking—sautéing onions, for example.

As I stood at the supermarket checkout with a basket of processed foods for research, I glanced over my shoulder and saw in line behind me a sweatsuit-attired suburban matron, not so different from me. I watched her unload from her cart multiple containers of frozen Toaster Strudel, Chocolate Chip Cookie Mix, French Toast and Popping Fresh Rolls and Iced Cinnamon Swirl Danish in shiny cardboard tubes. It shocked me to see the grocery choices of someone whose food values differed so greatly from mine. But to be honest, though I don't bring home those particular products, it's really a matter of degree: not only do we buy the not-so-occasional Lunchable in my family, we eagerly consume taco dinner kits, pop-up frozen yogurt, and macaroni and cheese in a box. Like many Americans, on most days my family dashes, and we take just about any help we can get.

WE AMERICANS LOVE our junk food. Twinkies are a case in point, with a history stretching back to the Great Depression and 500 million baked each year. In 2000 Hostess celebrated the 70th birthday of its most lucrative product with a cake 25 feet tall and 16 feet in diameter, containing 20,000 Twinkies. Appropriately outsized, perhaps, for a pastry that was included in the nation's millennium time capsule, representing "an object of enduring American symbolism." Rabid Twinkies fans flood Planet Twinkie, the product Web site, with recipies; representative is one for Twinkie Pie, which calls for twelve Twinkies, one premade pie crust, one spoon, and one bowl: place the Twinkies in the bowl and stir "until the desired consistency is reached." Pour it into the pie crust, and your dessert is good to go. The more gastronomically sophisticated might prefer the recipe for Kahlúa-drenched Twinkie-misu.

We've developed a deeply schizophrenic relationship with food. On the one hand we are wary of its natural properties, so frightened of sugars and carbohydrates and fats that we go to lengths to avoid them, inventing increasingly bizarre substitutes and engaging in dietary fetishes—determining to go wheat free, gluten free, carb free, fat free. I recently learned about ways summer diners can "cancer-proof" their backyard barbecues, on the principle, according to national food writer Jean Carpenter, that "high heat creates carcinogens in meat." Scientific research apparently demonstrates that mixing an equal amount of cherries or blueberries with the ground beef before grilling hamburgers suppresses certain chemicals that are linked to cancer, as does adding garlic, rosemary, or sage, or, astonishingly, accompanying your barbecue with tea as a beverage, either hot or iced. If you don't care to drink the tea you can simply marinate your steak or swordfish in it.

Yet despite the lengths to which we'll go to eat "healthfully," we feel it is our inalienable right to consume junk. Some even view it as un-American to advocate against commercial foods prepared with unhealthy ingredients or in an unhealthful manner. It's as if we are determined to streamline our at-home diets—when we cook at all—by broiling boneless, skinless chicken breasts rather than frying onion-smothered pork chops with mashed potatoes and brown gravy. Once we go out in the world, though, or eat the meals we don't cook but merely heat, we cling to our fat and sugar and preservative-laden processed food and fast food and soda and snacks.

Leaving behind home cooking has had grave health consequences. In recent years, America's struggle with obesity has been well-publicized. An estimated 61 percent of U.S. adults were overweight or obese in 1999, along with 13 percent of children and adolescents. Among preschoolers, 20 percent are overweight, more than double the number in 1970. Obesity among adults has doubled since 1980, and overweight among adolescents has tripled. These trends are associated with dramatic increases in such conditions as asthma and in Type 2 diabetes in children. Naturally, there is an economic cost of obesity, which the U.S. Surgeon General's Office put at about $117 billion in 2000.

Nutrition experts theorize that the switch in our "food environment" has played a major role in these developments. According to Dr. Marion Nestle and Dr. Michael Jacobson in *Halting the Obesity Epidemic: A Public Health Policy Approach,* "Food eaten outside the home, on average, is higher in fat and lower in micronutrients than food prepared at home." Americans, they report, "spend about half of their food budget and consume about one-third their daily energy on meals and drinks consumed outside the home." Centers for Disease Control Director Jeffrey P. Koplan blames the nation's fat epidemic on "the American lifestyle of convenience and inactivity." Today, it's customary even for educational institutions to serve fast food. The American School Food Service estimates that at least 30 percent of public high schools sell some kind of name-brand fast food. Wendy's and Burger King maintain franchises in major hospitals.

It's not only physical health that gets lost in the shift from food that is homemade to mass-produced. Children, say sociologists, experience much of their intellectual growth around the dinner table. With the decline in home cooking comes a reduction in the number of those healthy—and intellectually salutory—family meals.

It would be inaccurate to judge Americans only as junk food junkies. Countervailing forces fight the synthetic, now as always. It's still so common as to be almost a cliché for someone to recall the flavor of corn just picked from the field: all it needs is to ever so briefly be tossed in the pot, people say, to provide the most delicious eating experience imaginable. Few today can enjoy field-fresh corn, because few of us inhabit the rural parts of the country, let alone live alongside a field of ripe Silver Queen, but many feel wistful for it. One of the last remaining ways to taste really fresh produce is to grow it in an at-home vegetable garden. And homegrown vegetables are coveted. Every growing season, legions of tomato fanatics defy the dictates of the giant tomato growers, who develop fruit with a thick skin and blocky shape for maximum shipping efficiency. Backyard tomato farmers have totally different priorities: intense flavor and juiciness. I remember once bringing a big, golden-yellow heirloom tomato just picked from my garden when I met some people for dinner at a nice city restaurant. The maitre d' had it sliced and brought to the table on a platter, round golden slices like moons against the white china. That plain, simple fruit was fully as exquisite as the dishes that came out of the professional kitchen.

Sometimes Americans still want a traditional meal with all the trimmings, although we don't necessarily want to make it ourselves. No "Homestyle Bakes" will do on America's favorite holidays. An economical way to put the turkey and the trimmings on the table is to pick up a complete cooked dinner at Boston Market, the phenomenally successful homestyle chain that McDonald's acquired several years ago. Pricier alternatives also abound. One springtime I worked in the kitchen of an upscale caterer in a horsey Westchester community. In early spring the kitchen was swamped with orders for Easter dinners and Passover seders. The sous-chef and I were assigned by the owner to complete almost all the jobs, from tiny delicate crab cakes to rosemary potatoes, orange chicken to flourless brownies topped with miniature chocolate chips.

The brisket on order for one regular customer, the caterer announced, she must prepare herself. The procedure wasn't difficult. She rubbed the meat with handfuls of sea salt and coarse pepper and paprika, seared it, covered it with sliced onions, then poured tomato juice over the whole thing and braised it in a slow oven until it was spoon-soft. Why couldn't her kitchen staff be trusted with so simple a recipe? Because the family of the woman who ordered the dish knew it as "her" recipe and she wanted them to believe when she put it on the Passover table that she had cooked it herself. Only the caterer could be relied upon to know the exact degree of spice and tenderness this brisket needed year in, year out. The client insisted upon the appearance of homemade without the hassle.

Susan Lawrence, owner of a high-end catering business in suburban New York, reflected on the expectations of people who shop with her in an interview with *The Valley Table*:

> People who are fairly skilled cooks (which a lot of my customers are) really just don't have time, especially when it comes to entertaining, and are not only coming in for dinner for the family but also to pick up foods that will make their entertaining easier. Not that people aren't capable of cutting up vegetables, but it's a matter of do you have half an hour to spend cutting up all of those vegetables and making a beautiful crudité, not to mention having to go to the supermarket and buy everything.
>
> I think that as people's lives get busier and busier and people are more and more involved in working and taking care of their kids and doing a million other things, that they have less and less time to cook. I predict—I hope I'm right about this—that people are looking more and more for quality take-home foods that make their lives easier.
>
> Of course, there is an interest in foods that are healthy, but I see, even more importantly, that people want interesting comfort foods, you know, meatloaf and mashed potatoes. We're the new mom.

Lawrence's take-out business embodies her views, purveying rib-sticking macaroni and cheese and knockwurst and beans and pot roast alongside winter wheatberry and edamame salad in mirin vinaigrette. This New Mom represents food carefully prepared on a small scale by a company that grows its own herbs. Though she may produce hundreds of apple pies at Thanksgiving, each is given personalized attention, and the dough for each is rolled out and draped over the pie plate one at a time.

The business of upscale caterers experiences a major bump every major holiday as people choose to let a professional do the honors. Gourmet-shop menus sound like the fabulous ideal of a holiday spread, but after all there is one crucial difference—the food emerged from someone else's kitchen, not from yours. Not only does it lack the individuality that makes home cooking great, but in hiring someone else to put the meal together we deprive ourselves of the pleasure of doing so. Think of the film *Babette's Feast*, which culminates in a banquet that causes a spiritual conversion among the diners: who in fact derives more satisfaction from the creation of this remarkable spread, Babette or her dour, pinch-faced patrons?

When I was a child, my family drove to Pennsylvania Dutch country to have Thanksgiving dinner with other families up and down the long table of an Amish household. I remember the sideboard laden with roasted meats, fresh-baked bread, and egg noodles. We ate home-cured pickles, a profusion of fresh vegetables, and the dish that most impressed me, a tapioca pudding whose fat semiopaque pearls swam in a milky sauce running with vanilla. All the food looked almost magical at this feast, because of the way it was spread out over a white cloth, and because each and every dish was homemade. Already, in the late 1960s, the groaning board of that Amish family appeared exotic to a mainstream suburban child like me—possibly more exotic, since my father worked in advertising and brought home an inexhaustible supply of the Ring Dings and Yodels his clients produced. Today, when processed foods dominate the American diet, tourists continue to reach out for this nonsynthetic experience of food and of life, out-of-step as it might seem with their everyday consumption of processed food, fast food, and restaurant takeout.

The fact is that every day could more closely resemble the cherished holiday of Thanksgiving, when the air is filled with the spicy scent of pie and our meal is prepared in partnership with those we love. We don't need to deny ourselves the pleasure of cooking homemade foods or sharing them with family and friends. Family tensions might well lessen because there wouldn't be the pressure of squeezing all that emotional connection into just one day. We might not even overeat to the point of indigestion if we knew these weren't the last homemade mashed potatoes and gravy we were going to see for a year.

THE EDITORIAL-ADVERTISING MIX of shelter magazines reflects the current confusion about food. Readers find idealized depictions of old-fashioned home-cooked cuisine in cozy proximity with ads for the very products that are fast supplanting it. A summer issue of *Country Living* (June 1998), for example, features an article illustrated by photos of antique bread boxes, knotty-pine kitchen tables, vintage linens, and jewel-colored heirloom tomatoes. Alongside runs an ad that reads "Shortcut to Summer," across a photo of what now passes for strawberry shortcake—a tower of fruit, Sara Lee packaged pound cake, and Cool Whip nondairy topping. The same magazine runs a regular recipe feature called Country Cooking. Opposite appears an acid-green, full-page ad for Lunchables, with an exultant young boy holding aloft a Pizza Swirls kit beneath an emphatic banner: "Awesome Mom."

The cookbook publishing industry, having exploded over the course of the 1990s, now releases roughly a thousand new titles every year. With less cooking instruction from generation to generation, cookbooks play an important role in teaching the basics. With cooking itself on the decline, however, a cookbook becomes in large part a fantasy item. One author, Mark Miller of Santa Fe's Coyote Café, explained to *Restaurants USA* that "cookbooks are almost a substitution for a lost sense of culture. People want some other life than the one they're living, so they buy a cookbook with pictures and imagine themselves as part of that life."

TV food shows likewise reflect viewers' hunger for cooking from scratch. For many, these programs are like sitting in the virtual kitchen of a good friend, with its warmth and good tastes and smells. Bruce Seidel, vice president at the Food Network, whose viewership increased 32 percent in 2001, attributes the popularity of these shows to a generation deprived of similar experiences in their own kitchens as they were growing up, and who find in the programs "an opportunity for discovery."

*USA Weekend* writer Michele Hatty decided to study the Lebanese cuisine her mother has perfected, including fresh tabbouleh and dolmas and a buttery sweet dessert called betlawa. She explains the interest of her generation in reclaiming their food history. She writes,

> This desire to re-create Mother's cooking is not unique to my generation. But in an age where culture is ultra-homogenized, a McDonald's is on every corner and few live in the place where they grew up, we 20-somethings find one of the last ways we can concretely capture any heritage is by learning to make the meals we grew up with.
>
> Even Generation X's poster children nod to this desire. *Friends* devoted an episode to ditzy Phoebe's determination to replicate the cookies her grandmother used to make. In an attempt to help, Monica spends hours testing batch after batch of chocolate chip

cookies, altering them till she nails the heirloom taste. (In typical sitcom style, it turns out Phoebe's grandmother used the tried-and-true Nestlé Toll House recipe.) Humor aside, the truth is there: We want to taste the past while looking to the future.

Indigenous foods die when no one learns to cook them. Delicacies vary the world over, providing regional inhabitants with gratification in the way of identity as well as unique flavors. I don't particularly care for garlic-oil-bathed baby eels, for instance, but sophisticated Spanish tapas eaters prize them. Food scholars track the evolving gourmet fare of different civilizations. Raymond Sokolov, for example, reports in *Why We Eat What We Eat* that the pre-Columbian population of Mexico feasted upon salamanders, monkeys, and even steamed pond scum. The Aztec diet caught on with the invading Spaniards, who shaped the scum into cakes called cheese of the earth, which can still be found far, far off the beaten track. No matter how seemingly exotic, a culture's cuisine is its mainstay, and as domestic cookery weakens, retaining that cuisine proves challenging.

For some time now, gastronomic trends in America have reflected a yearning for tradition. Country-style is hip: simple dishes of fresh ingredients, braised or roasted or stewed. "The rustic quality draws us with a vicarious warmth and home, an opportunity to connect in a world that has become terribly confusing and scary," cookbook author Lynne Rossetto Kasper told a reporter. "Remember, too, that at a time when people are very concerned with their health and its relationship to what they eat, we have handed over the responsibility for our nourishment to faceless corporations."

As evidence of a vein of home cooking that still pulses against all odds, consider that the most popular food magazine in the U.S. is the decidedly low-tech Milwaukee-based *Taste of Home*, which features reader recipes and a devotion to plain and simple cooking from scratch. With a 4.5 million circulation, the publication out-paces *Bon Appétit, Gourmet,* and *Food & Wine* combined.

Paradoxically, Americans now spend about 75 percent of their waking hours in the kitchen. Home remodelers are furiously installing countertops of granite and teak, cherry cabinets, brushed stainless steel Sub-Zero refrigerators and family computer nooks. The new kitchen increasingly revives its old-fashioned function as a family gathering place. What it's not, according to industry experts, is a place to cook. "I don't know where people are eating, but people certainly aren't using high-end gourmet kitchens for cooking," said Jean Dimeo, editor of *Building Products* magazine. "All the spiffy appliances are just for show." Developer Mark Wade of Philadelphia reports that when his houses go up for resale, "the stoves have never been used and stainless-steel refrigerators big enough to park a minivan in are spotless. The microwaves, on the other hand, are covered with lots of fingerprints."

Given the plethora of tools that fly off the shelves of the cook-ware departments at Pottery Barn, Williams-Sonoma, and even Target, preparing food from scratch could be simple and common-sense. Cooking could be embedded in the fabric of everyday life as simply as the way the skillets fit their permanent sketched spots on the pegboard wall of Julia Child's famous kitchen (now appropri-ately ensconced at the Smithsonian Institution) instead of how it is now: effete, overdone, or too much of a chore to be bothered with.

At this point some reader has her hackles up. What do you want? she's muttering. Is it fair to expect down-home cooking from busy women who hold demanding jobs outside the home? Despite the daily use my kitchen gets, I still experience some emotional turbu-lence regarding the notion of my own domestic accountability. For example, I remember going to my Girl Scout co-leader's house for an early morning meeting. When she offered me warm, home-baked blueberry muffins to go with my coffee, I felt both surprise and discomfort. How did she have the time to bake muffins in the morning, when that truncated time in my household means rushing to shower, dress, grab cereal, and go to work? When was the last time I invited over a friend and served her something homemade? My gratefulness for my friend's gesture was somewhat overshadowed by the envious second-guessing churned up by a plate of muffins.

An accountant with a heavy work schedule told me about dining out with her husband and two teenagers one night a week. "We don't have time to cook every night, but I do want to have the kind of home life I had growing up," she said. "So we have rituals, but we scale back. We bring in bagels every Sunday and just relax. I guess we could cook together Friday rather than going out, but . . . all cook together? Then do the cleaning up? I don't think so. We enjoy going out. And don't we deserve it? So I guess that's a ritual, too." The rest of the week the family is "just too busy to eat all at the same time."

For this woman and others, finding time to cook is a subject of understandable irritation. The United States currently has the longest workweek among the industrialized nations, surpassing Japan. Sixty-two percent of Americans work on weekends, and another 32 percent bring work home. One study, commissioned by F-O-R-T-U-N-E Personnel Consultants, discovered that more than 80 percent of American workers born between 1945 and 1974 consider themselves to be workaholics. Women as much as men want their jobs and need the income they provide. It could easily be argued that the higher standard of living they are giving their families (or providing for themselves) is well worth the trade-off for anachronistic domestic crafts, especially peeling potatoes.

Between the 1920s and today, Americans bought the argument that we no longer have time to cook—and, even if we did have time, it was drudgery we'd rather avoid in preference of leisure activities. We use this phrase all the time: *kitchen drudgery*. What we don't realize is that it's a message promulgated by marketers for the processed food companies, beginning way back, almost a hundred years ago. Harvey Levenstein, in his book chronicling the social history of eating in America, cites the 1957 response of the president of Campbell's Soup when he was asked why it is that people want things so "highly packaged." "To save trouble," he said. "The average housewife isn't interested in making a slave of herself. When you do it day after day [cooking] tends to get a little tiresome, and the young housewife is really less interested in her reputation as a home cook today. . . . She doesn't regard slaving in the kitchen as an essential of a good wife and mother." Along the same lines, the American Can Company boasted that in the years 1951–1952, the use of frozen orange juice had saved American housewives 14,000 years of "drudgery." An inadvertent collaboration developed between the giant food companies and women eager to get out from under the feminine mystique.

Our foodways have been co-opted by food corporations, who sell a dream of home cooking with no effort. Manufacturers attempt to capitalize on peoples' stress about overwork and fears of being trapped in sex roles, and they have been phenomenally successful. Spend less time cooking, we are told, so you can spend more time with your family. If we cook *with* the family, however, the work is more equitable and we share the pleasure of preparing the meal.

The most dependable place to find real home cooking now is at the most upscale restaurants. Cooking from scratch is increasingly the purlieu of highly specialized schools, which people attend only if they are aiming for a job in the booming food preparation industry. As part of their effort to produce unforgettable meals, chefs of haute cuisine are returning to such traditions as home canning, performing the elaborate process of making cherry preserves, for example, while hardly anyone else "puts up" their own preserves anymore.

Fine restaurants increasingly plump up their menus with mashed potatoes and macaroni and cheese and rice pudding. One, Home, in New York City's Greenwich Village, has answered diners' interest in old-fashioned cuisine by publishing its recipes and even relating how to create condiments, such as ketchup, from scratch, something few home cooks have attempted since Heinz usurped the market before the turn of the century. At the supersophisticated Manhattan restaurant Ouest, chef Tom Valenti satisfies the appetites of Barbara Walters and other luminaries with the ultimate in upscale down-home fare: meat loaf. There are trendy places on both coasts at which nostalgic diners spend $6 to order the old familiar Swanson's TV dinner. At some restaurants a chef-jiggered homestyle delicacy can fetch a pretty penny: one chic Manhattan restaurant offers macaroni and cheese with seared foie gras, with an asking price of $28.50.

CHAPTER 7

# A Specialty

IN HER BRILLIANT, intimate study of a small group of homemakers in the mid-1990s, *Feeding the Family*, Marjorie DeVault tries to restore respect to the job of producing a household's cooked food by proposing a battery of new terms. "Provisioning," for example, is her word for the job of calculating and satisfying the food needs of a family. DeVault describes a crucial aspect of provisioning: personal attention to the individual tastes of the household. "The family is a place where people expect to be treated in a unique, personally specific way instead of anonymously, as they are often treated outside. Part of the work of feeding is to give this kind of individual attention. . . ." One way we punish people in our society is by depriving them of personalized attention: we once fed criminals on bread and water, and we now eliminate choices on the prison food line. Increasingly, however, we mete out such punishment to ourselves, by partaking in a consumer culture that obliterates individual tastes in favor of mass-produced sameness.

A perfect example is McDonald's, which from the outset built its business formula on standardization. Ray Kroc, the company founder, specified that each beef patty cooked in every McDonald's outlet would conform to these standards: 1.6 ounces in weight, 3.875 inches in diameter, with a quarter ounce of onion and a bun three and a half inches wide. "The minute you get into customizing," wrote

Kroc in his memoirs, "you're on an individual basis. The cost of the product is exactly the same, but the labor triples. We can't do that." With so powerful a profit incentive—McDonald's revenues in 1998 were $18 billion—it's doubtful that customization will grow more popular among the fast-food chains. In the American gulag of the future, everybody gets Twinkies and Ding Dongs, regardless of a preference for petit fours.

The extent to which food is standardized or personalized is a matter of sustenance that is spiritual as well as physical. Kitchen traditions are those we rely upon to sustain us in times of need. Never in human history has food been unimportant—in fact, most often, it has been all-important.

In her 1942 classic about cooking well despite wartime shortages, *How to Cook a Wolf*, M. F. K. Fisher writes of keeping hunger at bay by eating "intelligently and voluptuously" whether you are preparing kidneys or kasha. She proposes cooking techniques that use thrift without sacrificing flavor (making melba toast or zwieback of stale bread, baking many apples at once to save energy). In a revised edition printed after the war, she reflects:

> These petty tricks seem somewhat more so when gas flows through the pipes and firewood is available and electricity actually turns on with a button. But in each one of them there is a basic thoughtfulness, a searching for the kernel in the nut, the bite in honest bread, the slow savor in a baked wished-for apple. It is this thoughtfulness that we must hold onto, in peace or war, if we may continue to eat to live.

Shopping and preparing food in this age of affluence makes it difficult to recall the succor provided by the simplest ingredients in times of want. When we do cook from scratch today, it had better be brief. The number of minutes Americans are willing to spend making a recipe has dropped precipitously even in the past decade, from half an hour five years ago to twenty minutes today. Thanksgiving offers the only excuse for most Americans to "indulge" themselves in taking time to cook at home and to eat with family. Considering how out of practice people are, how cut off from the culinary traditions of our forebears, it's no wonder that calls to the Butterball hotline soar. We grant ourselves a long weekend out of the year to do what households have done throughout history: share food over a common table. Even when the desire is still there, we lack the knowledge, the sense of purpose, the organic connection to an age-old tradition. Why is such a connection important? Because without it, things fall apart, in the Yeatsian sense of the phrase. Our metaphors begin to break down. To what extent can "Chicken Soup for the Soul" be nurturing if the only chicken soup we know is freeze-dried and comes in a plastic container with a peel-off lid?

Barbara Ketchum Wheaton writes in *Savoring the Past* that in other centuries, "Foods, whether as raw materials, cooked dishes, or meals given to mark occasions, became an appropriate way of offering friendship, showing concern, and marking relationships among people." In eighteenth century France, Voltaire was famous for the excellence of his kitchens and grew artichokes, strawberries, onions, and lavender in his beloved country gardens at his estate, Les Délices. He and his friends exchanged gifts of food along with their letters: a dozen baskets of apricots, partridges, a wild boar.

The bounty reflected the time as well as his personal wealth— this, after all, was a period when in rural France the rosemary grew so huge it was cut for firewood, and dozens of varieties of butter were sold in the Parisian marketplace. In America, meanwhile, settlers grew tired of feasting on oysters as big as dinner plates and giant lobsters were considered trash fish. But it's not only true in eighteenth century Europe or America, but throughout the world in wildly disparate cultures, that the preparation and sharing of food has been central. In southern Africa, for example, the Bantu people call exchanging food "a clanship of porridge." It reminds me of the time I was on a boat in the Yucatan with new friends who made their living diving for lobsters. After they'd swum to the bottom of the bay and speared a lobster and surfaced to throw it into the boat we cracked the carapace and split the tail, then squeezed onto the flesh the juice of a cut lime. A mouthful of this just-caught meat cooked in citrus acid was the most incredible ceviche possible. It was also a friendship-cementing ritual.

There is power in provisioning that is sometimes overlooked. Women, as is well known, make the vast majority of purchasing decisions in families—but that women can affect the home larder in other dramatic ways is attested to by the housewife riots in turn-of-the-century New York that brought down the price of kosher meat, as well as the successful campaign by the environmental activist group Mothers and Others to eliminate the pesticide Alar in apple growing. Even in canning foods at home there is underestimated power. It sounds old-fashioned, like something homemakers have done for all time, but in actuality women didn't start putting up fruits and vegetables until the invention of the Mason jar well into the nineteenth century and not in earnest until World War II. Today the option seems more attractive than ever, as it gives the individual control over what's packaged. You get fresher food. You can invent what you like, relishes or jellies or sauce. And you know it contains only what you put in it, without the preservatives or "natural flavors" or food dyes typical of mass-produced processed food.

One anthropologist has described the importance of maize in American Pueblo culture: "When I take away corn from such people, I take away not only nutrition, not just a loved food. I take away an entire life and the meaning of life." The psychological, emotional, and spiritual benefits to the person who participates in the food culture of our country are in danger of being taken for granted. Consider those people who have a "specialty," whether for brownies or carrot cake or chili or smoked ribs or a cheese ball appetizer. It's usually something deceptively simple, classic. Go to a bake sale, a benefit for the church or the volunteer fire department. Covering the plasticized tablecloth are row upon row of homemade chocolate chip cookies, but one tray will stand out, with cookies that are the chewiest, the most buttery, the thickest with chunks (and usually the biggest, too—diameter trumps all in bake sale cookies, if not in all cookies). One contributor, it seems, has the touch. Anyone could achieve excellence in chocolate chip cookies, but she does so consistently.

In large part brilliant home cooking, as in all creative effort, comes from just showing up. Anyone can make great cookies from scratch. Only some people bother, and bother all the time, enough to get it right, and then, finally, contribute their batch to benefit the public good. Today the bake sale groaning board often includes cardboard boxes of frosted donut holes from Dunkin' Donuts, a well-meaning contribution from someone without the time or inclination to go the homemade route. Still some people, especially older women, find the time to set out delicacies from their home ovens. Men aren't exempt. My husband's molasses cookies, from "his" recipe—which can be traced to the label of the Br'er Rabbit bottle in the 1950s—are often donated to the class picnic or swim team bake sale. I've had many compliments from people who assumed they were mine when I transported the cookies to the event.

My friend Josefa has assembled "her" succulent meatless lasagna dozens of times. Susie has perfected "her" strawberry pie with an all-butter crust. My mother has had long experience with "her" cauliflower Nivornais, a cold dish bathed in mayonnaise-mustard dressing that invariably appears on the family's holiday table. She originally got the recipe out of the paper—in fact, not trusting her memory, she still uses the yellowed clipping to prepare the dish—but though it once came from the daily food column, the recipe still is one that "belongs" to her. I've telephoned her for it more than once.

My sister-in-law brings "her" silage salad (based on her mother's recipe, which no doubt came from a friend rather than a cookbook), a vinegary layered melange incorporating broken uncooked Ramen noodles and shredded napa cabbage, to count-less potluck suppers. In the Midwest, where she lives, silage salad appears on many a buffet table, and sometimes multiple versions of silage salad. Each is different. Mimi elevates the dish by increas-ing the butter in which she toasts the almond slivers and sesame seeds. And it's true: other versions are good, hers happens to be great. It's by experimentation and fixing the dish again and again, contributing it to the communal table over and over, that the recipe becomes one's own and, simultaneously, reaches some kind of apogee of homemade taste. The result is a gift to whoever con-sumes the dish but also to the cook, who experiences the tremen-dous but usually unremarked satisfaction of putting great food in the mouths of innumerable people, including those outside one's domestic circle. "There is nothing to make you like other human beings so much as doing things for them," in the words of the writer Zora Neale Hurston.

Fried chicken is "my" specialty, if I had to name one. Like many homemade specialties, the recipe originated with another home cook. Emily was a weekend guest at the house of a couple I knew. Emily's fried chicken was the perfectly crisp result of jointing what she described as "a pink-white chicken" and soaking the parts overnight in milk, then dredging them in flour seasoned with salt and plenty of fresh-ground black pepper. Do the frying in Crisco with a little bacon grease, heated just to the point when a pinch of flour thrown in spits. In her seventies when she passed along these instructions, Emily was a painter from down South, with elegant, long white hair. I never knew her well, and my friends have drifted away, but a part of her remains in my method for frying chicken. It's now "mine" in part because I've adjusted some ingredients and steps—substituting canola oil for Crisco, adding cayenne, frying the pieces uncovered—but also, more basically, because I am the one who cooks the chicken, I am the one who serves it, I am the one who makes certain the drumsticks are precisely golden enough, that they have just the right amount of peppery crunch and meaty juiciness. In turn, I hope another home cook will admire the recipe and with effort and practice and experimentation make it her own. This is what makes up the silken web of our domestic food culture, a part of our homeways that is strong enough to bridge communities, families, and generations, but also so easy to break when we lose interest in sharing food and sharing recipes—when we instead bring that familiar bucket of KFC to the church picnic.

Community cookbooks—self-published, spiral-bound, usually sold to benefit a local worthy cause—dedicate themselves to the craft of raising "everyday" food or "comfort food" to the heights of a mouthwatering perfection, based on the personal touch of the cook and using the satisfied communal consumption of the dish as a gauge of its success. Each recipe in the 1973 Cookbook of the Altoona United Methodist Church—which provides as a bonus table graces, Bible jokes, and clever line drawings—cites the individual who contributed it. Lucille Berggren gave her recipe for Coffee-Date-Nut Bread. The Asparagus & Ham Hot Dish came from Mary Foss. The Peanut Butter Cake originated with Nona Agema and, according to a note, is "Reverend Agema's favorite *soggy* cake."

One comprehensive volume of this type is the West Point Offi-cers Wives' Club Cookbook, the perfectly titled *Enough to Feed an Army*, many of whose recipes are easily multiplied to feed hun-dreds. Helen Blewett, National Military Family Association Repre-sentative, gives the following commentary about her "Almond Chicken Casserole":

> This recipe was given to me as a brand new Army bride by Ruth Bryant whose husband, COL Burnell "Bunny" Bryant, was MacArthur's Provost Marshal in the Philippines, SUPT of the NY Military Academy and brother of Bea Bryant, Cadet Hostess at WP for many years. The note that came with the recipe read, "Five of these and you could feed an army!" It's true! This recipe has fed thousands over a 30 year Army career.

The cookbook features a recipe for chili for 1,000. Another, for Cadet Mess Creamed Chopped Beef, contributed by Mess Chef Manuel Mendes, guides readers through cooking per person, per 100 persons and per 1,000 persons (the last requires 188 pounds ground beef, 22 1/2 gallons lowfat milk, and 27 pounds each of flour and butter). Following many of the recipes is a useful commentary about occasions when the dish is generally consumed and with what results.

With their call for locally appreciated ingredients and their firm emphasis on unpretentious food that will appeal to indigenous tastes, these cookbooks hold back the tide of culinary uniformity. Community cookbooks document the specialties of a region and preserve its passing ways, at least on paper, providing "social history you can eat," in the words of Jane and Michael Stern. Thus Sweet and Sour Groundhog holds historical interest at the least in *The Amelia County Cookbook* of 1977. The Extension Homemakers Club of Amelia also includes instructions for home-curing a Virginia ham, for roasting venison and wild turkey, and for grilling doves. These volumes focus attention not only on local foods but on local home cooks. Culinary expert John Edge, who drew on the region's plethora of "gravy-splattered, spiral-bound cookbooks" for his wonderful compendium, *A Gracious Plenty: Recipes and Recollections from the American South,* has said, "I look upon those books as the voice of an unsung people. Nobody is paying attention to those churchwomen who came together, those firemen who cooked Brunswick stew every Sunday."

The covered casserole featured in so many community cookbooks has enjoyed a dignified history in difficult times. Upon an illness or death in the family, people still pay visits bearing a tray of baked ziti or a loaf of home-baked bread. Sending around a prepared meal from the deli section of the local market, even if it's the gourmet food shop, wouldn't be the same.

Cooking one's specialty can sustain one's self during a crisis as much as it can others. The suffering friend of a friend, on the verge of a divorce, was called upon during the holiday season to make "her" fruitcake—three dozen miniature loaves of it—as gifts for residents of a local old-age home where she sometimes volunteered. After working late, she painstakingly draped the bourbon-soaked cheesecloth over the rich dark cakes into which she had earlier stirred jewel-like candied fruit and toasted nuts before baking. It was a Sisyphean labor that would fill many stomachs, and perhaps warm some hearts, though it would never restore her marriage. Later she acknowledged that as arduous as it had been, the baking of those thirty-six cakes was what got her through that anguished time.

Today, preparing quantities of ethnic delicacies for sale at fairs or benefits can lead to skirmishes over what constitutes "home-made." I spoke with a middle-aged woman who was taking part in preparations for a weekend Ukrainian fair to benefit her organization's community center. I bet the food will be good, I said. "There will be hundreds of pierogies for sale," she told me. "They will be good, but . . . not homemade." Not homemade? Weren't the ladies of the group making them from scratch to sell? "Well, yes," she said, "they will be making them, true." They'd be making the dough, she told me, and they'd be filling the dumplings, and they'd be boiling them. "But . . . they'll be using dehydrated potatoes rather than whole ones. And that's—that's just not the way I'd do it. Sure, they'll be good," she told me. "But I make *mine* homemade."

Cooking gets us through death and illness but it's sometimes hard to do the cooking that would mean our own therapy in tough times. A pulmonary doctor who treats acutely ill patients once told me that you can tell when a woman is on the road to recovery when she resumes putting on lipstick. So it is with cooking: cooking again and cooking well seem a sure sign of returning health.

One time, after a grave illness, I found I simply had no rhythm or balance in the kitchen. I had lost the culinary equivalent of a green thumb. There were embarrassing mistakes, including some I inflicted on guests, as I tried to produce delicious meals and ended up with inedible flops. Worse was the agony of losing the pleasure of engaging in this activity. I was plagued by a sense of foreboding that if I could not cook I would never get well. One friend did her best to reassure me, saying that when her grandfather died, her grandmother, a naturally superb cook, was hopeless in the kitchen for a long time afterward, but eventually saw her skills restored. Finally, as my health began to return, I baked an apple pie that emerged from the oven just the way a pie should. I put it on the table to cool and watched the sweet steam lift up through the vents in the crust like a benediction: *you will get well.*

A sense of the wellness and bounty of a bygone time permeates the older community cookbooks. One volume my mother-in-law passed on to me, benefiting a long-dismantled children's charity, dates to 1943. It too contains quantity recommendations, such as strawberry shortcake filling for 50 (six quarts berries after hulling), mashed potatoes for 60, and cocoa for 100. The ads proclaim a different era: SKRUDLAND PHOTO SERVICE of Chicago, Illinois, claims pride of place inside the front cover, offering enlarged oversize prints at four cents apiece. A page devoted to Kitchen Wisdom reveals distinctions between taste then and now regarding the preparation of vegetables—for boiling asparagus, for example, the rule of thumb cited is 30–50 minutes. Equally intriguing but not so alien from today is the poem tucked in opposite a recipe for gingerbread by Mrs. Franklin S. Dyrness of Quarryville, Pennsylvania. An eight-stanza lament, it begins by demanding:

> *Where has she gone, the old fashioned wife,*
> *With her good "old fashioned way,"*
> *Who made her bread and cakes and sang*
> *"From my home I will never stray"?*
>
> *Has she left this earth, will she never more*
> *Make the kitchen her biding place,*
> *Or has she changed like the world, we ask,*
> *And the rest of the human race?*

The verses go on to mourn the loss of a once familiar domesticity—a comfortable house with a yard and birdsong outside, the smell of bacon and biscuits cooking. Sixty years back, home cooks anticipated the disappearance of a way of life centered on a cuisine made from scratch. The kitchen, the heart of the home, was already threatened by fast-breaking changes, with the U.S. immersed in the Second World War. A community cookbook like this one in which home cooks archived their personalized culinary knowledge was a stay against the coming of the domesticity-deprived future. As the artificial, the processed, "home meal replacement," and fast food encroach ever further onto the values of the domestic hearth, cookbooks published by ordinary people still serve as something of a finger in that dike. The end of the sixty-year-old verse, though undeniably quaint, still resonates:

> *Oh, may the time come back again,*
> *We ask our household Fairy,*
> *The thing we wish to "have and hold"*
> *Is a kitchen large and airy.*

> *Where we cook and stew and boil and brew,*
> *And eat of our home made tarts,*
> *Where there'll be no lack of the good "cold pack,"*
> *And other home made arts.*

The importance of community cookbooks and the idea of having a specialty may be taken for granted in most quarters. Yet the capacity to share homegrown cooking knowledge is critical to our spirit, strength, and happiness as a society. It constitutes one sure protector of our homeways.

◯◯

HOT PINK, thickly frosted, and big as a backyard wading pool, the strawberry cake stood high on its silver cardboard circle and awaited its passage into the party. Six candles glowed on top, including one for my birthday girl's good luck. But the magic of this cake derived not only from the wishes granted when blowing out those tiny candles.

It was a delicious creation, loaded with berries and buttercream and jam, sweet to the point of teeth pounding. It also laid claim to a certain garish if inadvertent beauty, since the previous midnight as I hoisted the ample top layer above the first two, some parts slumped, others slid, and all needed generous amounts of icing if I was to spackle the cake back together. To mask the pits and slopes, ballerinas now danced among grottoes, fairy gardens, rolling hills, waterfalls, and gaudy spun sugar flowers.

It was fortunate the cake was huge, because both adults and children came back for second and third slices. From a baking standpoint, it's a forgiving recipe, almost foolproof (for which I, not much of a baker, am glad) and it tasted pretty good. But the attraction of the strawberry cake, I am convinced, the reason it made the party guests so happy, lay less in how it looked or tasted than in the fact of it's being *made from scratch.* And that has been its magic in celebrations ever since.

And yet . . . was the strawberry cake homemade? My mother had given me the recipe—an old family favorite, she told me, passed down from my great aunt. On closer inspection, this "homemade" cake called for white cake mix, frozen strawberries, and Wesson oil, along with its miracle ingredient, strawberry-flavored gelatin. The recipe came not from the distant past but a newspaper of the 1930s, probably reproduced from instructions on the back of a box of Jell-O. I have a copy of the clipping, which came from my grandmother's metal file box of well-used recipes. Like my strawberry cake, many of the recipes we treasure as old and passed-down can be traced to corporate test kitchens, disseminated through product packaging with the idea of drumming up sales.

In fact, what now constitutes "made from scratch" often includes artificial ingredients, and even the basics—flour, butter, sugar, and milk—are processed to an extent unknown before this century. There is really no cake that is completely natural—from chocolate chip pound cake to carrot cake—because virtually all the ingredients we blend to create it are processed to one degree or another. Today, a tomato soup cake recipe calling for canned Campbell's downloaded from the *Good Housekeeping* Web site may be as close to tradition as many people get. Or "Crazy Cake," described by one cyber-foodie as "old, old, old!" For this heirloom you sift dry ingredients into a square pan, make three holes with a spoon, put oil in one, vinegar in another and vanilla in the third, pour water over the top, and stir with a fork.

Like other aspects of history pertaining to the domestic lives of women, the history of cake baking comes down to us in fragments. Kitchen wisdom for centuries was transferred verbally from generation to generation rather than committed to paper. We do know that cake is millennia old. Once salt was employed in food preparation (before 17,000 B.C.), flour was ground (10,000 B.C), sugar was cultivated (6,000 B.C.), and olives were pressed for oil (around 6,000 to 5,000 B.C.), the ingredients for cake were available. Patties of crushed grains have been discovered among the remains of Neolithic villages, where these primitive tarts were cooked on hot stones.

For the ancient Egyptians, baking was an art, and to them we can credit the crucial development of ovens. Bread was so central to the Egyptians (they reputedly baked about fifty different varieties) that Herodotus called them "the Bread Eaters." Tombs were stocked with it, and sacred animals such as cats and wasps were fed on bread.

The early Greeks as well as the Egyptians created breads sweetened with honey. A recipe for cakes of nuts and honey has come down to us from Tyana of Crete. In Rome, "placenta" was the word for flat cake, one used as an offering at temples. Cato wrote a recipe for a honey-sweetened cheesecake in 75 A.D. Other Roman cakes incorporated barley, raisins, sweet wine, pomegranate seeds, and pine nuts, and some used yeast from the head of beer, called barm, as a leavening agent.

From the start, cakes have denoted celebration. Wedding cake dates from as early as first-century Rome, where the custom was to toss crumbs at the bride rather than cutting slices to serve. From the Middle Ages on, Europeans marked festival days with enormous fruitcakes called "great cakes."

Special-occasion cakes with equally ancient roots still exist as cultural artifacts throughout the world. At Mardi Gras in New Orleans, Twelfth Night revelers unveil a giant mock cake called a King Cake, which they pantomime slicing with wooden swords. Boxes distributed to guests contain either a morsel of cake or a silver bean on a chain. The "luck of the bean" will determine who will be crowned queen, a ritual dating back to the Roman Republic, when coins and fava beans were baked into cakes to determine mock royalty. Over the years Twelfth Night cakes grew larger, with one "Extraordinarily Large Twelfth Cake" advertised in 1811 London measuring 18 feet in circumference and reported to weigh "nearly half a ton." The edible cake that continues as an integral part of the Twelfth Night tradition today features brioche-like dough rolled with cinnamon and sprinkled with green, gold, and purple sugar.

The challenge to preserve what is beautiful, festive, and meaningful while adapting to societal changes has been met with remarkable success in the case of wedding cakes, whose power to amaze has not changed in hundreds of years. A memoirist named William Wirs described the bridal cake at a Williamsburg wedding in 1806:

> . . . It was past eleven when the Sanctum Sanctorum of the Supper-room was thrown open . . . and it was near twelve when it came to my Turn to see the Show. And a very superb one it was, I assure you. The Tree in the centre Cake was more simply elegant than anything of the Kind I remember to have seen. It was near four Feet high: the

Cake itself, the Pedestal, had a rich—very rich—Fringe of white paper surrounding it: the Leaves, Baskets, Garlands, &c., were all very naturally done in white Paper, not touched with the Pencil, and the Baskets were rarely ornamented with silver Spangles. At the Ends of the Tables were two lofty Pyramids of Jellies, Syllabubs, Ice-creams, &c.—the which Pyramids were connected with the Tree in the centre Cake by pure white Paper Chains, very prettily cut, hanging in light and delicate Festoons, and ornamented with Paper Bow-knots. Between the centre Cake and each Pyramid was another large Cake made for Use: then there was a Profusion of Meats, Cheesecakes, Fruits, &c., &c.

. . . All the Grandees of the Place were there.

The sheer fabulousness of an oversized cake continues to awe spectators. On his fiftieth birthday, President Bill Clinton was feted with a cake created by one of the finest bakers in New York City, William Greenberg. The 300-pound layer cake had a raspberry filling and vanilla buttercream frosting and was topped with an elaborate American flag. It fed 2,000 partygoers.

Italian bakers became highly sought after in Renaissance Europe and were hired to make an early version of sponge cake called "biscuit." During the French Revolution, an egg-rich cake known as "biscuit de roy" was baked in paper or tins and sliced at the table.

The technology of baking has changed over the years, of course. The flour industry was the first in America to undergo industrialization. The invention of new technology for grinding wheat late in the nineteenth century transformed home baking, as people now could purchase factory-made flour rather than having to farm wheat and bring it to the mill themselves. The availability of fresh butter also grew. Wood ovens replaced baking over an open hearth fire, which surely enhanced the flavor of delicate baked goods such as cakes.

Despite modernization, fine baking still required skill. Making yeast wasn't easy, nor was regulating an oven's temperature. To leaven a cake required huge quantities of eggs, which needed to be beaten hard and long to make a cake stand up, until it was discovered that baking powder could be used to enhance the rising capability of eggs.

Cake baking found itself central to the repertoire of the nineteenth century housewife, who derived real prestige from her skill in the kitchen. Women from every social class coveted new recipes for fancy cakes and other baked goods. Even if a housewife had servants she would often assign rote tasks and everyday meals to them, reserving the task of special-occasion baking for herself.

By the early twentieth century home bakers cultivated elaborate variations and exotic ingredients to produce ever more creative as well as toothsome varieties of cake. Then, however, food manufacturers recognized the potentially huge market for so well-loved a foodstuff. In 1953, Sara Lee was the first company to devise a method of baking, freezing, and shipping good-quality pound cake in the same foil pan. A pound cake in the freezer answered the need of time-pressed housewives who wanted to provide a traditional dessert for their families.

Prepackaged cake mixes also hit the market in the mid-1950s, at the height of the food industry's first convenience boom. Betty Crocker, the fictive female figurehead who dispensed advice via magazines and radio broadcasts on behalf of General Mills, was invented in the wake of World War II to reassure consumers that the company's products were safe and nourishing. So powerful was the allure of the Betty Crocker brand that in 1957, only a decade after their invention, sales of mixes had increased to over half the country's home-baked cakes.

Then the journey to cake mix dominance hit a snag. During the war, when staples such as butter grew scarce, homemade goods became more precious than ever and women derived an even greater pride from their baked creations (causing a surge in home baking similar to that which took place in home canning during the war years). When cake mix was first packaged, it only required adding water, but marketers soon realized that housewives were too attached to the home baking role to eliminate all hands-on work. The solution: change the formula to require water and one egg, with the aim of making home bakers feel that they were still "baking." To further enhance the image of creativity, packaged mix boxes suggested minor additions to the bare-bones recipe.

This tradition continues. Food editor Anne Byrn recently published a book called *The Cake Mix Doctor*. She extols the virtues of cake mix reliability, since mixes have been "road tested like those steel-belted tires on your car. They've been tested over and over in corporate kitchens to make them as friendly as possible, ready for slip-ups from the consumer." The only problem is disguising the chemicals that give these products a "cake-mix taste," but that can easily be done, she assures, by bolstering the batter with almond extract, coffee, orange zest, or bourbon. The popularity of the book is both a reminder that people want home-baked cakes in their lives and an indication of how homogenized our cooking has become.

Homemade cake evokes powerful associations. I often recall the white coconut cake under glass on the counter of a corner shop in a town near mine. Its handsome simplicity could have been the model for any number of paintings by America's most sensitive cake artist, Wayne Thiebaud. Last time I looked, the restaurant was closed with a For Lease sign in the window. Places with home-baked cake don't stay in business forever. Eat that coconut cake while you can.

High-end establishments, though, still cut the cake. A fad has elevated comfort food at retro chic eating establishments, so power diners may order cookies and milk or banana pudding to follow their pasta with squid ink. Nostalgic patrons line up at one cafe in New York's Greenwich Village that offers nothing but peanut butter sandwiches—twenty-nine varieties of them. No wonder the finest bakeries in America have begun to revive homestyle layer cakes made from family recipes.

Years ago I visited the apartment of a friend who was fixing a cake for her boyfriend's birthday. He sat in her tiny kitchen, talking to her as she beat the batter. At the time, it surprised me—rather than reserve the cake for later as a surprise, she chose to assemble it with its recipient in the room. Since then I have come to understand her action as a demonstration of love. "There is no spectacle on earth more appealing," wrote Thomas Wolfe, "than that of a beautiful woman cooking dinner for someone she loves." I think his observation applies even more profoundly to baking a cake for someone.

Red velvet cake, devil's food, angel's food, yellow cake, and fruit cake. Food historian John Egerton writes: "In the days when homemakers had ready access to fresh cream and eggs, cakes were the pride and joy of many a cook, and at times almost an insignia of status. Everyone in the neighborhood knew who made the best caramel or coconut or chocolate cake, and at community dinners those prized creations were the first to disappear." Not only do many bakers have a cake specialty, nearly every cake recipient has his "favorite." Children, of course, recognize it as a crucial distinction—who favors vanilla, who likes chocolate. For adults, as well, on our birthday if at no other time, we get the kind of cake we like best, if we're at all lucky. It's a way we have of expressing our caring for a person, that we know him well enough to plan for his birthday cake—whether it's made at home or by a bakery or restaurant— without having to ask whether he is a chocoholic or prefers caramel or strawberry. *On your birthday, you get the kind of cake you want*—that should be the law.

I once borrowed a good friend's cookbook and decided which cake to bake from the number of chocolate smears on the page. It was a connection between her and me, a leap from the domestic life of one woman to that of another, that will be familiar to anyone who has inherited a stash of beloved family recipes on well-thumbed index cards. That cake was a Palm Beach Chocolate Tube Cake, and the cookbook was by Maida Heatter, one of the foremost dessert experts of our time. Explaining why she persists in what she does—testing and retesting recipes, getting the perfect orange pound cake—Heatter has said, "For me, life's problems seem less important and easier to cope with while trussing a chicken, chopping onions, kneading a yeast dough, or icing a cake. And all seems well to me when popovers and soufflés rise to magnificent heights. My mother taught me that cooking is an act of love—and a beautiful, mountainous escape."

Over the last few generations, we've seen the dilution and disappearance of a priceless homemade cake tradition along with the domestic arts as a whole. I've seen the evolution in my own family, from my maternal grandmother and the sights and smells associated with her kitchen, to my mother, who was capable of baking a cake but preferred not to, to my generation, who with few exceptions don't want to and can't bake. Gastronome- and women-oriented Web sites offer encyclopedias of homey treats for the whole family, premised on the skills of the culinarily compromised. At iVillage.com's Recipe Finder, one Halloween recipe is for Black Cat Cupcakes, made exclusively with store-bought, synthetic ingredients: Oreos, chocolate cake mix, canned chocolate frosting, licorice, and jelly beans.

The decline of home baking has gone hand in hand with the expansion of commercial food processing. In a 2001 *New Yorker* cartoon, a peevish woman holding a box talks to her skeptical husband in the kitchen: "If I add water I'm cooking." In the future of culinary atrophy, the vocabulary of the home-baked will be lost from our daily lives. We may still insist upon the availability of cakes and other delicacies in supermarkets, bake shops, and restaurants. After a while, however, the source of professional bakers' and pastry chefs' inspiration and basic skills—the cakes baked for loved ones in private kitchens—will dim, and we won't have that connection.

A question that reveals our discomfort with the issue of cakes store-bought versus made-from-scratch is how much can be "outsourced" without losing the intimate nature of an occasion. Birthday-cake-wise, we wonder, what demonstrates responsible, sensitive parenting? Baking the cake and collecting just the right decorations (football candles, sugar Big Birds) from the local supermarket represents considerable commitment for some parents. Others easily justify purchasing a birthday cake at the best bakery in town, either because it surpasses the results a nonbaker could ever achieve, or because they lack the time to do it any other way. It makes total sense for some parents to buy a Carvel cake, since their child demands it anyway, and especially now that Carvel has made it so easy, with its "secret formula" soft ice cream cakes available for purchase in any supermarket. These cake-related dilemmas blend with equally stressful concerns: whether a busy parent must host the party at home, or hire the best party organizer to plan the celebration and select the entertainment, or even be physically present at the event.

What does it matter if someone chooses to make a cake, especially if there is questionable difference when you come down to it between baking it totally from scratch or starting with a mix? (Think of the strawberry cake.) Whose business is it if a busy person with job and family to juggle brings home a birthday cake from the Wal-Mart bakery, especially when a seven-year-old spends exactly one and a half minutes sitting down to consume the cake at any given birthday?

The evolution of our relationship to cake parallels that of our relationship to home and homemaking. Both alter almost imperceptibly from one era, one generation to the next, not because the changes are negligible but because we are too close to them to see the difference they make in our lives.

Domesticity is itself what Dickens called in *Martin Chuzzlewit* "a highly geological home made cake," layered with meaning and memory, flavored with intense emotions. As significant as changes in the home have been over recorded history, we have never been in such danger of losing it altogether. One at a time, the customs of homemaking have begun to drift away, as irrevocably as a wonderful recipe forgotten because no one ever thought it important enough to write down. Some of our domestic arts have been called into question verbally, but others, such as baking cake from scratch in a domestic kitchen, have simply been left by the wayside, co-opted by companies that market easy, time-saving products like powdered cake mixes.

To bake a cake at home from flour, butter, milk, and eggs (and sometimes a package of Jell-O) has become remote to most Americans, even perceived as a sort of relic of a hobby, something indulged in by people with too much time on their hands, an affectation. But cake is only one manifestation of the rest of our fading homeways. Dinner goes from freezer to microwave to mouth. Housework is detestable, a set of chores engaged in only by those who have no other choice. Crafts that once were central to the needs of the household and identity of the homemaker have vanished. Proof of their decline lies in the marginalized or laughable efforts of diehards who want to salvage any of these pieces of the home before they are swallowed up like a penny tossed down the deep well of the remembered past.

Food consumption naturally changes over time. So does our idea of the homemade, along with our conception of home itself, which nonetheless shares with the finest cake a fundamental simplicity, along with the complexity of its crumb. Yet no matter whether there's Jell-O in the mix, the cake made from scratch embodies the link between the person who creates it and the one who consumes it, between the carer and the cared for.

"FOOD IS WHO WE ARE in the deepest sense," writes Cara de Silva in an introduction to *In Memory's Kitchen,* a cookbook assembled by the women of the Nazi slave labor camp in Terezín, Czechoslovakía, during the Second World War. "And not because it is transformed into blood and bone. Our personal gastronomic traditions—what we eat, the food and foodways we associate with the rituals of childhood, marriage, and parenthood, moments around the table, celebrations—are critical components of our identities. To recall them in desperate circumstances is to reinforce a sense of self and to assist us in our struggle to preserve it."

*In Memory's Kitchen* is an extraordinary document that attests to the life-preserving effect of homemaking traditions. At Terezín—and at other camps—prisoners compiled handwritten cookbooks and so survived day to day when all they ate was potato peelings, thin broth, stale bread, and turnips. Keeping written records of the foods of their culture became an act of defiance, too, under unfathomably dangerous and debilitating conditions: a prisoner at Lenzing work camp in Austria used a propaganda leaflet for the Third Reich to inscribe a recipe; she scrawled the ingredients and step-by-step instructions across the photo of Hitler that served as the tract's frontispiece. The experience of sharing what little food they had and the memories of preparing food proved indelible for those who survived the war. Years later, one Terezín prisoner remembered a "Mrs. Windholz" and her efforts to bake a semblance of a "ghetto torte" made of bread, a little coffee, margarine, saccharine, "lots of good wishes and an electric plate" and wrote of how delicious it was.

It wasn't only dreaming about delicious fare when they were starving that nourished the prisoners of Terezín. It was mentally re-creating the culture of caring that is inseparable from food prepara-tion. Sustaining them also was the idea that eventually, even if they themselves did not survive, they would be able to *connect,* to con-vey, via these pathetic scraps of handwritten recipes, some of their heritage to their children. The incarnation of caring that defines homemaking can be as conducive to the mental health of the prac-titioner as it is to that of her beneficiaries.

One of the sturdiest home-cooking styles in United States today, that of the black community, arose out of conditions of incredible want during slavery and after. Many customs of the American home kitchen still alive today were born during these times of crushing need. During the Depression, corn bread, salt meat, sweet potatoes, sorghum, and occasionally a chicken com-prised the diet of Southern sharecroppers. Some survived on little but fatback and collard greens. At the same time, according to John Steinbeck's observation, dandelion greens and boiled pota-toes were the standard fare of migrant farm workers out West.

"We ate weeds," recalls one man quoted in a cookbook based on recipes from the Great Depression, "but my mother was such an innovative cook that to this day I still love those greens." As the folk saying goes, "hunger is the best sauce." Under severe duress, we tend to return to common practices of caring, and sometimes being reduced to the basics makes the end product even more sustaining. Writes Patience Gray in *Honey from a Weed,* her sensational travel and food memoir of time spent in some of the most intensely poor Aegean islands, "Poverty rather than wealth gives the good things of life their true significance. Home-made bread rubbed with garlic and sprinkled with olive oil, shared—with a flask of wine—between working people, can be more convivial than any feast."

One recent summer I traveled to a family camp in the North Woods of Minnesota, the kind of place where families return season after season, where kids live around the clock in their gritty bathing suits, spiders haunt the cabin corners, and the food served is simple but delicious. Guests were always welcome to help out in the kitchen.

Also visiting was a Lithuanian guest who had come to the U.S. a decade before. With brassy hair and a pleasant manner, she had too little fluency in English to communicate much with the other campers. However, for the days I was there one subject she spoke of constantly was her potato-apricot dumplings, from a recipe she brought from her homeland and that she cooked for the group as a ritual each summer at the camp. She would corner people asking them if they would meet her in the kitchen on the last afternoon to prepare the dumplings and seemed truly disappointed if a person said they couldn't or didn't want to.

Anticipation began to build. On the final day of our stay, a handful of volunteers peeled potatoes, boiled potatoes, mashed and kneaded and mixed potatoes for a hundred dumplings. One whole apricot was sealed inside each doughy package. After boiling, the dumplings were sizzled in butter and rolled in a drift of confectioner's sugar. As she had promised, a bite into the hot juicy center of each golden dumpling would be followed by an exclamation: Ah! Good!

Stuff ourselves though we did, scores of leftover dumplings remained. This she must have anticipated, having cooked the same dessert so many times for a group of the same size. But she did not seem to mind. Creating such a bounty had meaning beyond putting dessert on the table. These cannonball dumplings were a gift from her to her summertime friends, but also a strategy for keeping intact the memories of her upbringing. By teaching others to make them she ensured the preservation of her homeways.

At issue in this story and so many others is not only family recipes or particular household hints, but connection—to each other, to history, to our humanity. How well the food is cooked is finally less important than the human dynamics involved. A grandmother shows her love in serving meals that, although they may not rival the works of the great chefs, nonetheless embody "the redemptive power of the home," to borrow social historian Glenna Matthews's discerning phrase.

Americans' choices in terms of how involved they want to be with the culture of food making and eating and sharing are not going to be identical, nor should they be. For a long time, at a house where we lived that was nestled in an apple orchard, my husband and I hosted late, extravagant feasts on long tables under the moon-lit sky, meals we happily spent days planning for, provisioning for, and preparing. Those dinners enriched my life and maybe that of the people who shared our food and our company. But there's no need to go overboard, as I sometimes have, frying chicken for sixty-five or squiggling tarragon mayonnaise on a whole poached fish or cooking gallons of cucumber soup for a casual gathering of friends. While I put up rich sparkling raspberry jam, collecting the August fruit from wild bushes, you may not relish the idea of getting stuck by thorns, or even of hiking out into the woods. It's only a question of building on what it is you do like—of reclaiming the parts of homemade that satisfy you as an individual.

∞

AUTHOR LIZ EHRLICH writes in *Miriam's Kitchen* that her grandmother-in-law manages to keep a strictly kosher kitchen and concoct feasts with only a few tools: a spoon, a bowl, a skillet. The culinary base of nearly every dish she makes is the same simple combination, onions fried in oil with salt and pepper. When Ehrlich is studying at Miriam's feet she is learning not only a way to cook but a way to live. Authors Peter Farb and George Armelagos have succinctly assessed the value of passing culinary tradition to the next generation. "Each society's culture," they write, "is transmitted to children through eating with the family, a setting in which individual personalities develop, kinship obligations emerge, and the customs of the group are reinforced."

Soup kitchens exist to fill the stomachs of hungry, hurting people. But perhaps the food served is beneficial not only because it provides calories that keep the poor alive, but spiritually, insofar as it is made from scratch. For four years I served as head chef at a soup kitchen in upper Manhattan. There were many times when a guest leaned in the kitchen door on his way out to thank the kitchen crew—not just for dinner, but more specifically for a meal that tasted like home. There were always people eager to talk about similar dishes their wives or their mothers had prepared. Make no mistake—out of necessity, we concocted the plainest, least expensive meals imaginable, usually some casserole incarnation of ground beef or chicken thighs, but as much as possible we drew the line at using government-issue meatballs or the industrial-size metallic-tasting canned string beans. We would favor the more prep-intensive onions and peppers with fried fennel sausages or fresh corn or asparagus or chard direct from the wet wooden farm crate. Talking to the soup kitchen patrons reminded me that all of us, even those who live on the street, share a common culinary heritage based on the down-to-earth cooking of the home. The same idea was well articulated by the legendary food journalist Clementine Paddleford, who was once well known to American households. "We all have hometown appetites," she wrote. "Every other person is a bundle of longing for the simplicities of good taste once enjoyed on the farm or in the hometown [he or she] left behind."

At the soup kitchen, I sometimes doubted the possibility that our culture's culinary bonds would remain strong through future generations. I worked with a large corps of volunteers, mostly younger than I was, in their twenties and early thirties, brokers, publishing execs, corporate middle managers. I noticed that I could ask them to perform certain tasks—to season a chicken for baking, for example—and I would receive blank stares in return. As a group, they were kitchen illiterate. I grew accustomed to providing remedial education in cooking skills as I assigned them jobs: "You cut the carrots cross-wise, like this, with a knife like this one." I always felt as though I were explaining some arcane but interesting bit of alchemy. They were charmingly open to the experience, perfectly willing to learn, and quite unabashed about their ignorance.

When we teach our children the traditions of hearth and home, we convey to them a vital and expressly matriarchal way of strengthening the bonds of love. The kitchen, no matter how humble, lies at the heart of any culture, and the simplest homemade food is somehow undeniably, amazingly therapeutic. Take away cooking, and the aching heart goes still.

How might our homeways hold up in "desperate circumstances" similar to Terezín, say, or the Great Depression? How long could the memory of a Big Mac with fries sustain any of us? Some would enthusiastically claim that it could. But the trade-off being made in our culture—of something like a homemade torte exchanged for a burger cooked (literally) by a robot—has been accomplished without coherent challenge, without discussion or remark, without laying out the terms of the trade.

"The degree of slowness is directly proportional to the intensity of memory;" wrote Milan Kundera in his novel *Slowness*. "The degree of speed is directly proportional to the intensity of forgetting." What is your most evocative food memory? How far back does it take you? Proust, most famously, had his madeleines. I can still recall a crisp, succulent baked fish on a rowboat of a platter, surrounded by halved roasted garlicky new potatoes with a dish of buttery pencil-thin green beans on the side. It was my first trip to Europe, and our ten-speed bikes were parked in front of a restaurant way out in the French countryside, where we ate family style. I had never imagined food like this. I was fifteen, and the experience remains clearer in my mind than many things that happened in the past week. I can taste that memory, an extraordinary gift.

What is at stake here is the quality of our lives. In twenty, thirty, or forty years, we will be forced to go to a restaurant in an oxymoronic attempt to get a home-cooked meal. But the best restaurant chefs learned their craft from their mothers and grandmothers. Once we stop teaching our children to cook, we will have nothing to inspire future chefs or give them the skills they need. When we grow old, people of my generation will need nurturing. We can look forward only to institutionalized caring if our children haven't learned (from us) to care for their loved ones the old-fashioned way.

Yet other ways of learning to cook hold out promise, too, especially given a weakened intergenerational heritage. Twenty-five years ago, my college roommate taught me to roast a chicken. It wasn't what my parents expected from my education, or what I hoped to learn. Yet of all the things I got out of school, that lesson probably had the most lasting value.

Friends make excellent cooking coaches. One, Christine, imparted her technique for high-standing baking-powder biscuits. Sandra showed me how simple food can be made elegant by scattering herbs just so, at the edges of the platter. From Catrine I learned to mix a handsome pie crust from half whole-wheat and half white flour. We can absorb from friends what we didn't from our mothers or grandmothers.

We're less confident about cooking and less likely to undertake it if we feel ignorant of the basics. Now fewer and fewer young people get those lessons. A friend told me he came home one evening to find his younger sister trying to prepare dinner for herself, boiling a solid hunk of pasta that had become stuck together because she didn't know to give it a stir once she'd dropped it in the pot.

⚭

I RECENTLY SPENT some time teaching at a boarding school near where I live. Many students there are far from home—whether home is geographically distant (Japan and England) or semidistant (Colorado) or only distant emotionally, as with kids alienated from their families in New York City. The school makes efforts to create a home-like environment for the students, with dorm parents and weekend trips to the local mall.

The most striking attribute of homestyle living is the school's food service, which provides a bounty of prepared foods at every meal, from split pea soup to oatmeal cookies. Living away from their families, these kids probably eat better than 95 percent of kids in America who live at home—simply because they aren't permitted to leave campus at lunchtime and so aren't consuming fast food.

In the course of this class for high school seniors, we discussed an article on the meat-packing industry that went into some depth about the questionable nutritive value of McDonald's hamburgers. Enthusiastic would characterize their reaction—enthusiastically dismissive. "I don't care!" one student shouted. Proclaimed another, "I'm going out right after class to Mickey D's." "This can't be true," said one kid, "and if it is I don't believe it."

McDonald's has become so enshrined a piece of Americana that some people grow upset upon hearing the chain criticized. It actually represents a part of their life, their family experience, their childhood, their birthright, the way grandmother's special ragout does for someone raised in a different environment. "The paradox of McDonald's longevity," writes social critic Douglas Kellner, "is that an institution which destroyed tradition (that is, home cooking, individualized family restaurants, a balanced and healthy diet) has itself become tradition that accrues nostalgia and the aura of Americana—in part the result of McDonald's advertising campaigns." These kids will fight for their right to fast food.

Where does this leave the next generation of Americans? In other countries gastronomic education is not the sole responsibility of the individual household but treated as a matter of vital collective interest. In France, one week every school year is devoted to teaching elementary-school children that eating is about much more than survival. In this twelve-year-old program, 3,000 chefs visit classrooms around the country demonstrating cooking techniques. Adults, too, participate in an event known as "Semaine du Goût"—Taste Week—tromping out into the woods, say, to learn to distinguish edible herbs and mushrooms.

The French emphasis on food takes place year-round. A reporter for The New York Times describes the typical menu in a French day care center: "No sloppy Joes here. Not even a hint of a peanut butter and jelly sandwich," she reports. Instead the tots are served "a little cream of pumpkin soup, followed by baby lamb, new potatoes and crème fraîche on strawberries." Some French children even learn to bake pies in preschool. Europeans tend to understand that maintaining ties to culinary quality ensures the preservation of an important dimension of national character. "What is patriotism but the longing for the foods of one's homeland?" in the words of Chinese poet-statesman Lin Yutang.

In the U.S., some people are fighting to keep alive an awareness of food outside its plastic wrap and to nurture in kids a passion for cooking. Five years ago, the Berkeley culinary institution Chez Panisse developed a program called the Edible Schoolyard, which works in conjunction with the Martin Luther King, Jr. Middle School to help students see food through from seed to table. The

children plant, garden, harvest, cook, and eat what they grow
—whether it's cucumber sushi or Jerusalem artichoke fritters—as
part of the school's educational curriculum. Alice Waters of Chez
Panisse has described her aim in the program:

> When you are feeding someone else, you should be thinking about
> their nourishment, not about manipulating them or selling them
> something. Food is not a commodity, it is the most important thing
> we can give to each other. Feeding one another is the most basic,
> fundamental part of healthy and moral living. Offering people
> things that help them to grow, physically and spiritually—that's
> what parents and teachers should be offering our children. This
> should be the foundation of their moral education.

Oldways Preservation, likewise, an organization devoted to sustaining world food traditions against the onslaught of modern pressures, has developed a curriculum that teaches children to cook
international dishes. And at a gourmet cookware store called Sur
la Table, which has twenty-one locations nationwide, kids take
cooking courses in which they learn knife technique, baking and
roasting, and even to carve peacocks out of melon.

I am convinced that learning to cook teaches children worthwhile nonculinary values. My daughter, then seven, was in the
kitchen the day I baked a chocolate-pecan pie that won the annual
pie-baking contest in my village. The crust contained more butter
than I generally use, and once in the oven promptly began to melt.
Checking its progress, I was dismayed to see the edge I'd so carefully braided caving in toward the center of the pie. The crust had
already begun to create sinkholes at the pie's nutty edge. At first I
thought I would give up. Instead I pulled out the pie pan, worked
up some more dough to patch the rim, sculpted leaves and flowers
to cover the bad spots on the surface, and stuck the thing back in

to bake. The best thing about the experience was not the blue ribbon but that my daughter had seen a minor disaster get fixed, a
kitchen lesson with crucial application to the rest of life.

Usually, however, with the increasing culinary inactivity at
home and the disappearance of classroom home ec, children spend
little time in an actual kitchen. Most often, they get their only
cooking exposure playing house, an activity that despite changes in
the character of the home is ever-enthralling to small boys and
girls. Children bustle about their colorful play kitchens, instantly
serving up invisible "delicious soup." They happily shape Play-Doh
to be pancakes or birthday cake or hamburgers. Usually as they stir
their plastic pots and bake with their plastic pans there is also a collection of grocery items to play with. These too are plastic. Maybe,
given the synthetic lunch kits in schoolkids' backpacks and the
instant "homestyle" meals adults barely have time to prepare, this
is appropriate preparation for the world of food that awaits them
when they grow up. That Playskool range and oven and plastic produce the little girls and boys so enjoy might be the closest they ever
get to the real thing.

# CHAPTER 8

# Cloth Divas

IN HER LANDMARK STUDY of 1929, *Old Patchwork Quilts and the Women Who Made Them*, Ruth E. Finley relates a story drawn from her own domestic past. She describes the twelve pairs of linen sheets made by her grandmother's cousin, Aunt Thankful, "spun and woven from flax grown in the Connecticut hills" and now dispersed among her descendents. As did her twin sister, Thankful had sewn a dozen sheet sets for her dowry chest while waiting for her fiancé to return from war. The twin's lover returned, but Aunt Thankful's did not, and so she went unmarried and the unused sheets remained in the bridal trunk, "as smooth and fine and strong as the day they left her loom." The upper right-hand corner of each sheet, Finley recounts, bore tiny, delicate embroidery that showed the number of the sheet, a heart, and Thankful's initials, all rendered in cross-stitch, sewn with her own hair as thread. Aunt Thankful literally put herself into her work, like other domestic artists of the Victorian era who used locks of their hair and of those they loved to create evocative, often mournful framed landscapes.

"To know the history of embroidery is to know the history of women," wrote Rozsika Parker in her 1984 book, *The Subversive Stitch*. Women's physicality has always been intertwined with the domestic fiber arts. For thousands of years, women have put themselves into their work, only rarely deriving any compensation other than the satisfaction of creating beautiful objects that bring comfort and joy to those closest to them. More than any other domestic endeavor, the effort having to do with thread and yarn and cloth is captured in the phrase "labor of love."

I inherited a box packed with dozens of pieces of needlework produced by my great aunt and my grandmother and my great-grandmother and even the great-greats. These items are delicate yet durable, sturdy confections of lace and linen, embroidery, crochet, and tatting. They seem to me almost unimaginably intricate as products coming from the human hand, and equally striking for having, apparently, little practical purpose. What use did it have, this circular piece of cream-colored gossamer the size of a personal pizza, as deft, as spectacularly crafted, as it is? The only point, it would seem, was to create scads of handworked items that were in essence art for art's sake. Though a stiffly pressed doily might occasionally be laid across the back of a sofa or a runner placed down the middle of a polished oak dining room table when elegance required it, for the most part these circles and ovals and long rectangles, each more complex and refined than the next, served no function other than to be beautiful. Many probably spent years in a drawer, secret treasures like Thankful's hand-stitched sheets. Discovering these vintage handcrafted masterpieces gives me a new pride in my female ancestors, tangible evidence of their tremendous ingenuity. Handling these textiles—starch-yellowed and smoothed by another woman's iron in a nearly forgotten time—feels like making contact with an extremely fragile ghost.

Upon first opening the box, an invitation fell out from among the linens. It read:

*Miss Hattie Ward*
*Requests your presence at a*
*Thimble Party*
*Friday Feb. 16ᵗʰ 1900*
*From 2:30–5.*
*Please bring your needlework.*

A rusted needle pierces the corner of the card. This message offers a tantalizing glimpse into my family's past and the culture that elevated needlework to so high a day-to-day presence, at least in the lives of my female ancestors. But because no written log exists to document the creators of this collection, and none bears a signature, the people who crafted these tablecloths, napkins, doilies, and infant caps remain mysterious, as anonymous as the workers who erected the great pyramids of Egypt. In researching the culture that brought these linens forth as well as the myriad textiles found at antique stores and flea markets and in attics across America, I discovered the histories of some families that are more detailed than my own.

The Blair sisters, for example, of eastern Tennessee, wove coverlets and pieced quilts of purchased calico and handwoven linsey-woolsey. Quilt historians Bets Ramsey and Merikay Waldvogel delved into the Blairs' records of the late 1800s for a project that documented the quilting traditions of the state. This is a profile of special value, since the household apparently saved nearly every object they owned, from calico scraps and tools to photographs, a spinning wheel, and a letter proposing marriage. "A family tradition," write Ramsey and Waldvogel, "even says that they saved the string used to tie the youngest daughter's navel cord."

Eleven quilts remain among the artifacts inherited by the family's descendants. The batting for the Blair quilts was hand-carded, probably from cotton grown on the family's farm. Three unmarried Blair sisters earned money sewing for others along with their voluminous quilting and weaving. A photo depicts the elderly women seated in front of an unpainted farmhouse, thin in their close-fitted handwoven linsey dresses, their posture seemingly bent forward from years of stooping over a quilting frame.

Also saved by the Blairs are letters to the maiden aunts from a favorite niece. "Tell Aunt Nancy I was going to try my luck raising geese," she writes. "I have some eggs setting. I think maybe by age 21, I will have me a feather bed. I am piecing me a very pretty scrap quilt called Winding Blades. I can crochet, please send me some little pieces of crocheting for a sample. I want to make some pretty trimming for mine and Maggie's pantiletts."

It's a scene that until recently was a part of more peoples' lives than not, yet today there is seldom a young girl who can make a seam, let alone a quilt.

HUNDREDS, probably thousands, of spinning groups thrive in this country, with names like Nutmeg Spinners Guild, Bo Peep's Lost Sheep, Tsceminicum Spinners and Weavers, Ewe Alls–Bayou Yarn Benders, Friendship Spinners, Serendipity Spinners and Weavers, the Arachnids Spinning Guild, Leatherstocking Spinners, Dyed-in-the-Wool Weavers and Spinners Guild, Twisted Spinsters, Ewe Guys, Obsessive Spinners Society, and Golden Fleece Spinners Society.

Spinners rival fly fishermen in their devotion to their craft, with a few differences. Simplicity of the activity is one. Another is the sheer breadth of spinning's historical inheritance. Both its methods and materials reach back to prehistory. Some spinners today use spindle whorls just as they did back in Neolithic times. Spinning matches that convened at New England ministers' homes in the eighteenth century gave women precious time to socialize as they spun their stuff. Surrounding the craft proper lie its attendant occupations—raising heirloom breeds of livestock, for example, some of which are in danger of extinction, and refining and intensifying natural dyes, such as indigo, cochineal, and madder.

For thousands of years, spinning distinguished itself as an important means of determining a woman's destiny. It was at the center of her life and the life of the home. Spinning was so central to the identity of the medieval woman that even queens were often buried with spindles. Folktales about spinning back then were symbolic; many decreed that a girl's skill at the craft would endow her with riches beyond measure. In one of the Grimm brothers' stories, "The Spindle, the Shuttle, and the Needle," an orphan girl possesses only a humble house and the three implements in the title. Spinning, sewing and weaving are her life. Because of her talent, flax overflows the storerooms, and the townspeople clamor to buy the cloth and rugs she creates. A handsome prince rides by outside her window, but her eyes are cast modestly down. Her spindle takes off and ropes the prince back with golden thread to the girl's home. In the meantime the shuttle weaves a beautiful carpet for the floor, and the needle flits throughout the house beautifying windows and furniture. The prince is stunned by the domestic skills on display and instantly proposes. Once married and in the palace, she ensconces the spindle, needle, and shuttle in the treasure room where they belong.

No longer a labor engaged in by the vast majority of women, the work of spinning thread has evolved to be a rather esoteric pursuit of some of the most highly educated Americans, and as an occupation the craft is almost certainly more rare than assembling rocket parts. One favored site for those who want to spin professionally is the living history museum, a locale that still takes seriously the spectrum of fiber arts, from raising sheep to sheering and carding and cleaning and dying their wool, to spinning yarn and weaving completely natural fabric. The Department of Textiles at Plimoth Plantation makes an ideal workplace for artist Penny Clough, who received her Bachelor of Fine Arts in 3D Fibers from the Massachusetts College of Art. Specializing both in weaving large-scale rugs and in the really arcane craft of making felt, she explains that rather than create art for art's sake she "likes to make things that are usable." At Plimoth, when the museum hosts its Springtime Rare Breeds & Heirloom Seeds Weekend, Clough spends the day at a vintage spinning wheel, making yarn from the wool of Dorset Horn sheep bred in the site's program. The skeins she produces will be colored with dyestuffs from the seventeenth century—logwood and alkanet, black walnut hulls and cutch, osage orange and indigo—and knitted into hats, stockings, mittens, and undershirts for interpreters to wear at the 1627 Pilgrim Village. For a fiber enthusiast, a job at Plimoth is a coveted opportunity to immerse oneself in the craft life of nearly 400 years ago.

Not all spinning aficionados get to be so close to what they love. Fortunately for amateurs, sheep-to-shawl weekends have proliferated at the nation's historic sites. In addition, weekend seminars teach beginners and pros alike. The most venerable spinning convention is SOAR, the *Spin-Off* Autumn Retreat, sponsored for twenty years by the craft's most influential magazine. At the 2002 SOAR, workshop participants could choose to pursue the art of tassel making or spin Icelandic fleece, or they could, according to the course listing, learn to "spin bombyx and tussah silk cocoons, handkerchiefs and noil for rough-textured yarns, and brick and top for smooth yarns."

Some scholars assert that we lost more than a simple craft when hand-spinning grew unnecessary and faded from daily life. It was around the fire after the workday for hundreds upon hundreds of years that two companion activities took place: spinning yarn and storytelling. Though today we still refer to "spinning yarns," the organic oral tradition lies almost completely defunct aside from academic or professional storytellers. Walter Benjamin has explained: "Storytelling is always the art of repeating stories, and this art is lost when the stories are no longer retained. It is lost because there is no more weaving and spinning to go on while they are being told."

The work of spinning fiber into thread and weaving thread into cloth has always been associated with women, most likely, scholars imagine, because making textiles can be more easily combined than other jobs with minding children. More perishable than relics of metal or stone, only a minute portion of the stuff produced when women first began to make string and cloth has survived—a fossilized piece of twisted rope from 15,000 B.C., discovered in the Lascaux caves. More common finds have been Neolithic clay spindle whorls. Subsequent archeological discoveries include loom weights and even gold and silver spindles, from times when the implements of spinning were literally worth their weight in precious metals.

Creating cloth was a rich and noble tradition when Homer described the inhabitants of a wonderful island where Odysseus is shipwrecked:

And fifty serving women belonged to the house,
Some of whom grind on the millstone the ruddy grain,
While others weave at the looms and twirl their spindles
As they sit, restless as the leaves of the lofty poplar,
And the liquid olive oil runs down from the linen warps.
By how much the Phaiakian men are expert above all other men in
Propelling a swift ship on the sea, by thus much their women
Are skilled at the loom, for Athena has given to them beyond all
    others
A knowledge of beautiful craftwork, and noble intellects.

Part of the intellectual power of ancient women lay in their ability to "write" the record of their culture by weaving the most important stories of the day into textiles, whether bolts of cloth, royal tents or canopies, or tapestries for hanging in ancient temples. (A form of expression that, as a kind of precinematic documentary, was prized up through the Renaissance; Henry VIII owned 2,000 tapestries at the time of his death, many of which depicted "newsworthy" events, albeit in allegorical form.) To honor Athena, the patron goddess of weaving, at her annual citywide birthday festival called the Panathenaia, the women of Bronze Age Athens would present an enormous, elaborately decorated new wool *peplos* to the deity as thanks for protecting their city. So spectacular was the garment they wove—deep purple and saffron yellow, with intricate depictions of battles of the gods—that out-of-town tourists made special trips into town to witness the sacred dress. According to archeologist Elizabeth Wayland Barber's fascinating study of women and textiles, *Women's Work: The First 20,000 Years*, the most famous female statue in the world, the Venus de Milo, goddess of love, was originally a spinster. Imagining this icon with her arms reattached, Barber shows she held her left one high and a little back and the right one in front of her at chest level, her eyes cast down at the lower hand. "Modern art critics are not often aware of it," Barber explains, "but this was a pose painfully familiar to women in ancient Greek society. They spent many hours holding a distaff loaded with fiber high in the left while working the thread and needle with the more 'dexterous' right, out in front where it could be watched. This Aphrodite (or Venus, as the Romans called her) was spinning." For the Greeks, a spindle was an apt accoutrement for the goddess of love, as spinning symbolized the creation of new life.

Our language still reflects the intimate relationship between women and cloth. The "distaff side" indicates the female line of a family, while the less commonly used "spear side" refers to the male side. The ability to craft thread is a domestic talent that, along with weaving, has been said to jump-start civilization, making possible the development of rope, nets, sacks, and tethers. "Were it not for the spindle," asserts spinning authority Bette Hochberg, "Europe would have gone naked until the thirteenth century." For 9,000 years, she writes, the hand spindle "met all these human needs: clothing, household linens, uniforms for armies, cloth wrappings and cordage for packages, trappings for animals, rugs and tapestries, sails for ships." Elizabeth Barber concurs, calling string "the unseen weapon that allowed the human race to conquer the earth." Just as in fairy tales, the women of history spun flax (and wool, and cotton) into gold.

Mahatma Gandhi, who furnished spinning wheels to help Indian peasants become self-supporting, himself would spin half an hour each day. He called spinning a sacrament that helped to turn the spinner's mind "God-ward." For contemporary spinners, too, their craft can rise to a mystical experience. Consider the statement of Sheryl Taylor, a spinner and crocheter from Caledon East, Ontario, whose angora christening gown was featured in the March 1989 issue of *Spin-Off* magazine. She writes of breeding and raising French Angora rabbits. "Consider the raw angora wool," she says.

> It speaks in soft, aesthetic, delicate, palatial, and romantic tones. Yet, almost in contradiction, it presents itself as pure, simple, stable, and vigorous. It must convey these same messages after it is spun.
>
> With skillful manipulation, the angora wool can be guided and coerced in such a way that a structurally sound, balanced yarn, with virtually no shedding, can be spun. As many as 28 hours of exacting, intense labor are required to produce one ounce of fine two- or three-ply yarn. This is no modest achievement. [ . . . ]

Only now can the arduous task of knitting, crocheting, or weaving commence, to reach the highest level of craftsmanship. Seemingly insignificant details play an integral role. We will never be hurried or compromised. It is refreshing to realize that, in this day of plastics, disposables, and instant rewards, gifted hands can still capture the essence of historical perfection.

Accompanying her manifesto is a photo of the fuzzy, opalescent christening gown, dripping with glossy satin ribbons, floating against a bottomless black background.

DOMESTIC CRAFTS have a grand tradition in England, though many which were developed as cottage industries (a term derived from work performed in literal British cottages) are now virtually extinct: linen making, reed matting, hemp spinning, the making of velvets, blankets, pillow lace, and bed ticking. Until the twentieth century, the homes of English country folk were in many ways cruder than the stables and kennels of the gentry, but they sheltered an incredibly complex home craft tradition, one that nurtured ordinary people physically and emotionally. One craft that still exists in some form is knitting.

Invented in the East, the ancient art of knitting saw its rise in the British Isles. In Yemen, city of the Queen of Sheba, it is said that women have knitted forever and that the pattern on the serpent's back in Eden was knitted by Eve. The craft was spread to Tibet, then to Spain and other Mediterranean ports by Arab traders. By the Middle Ages, a "knitting cup" was raised at English weddings, and by the time of Elizabeth I the craft was a way of life. In the Channel Islands, as an example, so many of the island's men, women, and children took up the craze that laws were passed prohibiting knitting during harvest season. Elizabeth herself was passionately fond of hand-knit silk stockings, which the ladies of the court executed for her in the Spanish manner, on fine steel needles.

In the English countryside, knitting was as common as walking; in fact, knitters knitted and perambulated at one and the same time. Visitors to the island of Jersey in the nineteenth century remarked on the housewives plying their needles as they traversed the lanes to market. Women of Yorkshire were known to knit along the many miles to and from market to sell the knitted products of their households—and, still knitting, they carried back the worsted for the following week's work. Welsh women knitted as they went to fetch water, earthenware jugs balanced on their heads. In Richmondshire, men would knit while tending their herds. Lovers courted with their needles. It was said when a young couple married that if both were expert knitters, no matter what their shortcomings in housewifery or husbandry, they would get on in the world. Because being able to knit was a practical necessity as well as a skill worthy of respect, a bride's skill at the craft was included in her dowry. In some parts of Britain knitting still flourishes—children are still given needles at the age of four in the Shetland Islands, for example, in order to begin to imitate their mothers. Today, you can go on the Internet to buy a hand-knit Aram wool sweater in a centuries-old pattern.

Before the twentieth century, home-based crafts were by no means performed exclusively by women. It was male sailors who brought knitting to the British Isles, for example, and there evolved male-dominated knitting and hosiery guilds throughout Europe. Yet the perfection of needlecraft techniques as a domestic rather than a commercial function was the province of the housewife, which evolved as an essential and respectable role in Britain. Ann Oakley, the authoritative historian of British housework, posits a distinction between the housewife and the homemaker, which she calls a more "leisurely" interpretation of the job. For hundreds of years, there was significant pride to be derived from the day-to-day achievements of keeping house in Britain, including much having to do with cloth. Knitting and sewing were self-evidently essential work, as valuable to the survival of a family and as honored as the work typically performed by men. There even exists heroic housewife lore having to do with needlework, like the tale of the woman whose house came under siege by Parliamentary forces during the seventeenth century civil war: she directed the defense of her home and in the meantime stitched a set of bed hangings.

Knitting today in America is "more than a hobby or livelihood," wrote Nancy Bush, the great historian and teacher of knitting. "It is a means of binding my life together with the lives of all the knitters, men and women, who have knitted before me. . . ." Her sensibility carries more weight now than ever, since no practical requirement dictates the need for hand-knitted items. Knitting has gone from being beautiful as well as purposeful to being simply beautiful. Even millennial runway couture favors the handcrafted, and designers hire their aunts to execute the high-fashion angora-and-merino cloches that sell at the trendiest boutiques.

It is the process itself of working with needles and yarn rather than any high-fashion product that has cemented knitting's popularity. The repetition required in needlework engenders a form of focus that one doctor, Herbert Benson of Harvard Medical School, has called the "relaxation response," in which brain waves actually change to counter whatever stresses may affect a person. Heart rate, muscle tension, and blood pressure decrease as a result, and a feeling of serenity washes over the knitter. Hobbyists liken the sensation to one of deep meditation. The calming effect of knitting has been put to use both in classes of wiggly first graders and at Colorado's Limon Correctional Facility, where inmates make afghans, baby clothes, and toys in a program that helps them manage drug and alcohol problems. Uncle Ralph's Ugly Hats is a line produced by a seventy-four-year-old steel mill worker in rural Pennsylvania. The craft, he finds, helps relieve his chronic arthritis. "It's how I relax," he told a fashion reporter. "I watch football and crochet."

Other hand crafts have proven themselves equally therapeutic: one man told me that for the first five years he attended meetings of Alcoholics Anonymous, he would calm himself by hooking rugs. Weaving, too, is reputedly good for the spirit. Sister Bianca Haglich teaches the fundamentals of the loom at the Fiber Arts program of Marymount College in Tarrytown, New York. She has said that in the process of weaving, "you are constantly facing yourself and your choices" and that in this process "you become closer to your own soul."

Signs around us suggest that Americans are reawakening to the sense of groundedness and tactile satisfaction the fiber arts can bring to their lives in an increasingly uncertain world. Knitting stores, clubs, and classes have flourished as this millennia-old craft has rebounded in popularity, because people want texture in their lives that is literal as well as figurative. Today, 38 million U.S. women—that's more than one in three—knit or crochet, according to a survey conducted in 2000 by Research Incorporated, up from 34.7 million in 1994. Of this group, nearly two-thirds say their craft helps ease the stress in their lives. The biggest growth has taken place among young people—the number of knitters and crocheters under the age of thirty-five jumped from 3 percent in 1998 to 15 percent in 2000, a 400 percent increase. Some of these see larger meaning in a pair of clicking needles: the leader of a knitting workshop at a 2002 conference of young Southern women presented the art as a means of subverting the patriarchy.

For a generation yearning for a sense of community, knitting circles have become the new quilting bees. Women visit yarn shops not only to buy their skeins and patterns but to linger a few minutes or even a few hours, knitting companionably with fellow enthusiasts.

A New Jersey mother of two girls who proudly told me she was "not the domestic type—my husband does all the cooking!" went on to describe the part-time job she found at her local knitting store, which she valued not so much for the pay as the chance to kibbitz with fellow crafters. She had learned the skill years before but renewed her interest while caring for her ailing mother, sitting by her sickbed, taking whatever solace she could in the simple click of the needles and this modest act of creation. "It's calming," she said, "better than TV as a way of tuning out." It seems that some women feel comfortable embracing knitting even as they resist other traditional "feminine" roles.

For an essentially solo activity, knitting has become decidedly social. Daylong Knit-Outs, which combine teaching with fashion with old-fashioned craft camaraderie, now take place in thirty cities. The Craft Yarn Council of America, which sponsors each event, describes it as "a love-in for the yarn arts." In 1999, so many people showed up in New York City that the instructors in the teaching area had physically to fend them off.

Knitters and crocheters express their love in another way, too, by donating handworked blankets or hats or scarves to people in need. One of the most ambitious, called Warm-up America, has volunteers knit or crochet seven by nine inch sections that are then joined into afghans and donated to battered women's shelters, the homeless, victims of natural disasters, teen pregnancy homes, and AIDS facilities. Children often take part: the students in Pat McLeavy-Payne's Atlanta, Georgia third-grade class, calling themselves "the Knits of the Roundtable," come to school early once a week to work their sections while being read to aloud. A pair of celebrity afghans incorporating squares from Tyra Banks, Elizabeth Taylor, Bridget Fonda, and forty other stars has been auctioned on eBay, with the results going to benefit the New York Police & Fire Widows' & Children's Benefit Fund. In the ten years since the inception of Warm-up America, more than 80,000 afghans have been donated.

Knitwear as philanthropic gesture can be seen on a local level, too. In the village where I live, the high school's art instructor decided this year to create the Guys Varsity Knitting Team, whose members—brawny football players included—come together during ninth period to produce hats and scarves that go to the Seaman's Church Institute in New York City for sailors overseas. In England, a custom is for time-pressed congregants to donate a crocheted square or two to a box in their church as they enter for the service; the women with time to spare stitch them into blankets for battered women.

The persistently popular magazine *Real Simple* regularly runs such features as "Sweater Season," which offers a pattern for a "quick and easy sweater" that even a novice can knit and purl—articles that are nearly interchangeable with the instructional newspaper clippings and patterns I discovered among the needlework of my ancestors in Tennessee. At a recent community meeting, I witnessed two women, both high-powered professionals, busily knitting away, Madame Defarge–like, as they offered up their opinions on taxes and school bonds.

MAKING A QUILT has always been largely ritualistic, commemorative, and rooted in process. As much as providing physical warmth, virtually every quilt conveys spiritual warmth and a powerful sense of emotional connection. The artist and author Sue Bender captured this truth in her memoir of the mid-1970s, *Plain and Simple, A Woman's Journey to the Amish,* whose depiction of a voyage inward through the medium of the patchwork quilt resonated with the book-buying Americans to the extent that it made an unlikely best-seller. "I didn't know that when I first looked at an Amish quilt and felt my heart pounding that my soul was starving," she wrote, "that an inner voice was trying to make sense of my life. I thought I was going to learn more about Amish quilts, but the quilts were only guides, leading me to what I really needed to learn, to answer a question I hadn't yet formed: Is there another way to lead a good life?"

Part talisman, part flag, part comforter, quilts commemorate weddings and births and deaths; they record history and provide solace during hard times. On the American frontier fabric scraps would have provided rare color in the bleakly simple structures the settlers called home. The Great Depression saw a quilting craze, not only because families needed to make do but because producing beautiful objects blunted the pain women felt over the deprivations they suffered. Patchwork has even communicated messages when no other medium was safe: historians tell us that during the time of the Underground Railroad, quilts draped out of open windows or over clotheslines outside slave cabins showed well-known patterns—Wagon Wheels, Tumbling Boxes—ingeniously coded with routes for those making their way North, serving essentially as maps that guided escapees from one safe house to the next. And quilts have gone to war. Two were sent during the Civil War to the Union Army accompanied by these messages:

> My son is in the army. Whoever is made warm by this quilt, which I have worked on for six days and almost all of six nights, let him remember his own mother's love.

> This blanket was carried by Millie Aldrich, who is ninety-three years old, down hill and up hill, one and a half miles, to be given to some soldier.

Another note accompanies a hand-sewn pillow:

This pillow belonged to my little boy, who died resting on it; it is a precious treasure to me, but I give it up for the soldiers.

The art of quilting cloth can be traced back as far as 12,000 years ago, when the Egyptians and the Chinese quilted fabric for clothing, and later, during the Crusades, some European soldiers rode into battle wearing heavily quilted outfits for armor. That tradition continued in early America, when the word *quilt* referred as often to a woman's petticoat as to her bedspread. Accomplished nineteenth century girls of well-to-do families successfully completed a dozen quilts before embarking on their marriage quilt. Before the Civil War, enslaved women on Southern plantations sewed elegant quilts that drew heavily on African patterns, color schemes, and techniques to oblige their masters while piecing together humbler bed coverings out of the scraps at hand to warm their families. According to quilt historian Roderick Kiracofe, Mary Todd Lincoln's seamstress and confidante Elizabeth Keckley created ornate embroidered and appliqued quilts containing silken scraps from Mrs. Lincoln's gowns. Later she was able to buy her freedom with her needlework skills.

It's been said that patchwork, like the other fiber arts, makes sense as women's work because it's a job that can be accomplished piecemeal, in between tending to the cleaning and the cooking and the kids. Beyond any practical purpose, though, to work a quilt has always represented an opportunity for improvisation and even for reinvention in a world that increasingly seems to offer narrow opportunity for either. The explosion of quilting in the last quarter-century—the readership of *Quilter's Newsletter* jumped from 5,000 in 1969 to 300,000 in 1985—has been driven by these needs, as well as by waves of patriotic nostalgia. Currently, fourteen million Americans make quilts.

"I said to myself we need a memorial," said Cleve Jones,

the creator of the NAMES Project AIDS Quilt. "Then when the word quilt went into my brain, what I remembered was my grand-mother tucking me in with this quilt that was made by my great-great-grandmother and has been repaired by various grand-mothers and great aunts over the years. I immediately had a very comforting, warm memory and that was the key."

"Every experience deeply felt in life needs to be passed along," said Thomas Jefferson. "Whether it be through words or music, chiseled in stone, painted with a brush, or sewn with a needle, it is a way of reaching for immortality." Where AIDS disrupts and destroys, the immense and ever-growing AIDS Quilt assures the continuity between past and future. Jones intended the quilt to be not only an epic national memorial, but an object whose benefit would derive from the process of its making, with "quilting bees in little communities with all different kinds of people coming together." Marita Sturken, author of *Tangled Memories*, a study of the politics of memory, the Vietnam Veterans Memorial, and the AIDS Quilt, describes a major purpose of quilting historically as a means by which women "created forms of cultural memory." She places the quilt solidly within that tradition, as outsized as it is. Each three-by-six-foot panel, she points out, takes the shape and approximate size of a human form or of a coffin.

As of 2002, the quilt includes more than 45,000 panels from twenty-nine countries and has been viewed by over five million people. Anyone can contribute. Whenever it is displayed, funds are raised for local AIDS organizations that provide services and care for people with AIDS. Panels have incorporated spray paint, wedding rings, stuffed animals, photos, credit cards, even crema-tion ashes or blood. That it is a quilt connotes the qualities of nur-turing and protection, yet it is as well a defiant political statement of heroic proportions, one meant to call attention to the magni-tude of the AIDS crisis. In 1989, the year the Quilt was nominated for the Nobel Peace Prize, a promotional ad for the project called the sewing needle "the most important tool in the building of a national monument." The strength of the quilt lies in its dual identity as a public object and as a domestic icon, rendering it a "central site of healing" in the AIDS epidemic.

The AIDS Quilt is only the best known of thousands of other quilt projects created to express their makers' humanitarian ideals. In 1984, in a scheme just wacky enough to be hugely influential, the women of the Boise Peace Quilt Project asked one child from each state in the union to draw a picture representing their vision of peace. After translating the drawings into a quilt, the group asked that every U.S. senator spend a night sleeping beneath it and subsequently record their feelings in a document called a Peace Log. Another project driven by symbolism was the Shaken Baby Syndrome Memorial Quilt, displayed in Salt Lake City, Utah, whose infant photos both paid tribute to those who had died and "put a face on" the problem. Mothers Against Drunk Driving has sponsored hundreds of quilt memorials with blocks memorializing loved ones killed in crashes. On a local level, the students at the Hutchinson Elementary School in Pelham, New York, worked for a year with quilt artist Lisa Curran to design panels that explored what it meant to be part of a community for a quilt titled, "Weaving the Threads of Humanity."

Raffling off a quilt as a fundraiser represents another long-standing tradition. One such quilt, with a Cherry Basket design, was sewn by the ladies of the Raus Community in Bedford County, Tennessee, in 1863. Each block bears the name of its maker in pokeberry ink. The finished product was raffled off to benefit a local regiment of Confederate forces. Contributors weren't necessarily southern ladies on fainting couches. One, a Confederate spy named Mary High Prince, told later of how during Yankee looting raids the quilt was stashed in stumps for safekeeping.

Today quilts are less often raffled off for political causes than donated to charity. Yet the labor of innumerable seamstresses around the country receives slight public recognition: such projects warrant mention only in local newspapers if at all. In the winter of 2000, for example, the Jersey Shore Quilters of St. Peter's Church in Point Pleasant Beach, New Jersey, donated over 350 Christmas quilts to St. Gregory's Food Bank. Project Linus has more than 300 chapters in the U.S. that have as of January 2002 delivered over 400,000 homemade security blankets to seriously ill or traumatized children. During the war in Kosovo, a Boise, Idaho, hobby quilter named Jill Kuraitis proposed to a group called the Global Development Center that it start a drive for quilts to go to refugees—not only to keep them warm, but for use as direly needed makeshift tents. Victoria's Quilts, which donates to hospitals and to cancer patients, was the "warm solution" inspired by the founder's sister-in-law, who told of lying at the treatment center freezing after chemotherapy and guided by her philosophy of quilt-making: "People aren't perfect. Why do quilts have to be?" Some projects' scope remains strictly local: the Unity Church Piece by Peace Quilters deliver lap quilts to the Grapevine, Texas, group's local nursing home. In a town near mine, a group called Chappaqua Neighbors Club donated seven baby quilts crafted by its members to the ABC Project, which gets them to babies in distress and infants in war-torn countries. Quilts from Caring Hands in Oregon assembles quilts pieced from high-contrast fur, polar fleece, terry cloth, and velour to give to visually impaired children. The Snuggles Project, launched by the organization Hugs for Homeless Animals, gets homemade security blankets to abandoned pets in shelters. A group called Tiny Miracles asks volunteers to create quilt blocks as small as just over a foot square for preemies in local neonatal intensive care units. At Scottish Rite/Eglestone Hospital in Atlanta, children in the cancer ward choose the fabrics they want in their quilts—a modest expression of each terminal patient's individuality and one cherished by parents, who keep the quilt after their child's death.

The gritty reality of efforts like these bears small relation to another end of the quilt world, that of museum curators and collectors, which esteems each vintage patchwork piece as a lovely but untouchable art object to be hung flat against a pristine gallery wall. It differs also from the traditional familial quilt, the intimate, personal, one-of-a-kind gift of mother to child or grandmother to grandchild—a tradition that remains strong despite inexpensive and attractive knockoffs hawked by such retailers as Lands' End or Kmart.

None of those projects that get quilts to those in need are really essential. Organizations beg for donations of batting, thread, and fabric so that thousands of volunteers can invest their time to create quilts that could be easily replaced by much less costly and equally warm factory-made blankets of 100 percent synthetic fiber. Each of these quilts, crafted as part of a large-scale project, to ultimately be given to total strangers, is born so that we can give care to another when no other gesture will suffice, practical considerations be damned. That's what makes them amazing.

As technology races forward, it would seem that our interest in quiltmaking would drop away, that hi tech and low tech couldn't possibly continue to coexist. Oddly, that couldn't be further from the truth. In an unlikely development for so tactile, so traditional an art form, quilting has found a deep and comfortable niche in cyberspace. Scholar Susan Behuniak-Long explains the delicate balance that allows quilts to hold their own:

> Painstakingly cut, pieced, and sewn, they move in slow motion as the rest of the world reels ahead in fast-forward. But this is precisely the source of their value. In a highly mechanized world, quilts stand

as statements about social values and technological limits. While we grapple with the task of defining technological boundaries, quilters use a needle to stitch the line beyond which technology should not tread.

Quilts, she concludes, are "artifacts of the social need for connection."

∞

DOMESTIC CRAFTS have offered fertile ground for the interpretation of contemporary fiber artists. One of the best loved, Faith Ringgold, has for years interwoven her personal experience and her observations of the world in large-scale quilts that depict the urban experience with a sense of childlike wonder. The art object itself embodies the techniques of the female craft tradition, but so does the process through which the work is created: Ringgold's mother taught her the fundamentals of sewing and for many years collaborated with her on the assemblage of her nontraditional quilts.

In the 1970s, the American art scene was wrenched by the concerns and sensibilities of the women's movement. Since then, artists have employed sewing and weaving, dying and cloth, knitting, crocheting, and quilting, some in the service of pieces that critique the female sphere from which these fiber arts sprang. Faith Wilding launched a trend when she constructed a room-sized crocheted environment in 1971 for an art installation called Womanhouse. For that piece, she has explained, she drew upon the craft skills she learned as a girl—crocheting, weaving, knitting, embroidery, basketry, ceramics, leatherwork, and woodwork. "I was motivated," she has said, "by my research on women's work and lives in various cultures. I found that women's work of making homes and domestic environments has been pivotal (though largely unacknowledged) in the major cultural inventions of civilization." Judy

Chicago's 1978 work The Dinner Party encompasses the home-spun crafts of embroidery and quilting as well as hand-painted china plates in an effort to honor the great women of history.

Artists have also revived the fiber arts tradition to express their particular vision without any but an implicit reference to domesticity. The works of British bad-girl artist Tracey Emin, for example, draw attention because of their sensational subject matter—her installations incorporate soaked tampons, neon, rumpled bed sheets, and morning-after pills. Yet her best known pieces also draw on decidedly nonedgy domestic techniques. Emin's creations strike me as poignant reminders that no matter how far we move from the long-standing traditions of housewifery—and Emin continually acknowledges the nondomestic, blasted cultural landscape and moral grappling of her life—we can't seem to leave behind so enduring a vocabulary as the one that originates in our domestic craft traditions. In 1994, while traveling the U.S. and performing readings from her often harrowing autobiographical book *Exploration of the Soul—a Journey Across America* ("about me—my beginning—from the moment of my conception to the time I lost my virginity"), Emin displayed a chair given her by her ninety-three-year-old grandmother, the seat of which she decorated with embroidery, patchwork, and appliqué. She had decided, she said, that "this chair is my inheritance—an inheritance of my future." One especially disturbing 1999 piece of Emin's features a soiled patchwork background on which are emblazoned the words, "PYCHO SLUT" [sic] and in smaller letters "AND I DON'T HAVE TO TELL YOU ITS ALL TOO BEAUTIFUL." It's disturbing, of the moment, and, like all strong art, impossible to parse too specifically. What interests me is the visual link between this piece and an early twentieth century photo of a virtually identical battered patchwork bed cover in a bare-bones room, included in one encyclopedic review of British homemaking customs. No matter how we fall away from the cherished, hard-won traditions of the past, they are still there, in the background of our consciousness, grounding us, patiently awaiting our recall.

∞

AS A TEENAGER, I went for weekly lessons at the house of my weaving instructor, whose enormous wooden loom crouched in her workroom like a sleeping animal awaiting her touch to spring to life. Her lessons in threading the taut, perfectly even warp and in handling the polished shuttle were a private yet vital part of my adolescent years. In my room at home I practiced on a borrowed junior version of that gigantic loom, weaving a rough-textured cloth out of some rust-colored mohair and wiry blue wool I had selected. It was weirdly consoling, this remnant of antiquity—Penelope's craft plunked down in my troubled teenage suburbia.

My weaving mentor taught me to make baskets, too, and now, thirty years later, when I hike in the woods or drive by fields with the window rolled down I recall the scent of the sweetgrass we used. Exhilarated by the satisfaction of making things myself, I worked with my friend to weave our hammocks, festooning a defunct weight room in the high school basement with yards and yards of stiff white rope. During those years I pieced the first of several quilts with the Singer machine my parents gave me for a Christmas present. I don't think the quilt was especially beautiful to anyone but myself, but that didn't decrease the pleasure creating it gave me. As with the cloth I wove and the baskets I made, the materials and design for these objects were my choice alone, the execution my accomplishment, and, most important, the process mine to enjoy on a purely tactile level—the over and under of each damp reed with every round of the basket. Those elements marked the experience as intoxicating. At sixteen I sewed the simplest high-yoked nightgown, white flannel with blue roses, and I wore it until the fabric literally fell to shreds years later.

I think that observing my female elders early on may well have predisposed me to an especially avid curiosity about the domestic arts as I was growing up. Certainly there exists a more active hunger in some people to use their hands, to make yarn or cloth or knitted goods from scratch. You don't have to have a love of textiles in your marrow to begin. It's late in life, often, that people discover their passion for spinning, for weaving, for dying wool or knitting socks, crafts that frequently grow from pleasant pastimes into obsessions. To name only one niche, that of hand-sewn dolls, scores of enthusiasts join regional groups devoted to the craft of designing, sewing, and decorating small beings assembled of fabric, lace, and yarn. The organization in my area, the Cloth Divas Doll Club, has a membership composed of women "of a certain age," according to one of its members, "who approach doll-making as an art."

THE HANDMADE will not grow obsolete, simply because of the primal pleasure, intellectual satisfaction, and pride that derive from personal involvement in making something from scratch. The tactile experience of working with fiber only becomes more desirable as our culture offers fewer similar opportunities to create artifacts by hand. Dying wool soft green with lichens or gray-blue with pennies or rainbow shades with Kool-Aid satisfies a basic urge to invent, to transform, and it doesn't require the talent of Michelangelo or the fortune of a Medici to do so. Many experts in the textile field only discover their craft as mature adults. It shows that we don't have to be indoctrinated into the mysteries of the knitting needle during childhood to get the fiber arts in our lives later. Even in an age dominated by machines and by virtual technologies, textiles will live on.

As busy as I might be, too consumed with work to take the time to weave fabric or baskets, too busy with my family to remove the dusty cover from my patient old Singer, these pastimes await my rediscovery. The instigator may be a local drive for infant quilts or knitted hats for those in need. The day might come when the scent of a meadow makes going back to weaving baskets irresistible. Or perhaps I'll resume the crocheting my great aunt taught me, in that time not so long ago that is already nearly forgotten, simply to pass along the skill to my own daughter.

∞

# Afterword

THE LOAM OF her garden crumbles black, rich with dung from the horse stable under the massive age-silvered barn, and out of the soil spring the tall tops of onions, both purple and yellow, and cabbage about to head, and a profusion of other vegetables growing in ripeness. She works the ground in two broad strips, and each year pushes the boundaries a little farther, and every growing season she attacks the quack grass and renders the earth a bit finer, a bit easier to work. At harvest, with her mother, she'll put up vegetables in dozens of Mason jars, sterilizing them in a big kettle on the burnished black stove. She'll stow the onions and potatoes in the crowded cellar. Make salsa, even grind the blue corn for her specialty, hand-rolled tortillas. Out at the barn, her husband pours concrete to shore up its foundation, one in a series of tasks he's undertaken over the years to preserve the sagging structure. Their eighteen-year-old son assists, as does a neighbor in exchange for help on his own property. Both husband and wife go out to work every day, he as a psychologist and she a nurse, and despite their fatigue when they return they dedicate themselves to transforming the tiny farmhouse. New windows, walls, and shelving appear as abundantly as the onions in the garden.

Another home, this one in an well-heeled East Coast suburb. Wife and husband, both accomplished media professionals, reside with their little girl in a red brick fortress filled with handsome furniture, art, and decorative objects collected from the antiques venues he visits wherever he travels. The family spends a lot of time in the kitchen, which is as utilitarian as it is beautiful, having been remodeled with their active participation in the design process. While their daughter sits atop the counter and colors, she unpacks her briefcase and he fixes the family dinner, a delectable pasta alla mare.

Two men occupy the ground floor of a city brownstone. Its windows have bars to prevent break-ins from the street, and the apartment's light is gray and indirect. In its bareness, however, the decor is soothing—the contribution of one member of the couple, who configures and reconfigures this space as naturally as breathing and who has collected what furniture they have from trash bins and rummage sales, treasures that once were throwaways. His partner has the skill of cooking perfect rice, which often graces the table since they favor Japanese cuisine. Their shared passion lies in cultivating the scores of exotic rosebushes that fill the otherwise nondescript walled backyard.

That these domestic visions are utterly distinct makes sense, since though home is a universal need it is equally a creation that is highly individual. For that reason, suggestions about how we can begin to reclaim the pleasures of the American hearth must remain general. To consider how to restore the harmony, the fulfillment, of domesticity, I can only look to my wishes for my own life, since I as much as anyone am trapped in the somewhat muddled, less than satisfying style of homemaking that characterizes so many households today. My particular approach to domesticity is a complicated hybrid that combines attraction to the past (quality, pace), some kitchen and needlework skills of which I'm proud, guilt over not living up to the ideals embodied by our flavor-of-the-week domestic divas, a wincing sense of being crunched by lack of time, overwork, and community obligations, and just plain neglect as keeping house becomes a forgotten art. I do my best, but I don't feel totally comfortable in the skin of my home.

So, though I can't pretend to know all the answers, these are some shifts in the current domestic paradigm I know I would like to see.

The first is a new division of roles in the home. Just because women claim the important historical legacy of care for home and hearth does not mean we return to the past and lock women in to a new feminine mystique. In the current technologically sophisticated era the sexes can share the chores—and the satisfactions—of homemaking. Our psychological investment in rigid notions of who cares for the home results in women feeling trapped and men disinterested in taking part. We need to find, after the dated clarity of domestic roles in the past and the awkwardness of the present, a new happy medium.

I'd like to see relief from the guilt that plagues both those who make homemaking their primary occupation and those who leave the home for paid work. The psychological battle now underway between women of childbearing age who make different choices has no winners. Greater flexibility in work schedules, which of course depends upon employers but can be pushed along by employees' advocacy, would allow everyone to have a more grounded domestic life—and I don't mean exclusively parents. Somehow it's usually presumed that mothers are the only individuals who need "balance."

We'd all benefit from a new consensus that the basest housework is worthy of respect. Knee-jerk reactions still dominate when it comes to the more commonplace aspects of domesticity. Scrubbing the sink is considered gross, drudgery, beneath us. As humans, however, we create waste wherever we go; we benefit physically and psychically when we attend to keeping our homes and our world clean.

Freedom to resist the mass-produced would be another item on my wish list. Rejection of objects not fashioned by hand doesn't have to be unilateral—there is no special merit in tanning your own leather, say—but everyone should be able to experience the benefits of domestic craft. Our culture often seems to suggest that just because it's not necessary to do it yourself, because you can pay for a service, it's somehow preferable not to do it yourself. The same equation applies to making things: Poppin' fresh rolls seem inherently better than homemade rolls; a blouse off the rack preferable to one home sewn. It takes some discipline to get off the ever-chugging commercial engine. To start, we can at least be conscious of the choices we make.

These are all big changes. To make a start, I would most like to see every person perform just one small domestic act. It needn't be an elaborate Martha Stewart-authorized holiday wreath. Get the people you live with involved—your roommate, your grown kids, your husband, lover. Transpose roles. Men, shine the silver. Women, build a fire the way we used to do in ancient times. Children, mop the floor with your parents, or help prepare dinner. The poet Seamus Heaney has captured the magic of sharing mundane cooking chores in these lines about peeling potatoes with his mother when he was small:

> I remembered her head bent towards my head,
> Her breath in mine, our fluent dipping knives—
> Never closer the whole rest of our lives.

This is what we lose with Ore-Ida Shoestrings from the freezer.

Or do we? A woman in her twenties, raised with the ubiquity of fast and processed food, asked me whether a parent and child could not bond equally well over a juicy Whopper as with a home-cooked meal. I believe that the rewards of the experience are not the same, even though a trip to the fast-food emporium can certainly offer shared fun and ease and to many the comfort of a thoroughly familiar transaction. The difference I think derives from something very simple: the inherent, primal human satisfaction of preparing food from scratch, and making it together, on one's personal turf. The fast-food giants and chain restaurants, flush with advertising dollars, may gain some success in persuading us that those values don't matter. In the long run, though, the return of comfort and of craft is inevitable. Americans are fed up with lack of texture. The world is too threatening a place for people not to see the urgency of reclaiming the pleasures we are in danger of losing, and, along with them, the self-respect and balance and order that naturally follow. Finally, domesticity comes down to connection— with the past, with family, with community, and with the self.

# Notes

## Chapter 1: Heirlooms

2    The changing percentage of rural Americans comes from Susan Strasser's authoritative *Never Done: A History of American Housework* (New York: Pantheon Books, 1982), p. 11.

7    Simone de Beauvoir's assertion "We have seen what poetic veils . . . ," appears in *The Second Sex* (New York: Alfred A. Knopf, 1953).

8    The Yankelovich Partners survey citing eighty-seven percent of women polled believe that women are still the main family nurturers and saying that a majority of working and nonworking mothers mothers wish they were better parents is referenced in *Self*, December 1999.

10    *The Overworked American* contains crushing evidence of the overwork of both men and women, but especially of women. On p. 83, Juliet Schorr cites studies estimating that in addition to forty-plus hours on the job, full-time working mothers perform between twenty-five and forty-five hours of housework a week.

10    Virginia Valian was interviewed in *The New York Times*, August 25, 1998, for a profile by Natalie Angier called "Exploring the Gender Gap and the Absence of Equality."

12    Material on Betty Crocker's secret history is drawn in large part from David Gerard Hogan's *Selling 'Em by the Sack: White Castle and the Creation of American Food* (New York: New York University Press, 1997).

20    That the staff at Plimoth "did not wear the black clothing often associated with our pilgrim ancestors . . ." is noted by Candace Tangorra Matelic in "Through the Historical Looking Glass," *Museum News*, March/April 1980, pp. 35–45.

20    Children may attend camp at many historic sites. At Van Cortlandt Manor in Croton-on-Hudson, New York, preteens spend 4 days at "Summer-week," in which they work in an herb garden, fish, cook, make medicine, and practice reading a compass and map.

21    Witold Rybczynski's observations on nostalgia appear in *Home: A Short History of an Idea* (New York: Viking Penguin, 1986) pp. 214–15.

23    Pantry material from "Old-Style Pantry Making a Comeback," by Alan J. Heavens, October 21, 2001, Knight Ridder Newspapers.

24    *Brill's Content* of December 1998/January 1999 cites the circulation of women's service magazines versus newsmagazines.

25    Maya Plisetskaya discusses her stage entrance in her 2001 autobiography, *I, Maya Plisetskaya* (New Haven, CT: Yale University Press).

## Chapter 2: Hestia's Fire

30    Hestia receives attention from many historians of classical Greece. I found Sarah Pomeroy's work especially useful, along with that of Robert Graves and Ginette Paris.

31    The comments of Robert Graves on Hestia, on the tools used for tending sacred fires, and about the omphalos, the charcoal piled on the three-legged stool, appear in his *The Greek Myths*.

31    The prytaneia were the town halls of each city, and each had a public hearth that belonged to Hestia.

32    The Homeric Hymn #5, "To Aphrodite," re: Zeus gave Hestia "a high honor instead of marriage . . ." is quoted by Pomeroy in *Goddesses, Whores, Wives, and Slaves: Women in Classical Antiquity* (New York: Schocken Books, 1975), p. 6. Pomeroy follows by commenting that Hestia "was the archetypal old maid, preferring the quiet of the hearth to the boisterous banquets and emotional entanglements of the other Olympians."

33    Hestia as "the central planet" is discussed in Ginette Paris's *Pagan Meditations: Aphrodite, Hestia, Artemis* (Woodstock, CT: Spring Publications, 1997), p. 174.

33    Z. A. Abramova wrote of the "mistress of the home and hearth . . ." in "Paleolithic Art in the USSR," *Arctic Anthropology*, 4 (1967), cited in Riane Eisler's *The Chalice & the Blade* (San Francisco: HarperSanFrancisco, 1987, 1995), p. 219.

34    Pomeroy explores the idea that Greek-speaking invaders married off their gods to Cretan goddesses. She also discusses the family burial plot within the Athenian Agora, dating from the end of the eighth century to the middle of the seventh century B.C., where the young woman's skeleton was discovered.

37    "Time for Life," *The Surprising Ways Americans Spend Their Time*, by John Robinson of the University of Maryland and Geoffrey Godbey of Penn State University's College of Health and Human Development, is the source for the drop in hours spent per week on housework.

38    De Beauvoir characterizes the housewife's mind in *The Second Sex*.

39    Kathryn Allen Rabuzzi explores the nature of domesticity extensively in *The Sacred and the Feminine: Toward a Theology of Housework* (New York: Seabury Press, 1982).

39    The Donald Hall poem "Sew" appears in his *Old and New Poems* (New York: Ticknor & Fields/Houghton Mifflin, 1990).

39    Suzette Haden Elgin discusses housework in *The Language Imperative* (Cambridge, MA: Perseus Books, 2000).

39    Caring is examined by Marjorie DeVault in *Feeding the Family: The Social Organization of Caring as Gendered Work* (Chicago: University of Chicago Press, 1991).

40    Lydia Maria Child spoke of "the art of gathering up the fragments . . ." in *The American Frugal Housewife, Dedicated to Those Who Are Not Ashamed of Economy* (Boston: Carter, Hendee, and Co., 1833).

40    Helen Fisher discusses the kinship web in *The First Sex: The Natural Talents of Women and How They Are Changing the World* (New York: Random House, 1999).

42    Judi Appel is quoted in "Craving a Comfort Zone: Homespun Activities and Purchases Have New Appeal," by Leslie Kaufman and Julian E. Barnes, *The New York Times*, October 10, 2001.

42    Stephen Jay Gould shared the apple brown betty anecdote in an op-ed piece for *The New York Times*, "A Time of Gifts," September 26, 2001.

43    Arlie Hochschild's work speaks eloquently of the stresses that have led Americans away from the home and made its commodification so irresistible. *The Time Bind: When Work Becomes Home & Home Becomes Work* (New York: Metropolitan Books, 1997) is a thoughtful and important resource on the subject, as is Hochschild's book with Anne Machung, *The Second Shift: Working Parents and the Revolution at Home* (New York: Viking Penguin, 1989).

## Chapter 3: Domestic Saints

47    Emily Dickinson's comment is cited in *Never Done*, p. 62; from Millicent Todd Bingham, *Emily Dickinson's Home: The Early Years as Revealed in Family Correspondence and Reminiscences* (New York: Dover Publications, 1967), p. 117.

53    The description "were worn and altered and dyed and turned . . ." appears in Flora Thompson's haunting *Lark Rise to Candleford*, p. 32.

53    Throughout this discussion I draw on the wealth of details about the history of housewifery, especially practices of cleaning and fire building, to be found in Una A. Robertson's *The Illustrated History of the Housewife, 1650–1950* (New York: St. Martin's Press, 1997).

56    Hannah Robertson's comment is cited by Una Robertson, but it was originally from Hannah Robertson's *Young Ladies School of Arts*, Second Edition (Edinburgh: Wal. Ruddiman Junior, 1767), Part II, p. xii.

58    I draw on both the history of the "evening fireside gathering" known as a veillée and the origin of fairy tales and folktales that receive extensive

discussion in Robert Darnton's illuminating *The Great Cat Massacre and Other Episodes in French Cultural History* (New York: Basic Books, 1984).

61 Robert Delort's description of the role of youth in medieval culture appears on p. 61 of his *Life in the Middle Ages* (New York: Greenwich House, 1972).

64 The emphasis on cleanliness in Dutch households is treated both in Simon Schama's exhaustive *The Embarrassment of Riches: An Interpretation of Dutch Culture in the Golden Age* (New York: Vintage Books, 1987) and in Rybczinski's *Home*. Rybczinski's discussion of the Dutch house-cupboards appears on p. 62 of *Home*.

64 Information on museum attendance at "Art & Home" courtesy of The Newark Museum.

65 Beecher's quote, "A woman who has charge of a large household . . ." is cited in Margaret Horsfield's *Biting the Dust: The Joys of Housework* (New York: St. Martin's Press, 1998).

68 Lydia Maria Child's "The true economy of housekeeping . . ." appears on p. 3 of *The American Frugal Housewife*.

69 Catharine Beecher's biographer, Kathryn Kish Sklar, in *Catharine Beecher: A Study in American Domesticity* (New Haven CT: Yale University Press, 1973), says much about the domestic climate of the nineteenth century. I am quoting "and expect to be received as the heroine" from p. 152. The following quote from Beecher, "To American Women, more than any others, . . . ," is cited in the same book.

70 The anecdotes about Stowe and the grocery paper and about the reception of *Uncle Tom's Cabin* in the U.S. and in Europe come from Oliver Ransford's *The Slave Trade* (Wiltshire, Great Britain: Redwood Press Limited, 1971). Ransford describes *Uncle Tom's Cabin* as the mirror in which America could see itself on p. 234 of that book. Among other sources for the Stowe portrait I have drawn upon Joan D. Hedrick's *Harriet Beecher Stowe: A Life* (New York: Oxford University Press, 1994).

72 Glenna Matthews's assessment of Stowe's "moral authority" as a housewife appears in *Just a Housewife: The Rise & Fall of Domesticity in America* (New York: Oxford University Press, 1987), p. 34.

72 "It is a dark, sloppy, rainy, . . ." is quoted in *Harriet Beecher Stowe: A Life*, p. 169, and "I am but a mere drudge . . ." on p. 129.

73 Stowe's phrase "domestic saints" appeared in an article she published in *The Atlantic Monthly* in 1864 and was cited in Laura Shapiro's *Perfection Salad: Women and Cooking at the Turn of the Century* (New York: North Point Press, 1986), p. 11.

73 "There is one thing . . ." quoted in *Harriet Beecher Stowe: A Life*, p. 139.

73 "Come here and I will do . . ." is quoted on pp. 84–85 of Geoffrey C. Ward and Ken Burns' comprehensive *Not for Ourselves Alone: The Story of Elizabeth Cady Stanton and Susan B. Anthony* (New York: Alfred A. Knopf,

1999). "I have not time to look up statistics . . ." also comes from *Not for Ourselves Alone,* p. 74, as does "A home of one's own . . ." on p. 124 and "Do any of you cling to the old theory . . ." on p. 129.

75      Charlotte Perkins Gilman has been extensively profiled by Glenna Matthews, Susan Strasser, and other domestic historians. Her comments about her breakdown, "a charming home; a loving and devoted husband . . ." and her physician's advice I have borrowed from Matthews' *"Just a Housewife,"* pp. 135–36. Gilman's statement, "There is nothing private and special in the preparation of food . . ." and her determination to "make that world our home at last" I quote from Strasser's *Never Done,* p. 222.

77      Elsie de Wolfe's passage appeared in *The House in Good Taste* (New York: 1913), p. 5; I am quoting it from Adrian Forty's *Objects of Desire: Design & Society from Wedgwood to IBM* (New York: Pantheon Books, 1986), p. 104.

77      The cartoon of the gentleman on cleaning day appears in *Never Done,* p. 62.

77      Frances Trollope's comments on "changing house" can be found in the charming travelogue, *Domestic Manners of the Americans* (London: Century Publishing Co., 1984), p. 309.

78      Wharton draws this portrait of Mrs. Peniston in *The House of Mirth* (New York: Charles Scribner's Sons, 1969), p. 98, and lampoons Lily's resentment of soap on p. 101.

## Chapter 4: Home Ec 101

84      I found the statement by the president of Bryn Mawr in *Never Done,* p. 203, from a mention in Isabel Bevier and Susannah Usher, *The Home Economics Movement* (Boston: Whitcomb & Barrows, 1906), p. 15.

85      "When the boys learn to grow wheat . . ." is quoted in Laura Shapiro, *Perfection Salad: Women and Cooking at the Turn of the Century* (New York: North Point Press, 1986), p. 186.

85      Christine Frederick's statement, "Our greatest enemy is the woman with the career . . ." also appears in *Never Done,* p. 218. Strasser discusses home economists who "defined new tasks in mothering and in consumption" on p. 7.

86      The dedication of *The Home Cook Book* (I. Fred Waggoner, 1877) appears on p. 5, "There is no earthly reason . . ." on p. 6.

89      Much of my data on changing domestic technology at the turn of the century comes from *Home,* especially pp. 138–43, and also from *Objects of Desire.* Useful information on running water and bathrooms appears in *Never Done,* p. 103.

91      The economist who wrote that the "invention of the washing machine has meant more washing" was Hazel Kyrk, in *Economic Problems of the Family,* New York, p. 99; quoted in *Objects of Desire,* p. 211.

93      *The Flirt* by Booth Tarkington was published by Doubleday, Page, and Company, New York, 1913.

93    Sarah Orne Jewett's story "Tom's Husband" appeared in *The Atlantic Monthly* 49, February 1882.

95    "Service to their homes . . ." is on p. xv of Carlotta C. Greer's *Foods and Home Making* (New York: Allyn and Bacon, rev. ed. 1939). "No insects . . ." is on p. 13. Greer cites Frances Willard and also tells the anecdote about the college president stepping down.

98    All material by Nellie Kedzie Jones comes from an anthology of her columns edited by Jeanne Hunnicutt Delgado, *Nellie Kedzie Jones's Advice to Farm Women: Letters from Wisconsin, 1912–1916* (Madison, WI: State Historical Society of Wisconsin, 1973).

102    "Containing and controlling food . . ." from *Perfection Salad,* pp. 6–7.

## Chapter 5: A Broom of One's Own

110    All Peg Bracken excerpts are from *The I Hate to Housekeep Book: When and How to Keep House Without Losing Your Mind* (New York: Harcourt, Brace & World, 1962).

112    All Virtue Hathaway quotations come from Shirley Boccacio's "The Housework Poster Rip-Off," *Feminist Art Journal,* Summer 1974; Vol. 3, No. 2.

118    De Beauvoir comments on the psychology of the housewife in *The Second Sex,* pp. 451–54.

120    Sara Evans analyzes this period in *Personal Politics: The Roots of Women's Liberation in the Civil Rights Movement & the New Left* (New York: Alfred A. Knopf, 1979), pp. 193–201.

121    Her comments about the ghost haunting young women appear on p. 39 of Ruth Rosen's *The World Split Open: How the Modern Women's Movement Changed America* (New York: Viking Penguin, 2000). The 1970 poster legends are cited by Rosen, p. 92.

121    Nathaniel Hawthorne quote from "The Old Manse" appears in *Mosses from an Old Manse.*

125    Hayden's passage from *The Grand Domestic Revolution: A History of Feminist Designs for American Homes, Neighborhoods, and Cities* (Cambridge, MA: The MIT Press, 1995) can be found on p. 307.

126    The interpretation of the change in domestic work ("The pre-industrial rural home was a tiny manufacturing center . . .") appears in Barbara Ehrenreich and Deirdre English, *For Her Own Good: 150 Years of the Experts' Advice to Women* (New York: Anchor Press, 1978), in the chapter called "Microbes and the Manufacture of Housework."

128    Joan Didion drew this portrait of the era's typical earth mother in "Slouching Towards Bethlehem," in her collection of the same title, published by Dell in 1968.

130    William Beer's comment comes from his *Househusbands: Men and Housework in American Families* (1983) and was quoted in *Biting the Dust,* p. 224.

134    "Maid to Order: The Politics of Other Women's Work," by Barbara Ehren-
       reich, appeared in *Harper's Magazine*, April 2000, and was later published
       as part of her book *Nickel and Dimed: On (Not) Getting By in America*.

135    "Confessions of a Closet Homemaker: Slaving over a hot stove is my great-
       est delight, and my deepest shame" was the title of Carolynn Carreno's
       thought piece for *The New York Times Magazine*, April 30, 2000. "A Salute
       to Housekeeping: Take Pride in Your Abilities to Maintain a Nice Home,"
       by Cheryl Laridaen in *The Post-Crescent* of Appleton, Wisconsin, October
       16, 1999, begins "I have a confession to make. I am a closet homemaker."

136    Cheryl Mendelson's observations come from *Home Comforts*.

139    Whitman's line come from *To Think of Time*.

140    Marilyn Monroe quote from "Marilyn: The Woman Who Died Too Soon,"
       Gloria Steinem, in *The First Ms. Reader*, edited by Francine Klagsbrun,
       1972.

142    Peg Bracken's remembrance of kitchens past  appears in *A Window Over the
       Sink: A Mainly Affectionate Memoir* (New York: Harcourt Brace Jovanovich,
       1981), Chapter 5.

## Chapter 6: The New Mom

147    In *My Mother and I* (New York: MacMillan Company, 1919), Elizabeth
       Stern writes "I can never remember . . ." on p. 21, "What an embarrassing
       moment! . . ." on p. 90, and "So mother went out . . ." on p. 167.

149    Kraft product information is listed on the company website. Other pack-
       aged food innovations are discussed in "Ketchup, Jell-O and other millen-
       nial milestones" by Carolyn Wyman and Bonnie Tandy Leblang, *The
       Arizona Republic*, December. 29, 1999, and "The Tastiest Century: Time-
       line," *USA Weekend*, November 12–14, 1999.

150    Bonnie Liebman's comments as well as useful statistics on Lunchables
       appeared in "Are Lunchables Good for Kids?" Carole Sugarman, *Washing-
       ton Post*, September 29, 1999.

150    Uncrustables information comes from Stephanie Thompson, "Homemade
       (Frozen) Goodness: Smucker's Ices PB&J Sandwich," *Advertising Age*, May
       1, 2000.

152    The dodo comment by Carrie Chapman Catt originally appeared in "An
       Eight-Hour Day for the Housewife—Why Not?" *Pictorial Review* (Novem-
       ber 1928); it was cited in *Just a Housewife*, p. 143.

152    Gerry Thomas, the inventor of the TV dinner tray, was quoted in an article
       called "TV dinner tray developer is hot stuff" by Walter Berry for the Asso-
       ciated Press.

152    The president and chief executive officer of the National Restaurant Asso-
       ciation feels good about the HMR trend. He has commented: "Hard-work-
       ing individuals are looking for ways to make their lives a little easier, and

tableservice restaurants are responding by providing high-quality meals in a convenient manner. Ordering takeout or delivery instead of cooking allows people to spend more time with family and friends, and less time in the kitchen after a long day." His statement appeared in a news release from the NRA on July 27, 2000.

153    NPD Group, a marketing information firm, found in its fourteenth annual study of American eating patterns that fast-food franchises accounted for more than eighty percent of growth in restaurant meals purchased in the past five years. Homemade meals, in the meantime, fell to a record low of 917 per person, compared with 933 in 1990. However, more than half of restaurant-purchased meals were consumed outside the restaurant, and eighteen percent were ordered at the drive-in window.

153    The estimate that fifty-six percent of all meals cooked in North America include one or more homemade items appears in 1999 program materials published by Weight Watchers International.

157    "Meals made from scratch . . ." is quoted by Hallie Forcinio in "Mapping Out a Safety Net," *Prepared Foods*, February 1999.

157    The percentage of Americans using their stoves and the Balzer quote and statistics appeared in *The Wall Street Journal*, March 1, 2002.

159    The M. F. K. Fisher passage "It does not cost much . . ." can be found on p. 247 of her collected works, *The Art of Eating* (New York: Macmillan Company, 1937).

161    Jeff Sandore quoted by Dale D. Buss in "Matters of Convenience," *Food Product Design*, June 1997. Information about techniques for creating and preserving flavor comes both from Dale Buss and from "Soup's On!" by Laura A. Brandt in *Prepared Foods*, May 2000.

162    Savory flavors information from Linda M. Ohr's "Savory Flavors Hit the Tough Notes," *Prepared Foods*, July 1998.

163    All Twinkie product information comes from Planet Twinkie.

164    Jean Carpenter's "Cancer-proof your barbecue" appeared in *USA Weekend*, June 29–1, 2001.

164    Statistics on overweight adults in 1999 provided by the U.S. Department of Health and Human Services in "Overweight and Obesity Threaten U.S. Health Gains," *HHS News*, December 13, 2001. Statistics on the number of preschoolers overweight today compared to 1970 appear in "Diagnosis: Supersize," Howard Markel, *The New York Times*, March 24, 2002. The U.S. Surgeon General's Office estimate of the cost of obesity in 2000 appears in the fact sheet, "The Surgeon General's Call to Action to Prevent and Decrease Overweight and Obesity.".

165    Comments on food consumed outside the home appear in *Halting the Obesity Epidemic: A Public Health Policy Approach*, Marion Nestle, Ph.D., M.P.H., and Michael F. Jacobson, Ph.D., *Public Health Reports*, Vol. 115, January/February 2000.

165     Jeffrey P. Koplan is quoted in "Hog Nation: U.S. Wallows in Obesity," *Earth Island Journal*, Spring 2000, Vol. 15, No. 1.

166     Boston Market's slogan is "food worth slowing down for," and its corporate materials explain the "Boston Market Concept": "Boston Market Corporation recognizes that in an increasingly fast-paced world, more and more people are pressed for time and looking for ways to make their lives easier. Many consumers want an alternative to cooking that allows them to slow down and spend more time with their family and loved ones. Boston Market restaurants offer fresh, delicious, home-style meals just like you would prepare and serve at home if you had the time—without the hassle of preparation and clean-up."

167     The Susan Lawrence passage was included in "Tastemakers 2000," *The Valley Table: The Magazine of Hudson Valley Farms, Food and Cuisine*, February–April 2000. Another caterer for the well-heeled, Hay Day Market, offers a decidedly homey Christmas meal-to-go featuring turkey, "traditional" bread stuffing, mashed potatoes, peas and baby onions, succotash, and the fixin's of gravy and cranberry relish.

170     Cookbook material from both Joan Acocella, "American Pie," *The New Yorker*, December 6, 1999, and David Belman, "200 Years of Cooking by the Book: The American Cookbook Celebrates Its Bicentennial," *Restaurants USA*, November 1996.

170     Food network data and Bruce Seidel observation from "Keenly Watched Pots," Bridget Byrne, *The Daily News*, June 24, 2002.

170     Michele Hatty's article "Tabbouleh or not tabbouleh?" was published in *USA Weekend*, April 6, 2001.

171     Lynne Rossetto Kasper was quoted in "Rustic Revival," by William Rice, *The Journal News*, November 3, 1999.

172     Waking hours in the kitchen courtesy of Joanne Furio, "Itchin' for a New Kitchen," *The Journal News*, June 8–9, 2002.

172     Jean Dimeo's and Mark Wade's thoughts are expressed in "Does what room we eat in have to do with how we eat?" Alan J. Heavens, *The Journal News*, December 2, 2001.

173     F-O-R-T-U-N-E Personnel Consultants commissioned Community Research to conduct the study.

174     The Campbell's Soup president's comment and frozen orange juice theory are cited in Harvey Levenstein's *Paradox of Plenty: A Social History of Eating in Modern America* (New York: Oxford University Press, 1993), pp. 108–109.

## Chapter 7: A Specialty

177     DeVault discusses "Knowledge of the individual" throughout *Feeding the Family*. Jeremy Rifkin quotes Kroc in "Anatomy of a Cheeseburger," *Granta* 38 (Winter 1991).

178      Passage on cooking well by M.F.K Fisher appears on p. 203 in *The Art of Eatin*

179      The statistics on the minutes Americans were willing to spend making a recipe five years ago versus today come from *Health* magazine, September 1999.

179      When we do bake for the holidays, it seems we only make the time to do so by squeezing it in among the other responsibilities we have. I found one study especially provocative, by the Land O'Lakes Holiday Bakeline, which examined when Americans bake for the holidays. Nearly a quarter of respondents do no baking whatsoever. Consider those who do, however: the study found that only 3.4 percent of holiday bakers are able to take a day off from work to prepare food for a holiday. Another 11 percent go at it all day and all night in a baking marathon. What I found most interesting is that 53 percent do their baking between the hours of 9 p.m. and 6 a.m.

179      The essayist Felix Platter described the rosemary, thyme, and marjoram that grew wild in the fields around Montpelier, where he had traveled to study medicine, according to Barbara Wheaton in *Savoring the Past: The French Kitchen and Table from 1300 to 1789* (Philadelphia: University of Pennsylvania Press, 1983). She also recounts the gifts exchanged by Voltaire's circle, p. 219.

180      The Bantu "clanship of porridge" is described in Peter Farb and George Armelagos' *Consuming Passions: The Anthropology of Eating* (Boston: Houghton Mifflin Company, 1980), p. 7. The book also cites the maize comment by Dorothy Lee on p. 4.

184      Jane and Michael Stern's "Doing Good by Cooking Well," in *Gourmet*, November 1998, is a nice piece on the community cookbook phenomenon.

185      Edge made the comment in "A mostly tasteful debate on Southern cooking," by Wendell Brock, *The Arizona Republic*, November 10, 1999. Devotees of Southern cuisine have banded together under the auspices of the University of Mississippi's Center for the Study of Southern Culture to produce an annual Southern Foodways Symposium that celebrates favorites of home cooking, such as fried chicken, collards, and boiled peanuts. Edge is the symposium director.

185      On the power of fruitcake we have this passage from Truman Capote's "A Christmas Memory," 1956: "The black stove, stoked with coal and firewood, glows like a lighted pumpkin. Eggbeaters whirl, spoons spin round in bowls of butter and sugar, vanilla sweetens the air, ginger spices it; melting, nose-tingling odors saturate the kitchen, suffuse the house, drift out to the world on puffs of chimney smoke. In four days our work is done. Thirty-one cakes, dampened with whiskey, bask on window sills and shelves." The passage appears in John Egerton's evocative cookbook, *Southern Food: At Home, on the Road, in History* (Chapel Hill: University of North Carolina Press, 1993).

190    I found fascinating pieces of cake history on the Internet: details on wedding cakes at www.cakesbysam.com, on king cake from Randazzo's Camelia City Bakery at www.kingcakes.com, and general background in an article called "The Peerless Cake Baker: The Surprising History of the Cake," by Helen Stringer. The description of the bridal cake by William Wirt was excerpted in a faux colonial cookbook available from the Colonial Williamsburg Foundation, called *The Williamsburg Art of Cookery.*

194    Anne Byrn warned Knight-Ridder reporter Cathy Thomas about "cake-mix taste" for her article "Easy Prescriptions for Doctoring Cake Mixes" on May 31, 2000.

195    The comfort food trend has caught on at any number of New York restaurants. Cookies and milk entice diners at Moomba, Tapika, Metrazur, Cucina & Company, and Atlas, among others. Bakeries known for their bread have begun producing old-fashioned layer cakes (the one at Ecce Panis is priced at $30).

195    The Thomas Wolfe "spectacle" quote is from *The Web and the Rock.*

195    Egerton's comment about cakes appears in *Southern Food: At Home, on the Road, in History.*

196    The Maida Heatter statement "For me, life's problems . . ." appears in *Maida Heatter's Book of Great Desserts* (New York: Alfred A. Knopf, 1977), p. ix.

199    Cara de Silva's commentary on the powerful material in *In Memory's Kitchen: A Legacy from the Women of Terezín* (Northvale, NJ: Jason Aronson, 1996) is remarkable, as are the recipes themselves.

200    Steinbeck's observations are cited in *Paradox of Plenty,* p. 60.

200    "We ate weeds . . ." and other sobering reflections fill the spiral-bound pages of an unusual series of cookbooks: *Stories and Recipes of the Great Depression of the 1930's,* Volumes I, II, and III by Janet Van Amber Paske, Home Economist (Neenah, WI: Van Amber Publishers, 1986).

200    For an appreciation of all that is made from scratch, Patience Gray may be unsurpassed. This passage appears on p. 12 of *Honey from a Weed: Fasting and Feasting in Tuscany, Catalonia, The Cyclades and Apulia* (New York: Harper & Row/Prospect Books, 1987).

207    Douglas Kellner's discussion of the fast-food giant appears in "Theorizing/resisting McDonaldization," p. 199 in Barry Smart, ed., *Resisting McDonaldization* (London: Sage Publications, 1999).

207    The "No sloppy joes . . ." observation belongs to Suzanne Daley in "With ABC's of Dining, France Raises Epicures," *The New York Times,* October 27, 2001.

208    Concerning Alice Waters' emphasis on moral education, it is fascinating that surveys by the National Center on Addiction and Substance Abuse at Columbia University have consistently found that the more often twelve- to seventeen-year-olds have dinner with their parents, the less likely they

are to smoke, drink, or use illegal drugs. Also, a study that included 16,000 children of nurses, published in *Archives of Family Medicine* in March 2000, found that children who shared sit-down family meals were one and a half times as likely to eat five servings of fruits and vegetables every day as those who rarely ate with their parents. The children were between the ages of 9 and 14.

## Chapter 8: Cloth Divas

211   The Aunt Thankful anecdote is one of many wonderful stories in Ruth Finley's 1929 classic *Old Patchwork Quilts and the Women Who Made Them* (McLean, VA: EPM Publications, 1992).

211   Rozsika Parker's assertion appears in *The Subversive Stitch: Embroidery and the Making of the Feminine* (London: Women's Press, 1984), p. 5.

213   The Blairs are profiled by Bets Ramsey and Merikay Waldvogel in *The Quilts of Tennessee: Images of Domestic Life Prior to 1930* (Nashville, TN: Rutledge Hill Press, 1986).

217   Walter Benjamin is quoted in Darnton's *The Great Cat Massacre*, p. 106.

218   Scholar Elizabeth Wayland Barber exhaustively depicts spinning in antiquity in *Women's Work: The First 20,000 Years: Women, Cloth, and Society in Early Times* (New York: W. W. Norton & Company, 1994). Sarah Pomeroy also describes the ancient importance of fiber to this culture, telling us in *Goddesses, Whores, Wives, and Slaves* on p. 199 that "The old-fashioned Roman bride wreathed the doorposts of her new home with wool." She also discusses the peplos in some depth.

219   Some years ago, Bette Hochberg self-published a small book, *Spin Span Spun: Fact and Folklore for Spinners* (1979), which continues to serve as a rich source about spinning history.

222   Nancy Bush's cult classic *Folk Socks* features an extensive history of the craft of knitting.

222   Benson has written a book called *The Relaxation Response* (New York: Avon Books 2000), first published in 1976.

223   Sister Bianca was profiled by Mary Greenfield in *The New York Times*, "Teaching the Spiritual Art of Weaving," November 5, 2000.

225   Bender's *Plain and Simple: A Woman's Journey to the Amish* (San Francisco: HarperCollins, 1991) still constitutes an affecting read.

226   The hand-written notes cited here are discussed in Sandi Fox, *For Purpose and Pleasure: Quilting Together in Nineteenth-Century America* (Nashville, TN: Rutledge Hill Press, 1995), p. 101.

227   As of 1997 fourteen million Americans made quilts.

227   Cleve Jones discusses the inspiration of his grandmother in Marita Sturken's *Tangled Memories: The Vietnam War, the AIDS Epidemic, and the Politics of Remembering* (Berkeley: University of California Press, 1997),

p. 191, but was originally quoted by Gary Abrams, "AIDS Quilt Comforting U.S. Grief," *Los Angeles Times*, March 22, 1988.

229    The quilt stump story appears on p. 23 of *The Quilts of Tennessee*.

230    I found useful descriptions of grassroots quilting groups on the Internet, on the many elaborate quilting websites. Hickory Hill Quilts, for one, features a lengthy page called "Good Works" that lists project after project for those interested in contributing their time.

231    Susan Behuniak-Long's comment comes from her web essay on technology and quilting at xroads.virginia.edu.

232    Faith Wilding has written an illuminating essay about domestic imagery and techniques, "Monstrous Domesticity," which can be found at www.art.cfa.cmu.edu.

# Sources

Allen, Elaine. *Watkins Household Hints* (Newark, NJ: J. R. Watkins Co., 1941).

Anderson, Jean. *The Grassroots Cookbook: Great American Recipes from Kitchens Across the Land* (New York: Doubleday, 1992).

Apuleius, trans. by Lindsay, Jack. *The Golden Ass* (Bloomington, IN: Indiana University Press, 1962).

Bank, Mirra. *Anonymous Was a Woman* (New York: St. Martin's Press, 1979, 1995).

Barber, Elizabeth Wayland. *Women's Work: The First 20,000 Years: Women, Cloth, and Society in Early Times* (New York: W. W. Norton & Company, 1994).

Bay Laurel, Alicia. *Living on the Earth* (New York: Vintage Books, 1971).

Bender, Sue. *Plain and Simple: A Woman's Journey to the Amish* (San Francisco: HarperCollins, 1991).

Bracken, Peg. *The I Hate to Cook Book* (Greenwich, CT: Fawcett Publications, 1960).

Bracken, Peg. *The I Hate to Housekeep Book: When and How to Keep House Without Losing Your Mind* (New York: Harcourt, Brace & World, 1962).

Bracken, Peg. *A Window Over the Sink: A Mainly Affectionate Memoir* (New York: Harcourt Brace Jovanovich, 1981).

Bush, Nancy. *Folk Socks: The History & Techniques of Handknitted Footwear* (Interweave Press, 1995).

Bynum, Victoria E. *Unruly Women: The Politics of Social & Sexual Control in the Old South* (Chapel Hill: University of North Carolina Press, 1992).

Carter, Susannah. *The Frugal Colonial Housewife* (originally published in 1742) (New York: Dolphin Books, 1976).

Child, Lydia Maria. *The American Frugal Housewife, Dedicated to Those Who Are Not Ashamed of Economy* (Boston: Carter, Hendee, and Co., 1833).

Chira, Susan. *A Mother's Place: Taking the Debate About Working Mothers Beyond Guilt and Blame* (New York: HarperCollins, 1998).

Clayton, Bernard. *Cooking Across America* (New York: Simon & Schuster, 1993).

Coontz, Stephanie. *The Way We Never Were: American Families and the Nostalgia Trap* (New York: Basic Books, 1992).

Coontz, Stephanie. *The Way We Really Are: Coming to Terms with America's Changing Families* (New York: Basic Books, 1997).

Copper, Arthur. *The Household Searchlight Homemaking Guide* (Topeka, KS: The Household Magazine, 1937).

257

Cowan, Ruth Schwartz. *More Work for Mother: The Ironies of Household Technology from the Open Hearth to the Microwave* (New York: Basic Books, 1983).

Darnton, Robert. *The Great Cat Massacre and Other Episodes in French Cultural History* (New York: Basic Books, 1984).

De Beauvoir, Simone. *The Second Sex* (New York: Alfred A. Knopf, 1953).

Delgado, Jeanne Hunnicutt, ed. *Nellie Kedzie Jones's Advice to Farm Women: Letters from Wisconsin, 1912–1916* (Madison, WI: State Historical Society of Wisconsin, 1973).

Delort, Robert. *Life in the Middle Ages* (New York: Greenwich House, 1972).

De Pauw, Linda Grant, and Conover Hunt. *Remember the Ladies: Women in America 1750–1815* (New York: A Studio Book, Viking Press, published in association with the Pilgrim Society, 1976).

De Silva, Cara, ed. *In Memory's Kitchen: A Legacy from the Women of Terezín* (Northvale, NJ: Jason Aronson, 1996).

DeVault, Marjorie L. *Feeding the Family: The Social Organization of Caring as Gendered Work* (Chicago: University of Chicago Press, 1991).

Didion, Joan. *Slouching Towards Bethlehem* (New York: Dell Publishing, 1968).

Donovan, Mary, Hatrak, Amy, Mills, Frances, and Shull, Elizabeth. *The Thirteen Colonies Cookbook* (New York: Praeger, 1975).

Edge, John T. and Rolfes, Ellen. *A Gracious Plenty: Recipes and Recollections from the American South* (New York: Putnam, 1999).

Egerton, John. *Southern Food: At Home, on the Road, in History.* (Chapel Hill: University of North Carolina Press, 1993).

Ehrenreich, Barbara and English, Deirdre. *For Her Own Good: 150 Years of the Experts' Advice to Women* (New York: Anchor Press, 1978).

Ehrlich, Elizabeth. *Miriam's Kitchen* (New York: Penguin Books, 1997).

Eisler, Riane. *The Chalice & the Blade* (San Francisco: HarperSanFrancisco, 1987, 1995).

Evans, Sara. *Personal Politics: The Roots of Women's Liberation in the Civil Rights Movement & the New Left* (New York: Alfred A. Knopf, 1979).

Evans, Sara M. *Born for Liberty: A History of Women in America* (New York: Free Press, 1989).

Falick, Melanie D. *Knitting in America: Patterns, Profiles & Stories of America's Leading Artisans* (New York: Artisan, 1997).

Farb, Peter and Armelagos, George. *Consuming Passions: The Anthropology of Eating* (Boston: Houghton Mifflin Company, 1980).

Finley, Ruth E. *Old Patchwork Quilts and the Women Who Made Them* (McLean, VA: EPM Publications, 1992).

Fisher, Helen. *The First Sex: The Natural Talents of Women and How They Are Changing the World* (New York: Random House, 1999).

Fisher, Katharine A. *Good Meals and How to Prepare Them: A Guide to Meal-Planning Cooking and Serving* (New York: International Magazine Company, 1927).

Fisher, M. F. K. *The Art of Eating* (New York: Macmillan Company, 1937).

Fishwick, Marshall, ed. *Ronald Revisited: The World of Ronald McDonald* (Bowling Green, OH: Bowling Green State University Popular Press, 1983).

Fitton, J. Lesley. *Cycladic Art* (Cambridge, MA: Harvard University Press, 1990).

Flexner, Eleanor and Fitzpatrick, Ellen. *Century of Struggle: The Women's Rights Movement in the United States* (Cambridge, MA: Belknap Press, Harvard University Press, 1996).

Florman, Monte and Florman, Marjorie. *How to Clean Practically Anything* (Yonkers, NY: Consumer Reports Books, 1992).

Forty, Adrian. *Objects of Desire: Design & Society from Wedgwood to IBM* (New York: Pantheon Books, 1986).

Fox, Sandi. *For Purpose and Pleasure: Quilting Together in Nineteenth-Century America* (Nashville, TN: Rutledge Hill Press, 1995).

Fox-Genovese, Elizabeth. *Within the Plantation Household: Black and White Women of the Old South* (Chapel Hill: University of North Carolina Press, 1988).

Friedan, Betty. *The Feminine Mystique, Tenth Anniversary Edition* (New York: W. W. Norton & Company, 1974).

Fussell, Betty. *I Hear America Cooking: The Cooks and Recipes of American Regional Cuisine* (New York: Penguin Books, 1997).

Genovese, Eugene D. *Roll, Jordan, Roll: The World the Slaves Made* (New York: Vintage Books, 1976).

Gentry, Francis G., ed. *German Medieval Tales* (New York: Continuum, 1983).

Getz-Preziosi, Pat. *Early Cycladic Sculpture: An Introduction* (Malibu, CA: J. Paul Getty Museum, 1994).

Glasse, Hannah. *The Art of Cookery Made Plain and Easy* (Alexandria, VA: Cottom and Stewart, 1805).

Grahame, Kenneth. *The Wind in the Willows* (New York: Ariel Books/Henry Holt and Company, 1980).

Gray, Patience. *Honey From a Weed: Fasting and Feasting in Tuscany, Catalonia, the Cyclades and Apulia* (New York: Harper & Row/Prospect Books, 1987).

Greer, Carlotta C. *Foods and Home Making* (New York: Allyn & Bacon, 1939).

Haden Elgin, Suzette, Ph.D. *The Language Imperative* (Cambridge, MA: Perseus Books, 2000).

Heatter, Maida. *Maida Heatter's Book of Great Desserts* (New York: Alfred A. Knopf, 1977).

Hedrick, Joan D. *Harriet Beecher Stowe: A Life* (New York: Oxford University Press, 1994).

Height, Dorothy I. and the National Council of Negro Women, Inc. *The Black Family Dinner Quilt Cookbook* (New York: A Fireside Book/Simon & Schuster, 1993).

Heloise. *Heloise's Housekeeping Hints* (Englewood Cliffs, NJ: Prentice-Hall, 1962).

Heloise. *Heloise's Kitchen Hints* (Englewood Cliffs, NJ: Prentice-Hall, 1963).

Heloise. *All Around the House* (New York: Pocket Books, 1967).

Hewlett, Sylvia Ann. *A Lesser Life: The Myth of Women's Liberation in America* (New York: William Morrow, 1986).

Hewlett, Sylvia Ann. *When the Bough Breaks: The Cost of Neglecting Our Children* (New York: Basic Books, 1991).

Hochberg, Bette. *Spin Span Spun: Fact and Folklore for Spinners* (Santa Cruz, CA: Bette and Bernard Hochberg, 1979).

Hochschild, Arlie Russell, with Anne Machung. *The Second Shift: Working Parents and the Revolution at Home* (New York: Viking Penguin, 1989).

Hochschild, Arlie Russell. *The Time Bind: When Work Becomes Home & Home Becomes Work* (New York: Metropolitan Books, 1997).

Hogan, David Gerard. *Selling 'Em by the Sack: White Castle and the Creation of American Food* (New York: New York University Press, 1997).

Horsfield, Margaret. *Biting the Dust: The Joys of Housework* (New York: St. Martin's Press, 1998).

Hosmer, Jr., Charles B. *Presence of the Past: A History of the Preservation Movement in the United States Before Williamsburg* (New York: G.P. Putnam's Sons, 1965).

Hoy, Suellen. *Chasing Dirt: The American Pursuit of Cleanliness* (New York: Oxford University Press, 1995).

Inness, Sherrie A., ed. *Kitchen Culture in America: Popular Representations of Food, Gender, and Race* (Philadelphia: University of Pennsylvania Press, 2001).

Isbell, Robert. *The Keepers: Mountain Folk Holding on to Old Skills and Talents* (Winston-Salem, NC: John E. Blair, 1999).

Jones, Evan. *American Food: The Gastronomic Story* (New York: E. P. Dutton, 1975).

Kamman, Madeleine. *When French Women Cook* (New York: Atheneum, 1983).

Kimball, Gayle, ed. *Women's Culture: The Women's Renaissance of the Seventies* (Metuchen, NJ: Scarecrow Press, 1981).

Kiracofe, Roderick. *The American Quilt: A History of Cloth and Comfort 1750–1950* (New York: Clarkson Potter, 1993).

Klatch, Rebecca E. *Women of the New Right* (Philadelphia: Temple University Press, 1987).

Krondl, Michael. *Around the American Table: Treasured Recipes and Food Traditions from the American Cookery Collections of the New York Public Library* (Holbrook, MA: Adams Publishing, 1995).

Kundera, Milan. *Slowness* (New York: HarperPerennial, 1996).

Lasch, Christopher. *Women and the Common Life: Love, Marriage, and Feminism* (New York: W. W. Norton & Company, 1997).

Lassiter, William Lawrence. *Shaker Recipes and Formulas for Cooks and Homemakers* (New York: Bonanza Books, 1978).

Lefkowitz, Mary F. and Fant, Maureen. *Women in Greece and Rome* (Toronto: Samuel-Stevens, 1977).

Leon, Vicki. *Uppity Women of Ancient Times* (Berkeley, CA: Conari Press, 1995).

Levenstein, Harvey. *Paradox of Plenty: A Social History of Eating in Modern America* (New York: Oxford University Press, 1993).

Lightman, Marjorie and Lightman, Benjamin. *Biographical Dictionary of Ancient Greek & Roman Women* (New York: Checkmark Books/Facts on File, Inc., 2000).

Luxemberg, Stan. *Roadside Empires: How the Chains Franchised America* (New York: Viking Penguin, 1985).

Markham, Gervase. *The English Housewife: Containing the Inward and Outward Virtues Which Ought to Be in a Complete Woman* (Montreal: McGill-Queen's University Press, 1986).

Maron, Mindy. *The Secret to Tender Pie: America's Grandmothers Share their Favorite Recipes* (New York: Ballantine Books, 1997).

Marshall, Melinda M. *Good Enough Mothers: Changing Expectations for Ourselves* (Princeton, NJ: Peterson's, 1993).

Matthews, Glenna. *"Just a Housewife": The Rise & Fall of Domesticity in America* (New York: Oxford University Press, 1987).

McKenna, Elizabeth Perle. *When Work Doesn't Work Anymore: Women, Work, and Identity* (New York: Delacorte Press, 1997).

Mintz, Steven and Kellogg, Susan. *Domestic Revolutions: A Social History of American Family Life* (New York: Free Press, 1988).

Morgan, Robin. *Sisterhood Is Powerful: An Anthology of Writings from the Women's Liberation Movement* (New York: Vintage Books, 1970).

Moynihan, Ruth Barnes. *Rebel for Rights: Abigail Scott Duniway* (New Haven, CT: Yale University Press, 1983).

Oakley, Ann. *Woman's Work: The Housewife, Past and Present* (New York: Pantheon, 1974).

Oppenheimer, Jerry. *Just Desserts* (New York: Avon Books, 1997).

Olsen, Tillie. *Tell Me a Riddle* (New York: Delta, 1960).

Palmer, Phyllis. *Domesticity and Dirt: Housewives and Domestic Servants in the United States, 1920–1945* (Philadelphia: Temple University Press, 1989).

Papachristou, Judith. *Women Together: A History in Documents of the Women's Movement in the United States* (New York: A Ms. Book/Alfred A. Knopf, 1976).

Paris, Ginette. *Pagan Meditations: Aphrodite, Hestia, Artemis* (Woodstock, CT: Spring Publications, 1997).

Plante, Ellen M. *Women at Home in Victorian America: A Social History* (New York: Facts on File, 1997).

Pomeroy, Sarah B. *Goddesses, Whores, Wives, and Slaves: Women in Classical Antiquity* (New York: Schocken Books, 1975).

Rabuzzi, Kathryn Allen. *The Sacred and the Feminine: Toward a Theology of Housework* (New York: Seabury Press, 1982).

Ramsey, Bets and Waldvogel, Merikay. *The Quilts of Tennessee: Images of Domestic Life Prior to 1930* (Nashville, TN: Rutledge Hill Press, 1986).

Ransford, Oliver. *The Slave Trade* (Wiltshire, Great Britain: Redwood Press Limited, 1971).

Redstockings of the Women's Liberation Movement. *Feminist Revolution* (New York: Random House, 1978).

Reid, Richard. *The Shell Book of Cottages* (London: Michael Joseph, Ltd., 1986).

Roan, Nancy and Donald. *Lest I Shall Be Forgotten: Anecdotes and Traditions of Quilts* (Green Lane, PA: Goschenhoppen Historians, 1993).

Robertson, Una A. *The Illustrated History of the Housewife, 1650–1950* (New York: St. Martin's Press, 1997).

Root, Waverly and de Rochemont, Richard. *Eating in America: A History* (New York: Ecco Press, 1995).

Rose, Peter G., transl. and ed. *The Sensible Cook: Dutch Foodways in the Old and the New World* (Syracuse, NY: Syracuse University Press, 1989).

Rosen, Ruth. *The World Split Open: How the Modern Women's Movement Changed America* (New York: Viking Penguin, 2000).

Rosenzweig, Roy and Thelen, David. *The Presence of the Past: Popular Uses of History in American Life* (New York: Columbia University Press, 1998).

Rowbotham, Sheila. *A Century of Women: A History of Women in Britain and the United States* (London: Penguin Books, 1999).

Rybczynski, Witold. *Home: A Short History of an Idea* (New York: Viking Penguin, 1986).

Schama, Simon. *The Embarrassment of Riches: An Interpretation of Dutch Culture in the Golden Age* (New York: Vintage Books, 1987).

Schlosser, Eric. *Fast Food Nation: The Dark Side of the All-American Meal* (New York: Houghton Mifflin, 2001).

Schor, Juliet B. *The Overworked American: The Unexpected Decline of Leisure* (New York: Basic Books, 1991).

Shapiro, Laura. *Perfection Salad: Women and Cooking at the Turn of the Century* (New York: North Point Press, 1986).

Sheraton, Mimi. *From My Mother's Kitchen: Recipes & Reminiscences* (New York: Harper & Row, 1979).

Sklar, Kathryn Kish. *Catharine Beecher: A Study in American Domesticity* (New Haven, CT: Yale University Press, 1973).

Smart, Barry, ed. *Resisting McDonaldization* (London: Sage Publications, 1999).

Snow, Stephen Eddy. *Performing the Pilgrims: A Study of the Ethnohistorical Role-Playing at Plimoth Plantation* (Jackson: University Press of Mississippi, 1993).

Spruill, Julia Cherry. *Women's Life and Work in the Southern Colonies* (New York: W. W. Norton & Company, 1998).

Stacey, Michelle. *Consumed: Why Americans Love, Hate, and Fear Food* (New York: Simon & Schuster, 1994).

Stern, E. G. *My Mother and I* (New York: MacMillan Company, 1919).

Stowe, Harriet Beecher. *Three Novels* (New York: Viking Press, 1982).

Strasser, Susan. *Never Done: A History of American Housework* (New York: Pantheon Books, 1982).

Stratton, Joanna L. *Pioneer Women: Voices from the Kansas Frontier* (New York: Simon & Schuster, 1981).

Sturken Marita. *Tangled Memories: The Vietnam War, the AIDS Epidemic, and the Politics of Remembering* (Berkeley, CA: University of California Press, 1997).

Swan, Susan Burrows. *Plain & Fancy: American Women and Their Needlework, 1650–1850* (Austin, TX: Curious Works Press, 1995).

Tatar, Maria. *The Hard Facts of the Grimms' Fairy Tales* (Princeton, NJ: Princeton University Press, 1987).

*The Home Cook Book* (I. Fred Waggoner, 1877).

*The Old West: The Women* (New York: Time-Life Books, 1978).

Thom, Mary. *Inside Ms.: 25 Years of the Magazine and the Feminist Movement* (New York: Henry Holt and Company, 1997).

Thomas, Mary. *Mary Thomas's Knitting Book* (Mineola, NY: Dover Publications, 1972).

Thompson, Flora, *Lark Rise to Candleford: A Trilogy* (New York: Penguin USA, 1996).

Tobin, Jacqueline L. and Dobard, Raymond G., Ph.D. *Hidden in Plain View: A Secret Story of Quilts and the Underground Railroad* (New York: Doubleday, 1999).

Trollope, Frances. *Domestic Manners of the Americans* (London: Century Publishing Co., 1984).

Ulrich, Laurel Thatcher. *The Age of Homespun: Objects and Stories in the Creation of an American Myth* (New York: Knopf, 2001).

Ulrich, Laurel Thatcher. *Good Wives: Image and Reality in the Lives of Women in Northern New England 1650–1750* (New York: Vintage Books, 1991).

Van Amber Paske, Janet. *Stories and Recipes of the Great Depression of the 1930s, Volumes I, II, and III* (Neenah, WI: Van Amber Publishers, 1995).

Vidal, John. *McLibel: Burger Culture on Trial* (New York: New Press, 1997).

Visser, Margaret. *Much Depends on Dinner: The Extraordinary History and Mythology, Allure and Obsessions, Perils and Taboos of an Ordinary Meal* (New York: Collier Books, 1986).

Vlach, John Michael. *Back of the Big House: The Architecture of Plantation Slavery* (Chapel Hill: University of North Carolina Press, 1993).

Ward, Geoffrey C. and Burns, Ken. *Not for Ourselves Alone: The Story of Elizabeth Cady Stanton and Susan B. Anthony* (New York: Alfred A. Knopf, 1999).

Wharton, Edith. *The House of Mirth* (New York: Charles Scribner's Sons, 1969).

Wheaton, Barbara Ketcham. *Savoring the Past: The French Kitchen and Table from 1300 to 1789* (Philadelphia: University of Pennsylvania Press, 1983).

White, Joyce. *Soul Food: Recipes and Reflections from African-American Churches* (New York: HarperCollins, 1998).

Williams, Susan. *Savory Suppers and Fashionable Feasts: Dining in Victorian America* (New York: Pantheon Books, in association with the Strong Museum, 1985).

Young, Carrie, with Felicia Young. *Prairie Cooks: Glorified Rice, Three-Day Buns, and Other Reminiscences* (Iowa City: University of Iowa Press, 1993).

Zipes, Jack. *The Trials and Tribulations of Little Red Riding Hood* (South Hadley, MA: Bergin & Garvey Publishers, 1983).

# Acknowledgments

Some great editors shepherded this book through to publication. Elizabeth Maguire understood the vision embedded in the proposal and took this project on board. Philip Rappaport oversaw some of the nuts and bolts that make book ideas published realities. Finally, the conscientious and talented Elizabeth Stein helped bring these words to life.

I am tremendously grateful to Betty and Steve Zimmerman for the invaluable support they gave during the writing of *Made from Scratch*. Andy Zimmerman, Peter Zimmerman, and Suzanne Levine continually furnished encouragement and ideas.

To thank everyone who fueled my thinking on this subject is not possible. I call out some who both taught me about the value of home and whose deep friendship supported me during this process: Christine Gilmore, Debbie Levitt, Josefa Mulaire, Sandra Robishaw, and Lisa Senauke.

I must acknowledge the important contribution of Nancy Lubell, who at a crucial juncture commanded that I write just one page.

I am indebted to Betsy Lerner, my longtime friend and champion, who was there from the beginning and whose read of an early draft helped made this a better book. If I could bottle her combination of sensitivity and smarts I'd make a fortune.

Maud Reavill energetically enhanced my own domestic joy while patiently awaiting my return from the computer, and helped me with wording choices when I was stuck.

My husband and partner and mentor Gil Reavill also demonstrated tremendous patience. He believed in this project, and nurtured my spirit through some precipitous ups and downs. I am grateful for, as much as anything, Gil's willingness to let go when it was time.

# About the Author

Jean Zimmerman's books include *Raising Our Athletic Daughters: How Sports Can Build Self-Esteem and Save Girls' Lives* with Gil Reavill, and *Tailspin: Women at War in the Wake of Tailhook.* She lives with her family in Westchester County, New York.